**WITHDRAWN
UTSA LIBRARIES**

KENNIKAT PRESS SCHOLARLY REPRINTS
Ralph Adams Brown, Senior Editor

Series In
IRISH HISTORY AND CULTURE
Under the General Editorial Supervision of
Gilbert A. Cahill
Professor of History, State University of New York

St. Audoen's Arch—one of the Old Gates of the
City—where many of the Guilds had
their meeting place.

The Guilds of Dublin

BY JOHN J. WEBB, M.A., LL.D.
*Barrister-at-Law. Lecturer in
Municipal History at
University College
Dublin*

KENNIKAT PRESS
Port Washington, N. Y./London

THE GUILDS OF DUBLIN

First published in 1929
Reissued in 1970 by Kennikat Press
Library of Congress Catalog Card No: 76-102630
SBN 8046-0806-7

Manufactured by Taylor Publishing Company   Dallas, Texas

KENNIKAT SERIES IN IRISH HISTORY AND CULTURE

Contents

		Page
Chapter I.	The Guild Merchant	1
Chapter II.	The Craft Guilds	53
Chapter III.	A Tudor Account Book	79
Chapter IV.	The Common Council and the Guilds	103
Chapter V.	The Guild Merchant in the Seventeenth Century	133
Chapter VI.	The Craft Guilds in the Seventeenth Century	177
Chapter VII.	The Break-up of the Guilds	241
Appendix	Deed of Assignment of Property of Guild of St. Luke	285
Subject Index		289
Index of Names		295

Authorities

Gilbert : *Historic and Municipal Documents of Ireland.*

Gilbert : *Calendar of the Ancient Records of Dublin.*

Transcript of Charters and Documents of The Guild of the Holy Trinity or Merchants' Guild of Dublin. Transcribed in 1867 for J. T. Gilbert.

Another Transcript of same in British Museum Library (Egerton MSS.).

Original Records of the Fraternity of Barbers and Chirurgeons of the Guild of St. Mary Magdalene (Library of Trinity College, Dublin).

Original Records of Guild of Felt Makers (formerly in Public Record Office, Four Courts, Dublin. Destroyed in the year 1922).

Original Records of the Guild of Goldsmiths.

Original Records of the Guild of Painter-Stainers and Stationers, or Guild of St. Luke the Evangelist.

Transcript of Records of the Guild of Tailors, or Fraternity of St. John the Baptist (Transcribed for J. T. Gilbert).

Report of Municipal Corporations (Ireland) Commission, 1835.

Gross : *The Gild Merchant.*

Monck Mason : *De Rebus Eblanae.*

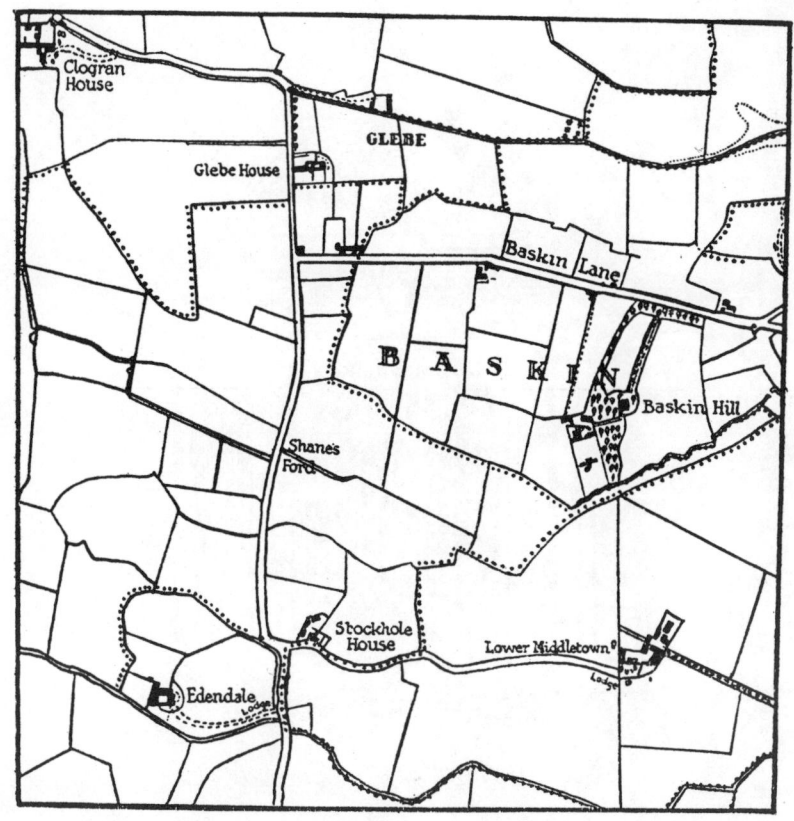

The Lands of Baskin.   See Chapter III.

Entrance to The Tailors' Hall, Back Lane

CHAPTER I.

THE GUILD MERCHANT.

The Guilds of Dublin

CHAPTER I.

The Guild Merchant

DURING the seven and a half centuries which elapsed between the expulsion by the Normans of the last Scandinavian ruler of Dublin and the setting up of a native government having its seat of power in the city, there are few features in the history of Dublin of such intense human interest as the story of the daily round of work of the merchants and craftsmen who formed the body of the citizens. In these pages an attempt is made to illustrate this feature of civic life.

Throughout the length and breadth of Western Europe the business of buying and selling merchandise and the activities of handicraftsmen were organised in the later mediaeval period on the same general lines. In France and Spain and Italy, in the Netherlands, in England and in Germany, the merchants of every important town became associated in fraternities or brotherhoods, the main purpose of which was to secure to the brethren a monopoly of the profits of trading. In these associations the merchant body waxed strong and wealthy, and became the most powerful element in the town. Somewhat later in date than the merchants, the craftsmen engaged in the more important industries organised themselves in associations modelled upon that of the merchants. The keynote of the system was exclusiveness. The craftsmen thus organised had as their object the monopoly of their particular craft. When the system became perfected none but members of the merchant guild could lawfully buy or sell merchandise in the district, none but members of the craft guilds could lawfully practise an organised craft. The establishment of Norman rule led to the introduction of this system into many of the towns of Ireland. Nowhere in Ireland was the system more firmly established or more fully developed than in Dublin.

In the year 1192 Prince John, son of Henry II. of England, granted to the citizens of Dublin a charter conferring upon them many rights and privileges. One of the rights granted by him was that the citizens should have all their reasonable guilds, as the burgesses of Bristol had, and in the most advantageous manner. As King, he confirmed this right by charters granted to the citizens in the years 1200 and 1215 respectively.

Origin of Guilds.

Prince John's Charter of the year 1192 contains the earliest specific reference to the Dublin Guilds. The right to establish guilds in Dublin may, however, be traced to the grant by Henry II., in the year 1171, to his men of Bristol of the city of Dublin, to be inhabited and held by them from him and his heirs with all the liberties and free customs which they had at Bristol and throughout his entire land. Amongst the liberties enjoyed by the burgesses of Bristol was that of organising themselves into guilds, as appears from a charter quoted by Gross in " The Gild

Merchant," which granted that the burgesses of Bristol should have all their reasonable guilds such as they had in the time of Robert and William, Earls of Gloucester (1109-1173).

The right to set up a guild organisation was early availed of by the citizens of Dublin. Records of the Guild of the Merchants date back to the end of the twelfth century. In the archives of the Dublin Corporation is preserved a Roll of Names which Sir John Gilbert has identified as being the Roll of the Guild Merchant of the twelfth century. The Roll consists of six membranes, inscribed with names in double columns on front and back, and contains over sixteen hundred names. This important document is printed in Gilbert's "Historic and Municipal Documents of Ireland." This "roll of names" formed the wrapper of a bundle of parchments which Gilbert found in the year 1866 in the Muniment Room of the Dublin Corporation. The bundle contained in addition to a Roll of Free Citizens of Dublin admitted during the period A.D. 1225-1250 thirty-six membranes containing names of members of the Guild Merchant admitted in the twelfth and thirteenth centuries. While the six membranes which formed the wrapper of the bundle are all undated and without a heading, as are some of the membranes found within, and their identification by Gilbert as being portion of the Roll of the Guild Merchant might be challenged, no doubt whatever exists as to the remaining membranes. Three of these membranes bearing date A.D. 1226, 1256 and 1257 respectively, are reproduced in "Historic and Municipal Documents." From the Roll it is possible to learn the names of those who followed the art of merchandise, or practised handicrafts in Dublin seven hundred years ago.

The members of the Guild are described by their Christian names, with the addition of (1) a surname, (2) the name of a trade, (3) the name of a town, (4) the relationship to another person, or (5) a personal attribute. In some cases a double description is given.

The membrane for the year 1226 contains the following heading and list of names:—

"Hii subscripti intrauerunt in gillemercaturam, Roberto Pollard et Petro de Ballimor, existentibus prepositis; anno regni regis Henrici decimo:"

MATHEUS DE DUNI.
STEPHANUS RUSSEL.
WALTERUS DE KERDIF,
    FRATER RICARDI BRUN.
ROBERTUS DE DALTUNE.
RICARDUS DE GLOUERNIA.
SIMON DE LICHEFELD.
NICOLAUS DE KENT.
ALANUS DE FORNEIS.
WILLELMUS DE TRUM.
OLIVERUS DE NICHOL,
    AURIFABER.
WALTERUS DE OXONIA
PHILIPPUS THE ROPERE;
RICARDUS BAKUN.
NICHOLAUS DE LONDON.
SAGGERE, FILIUS GAME.
RICARDUS DE EXCESTER.
ANDREAS DE HUNTEDUNE.

WILLELMUS CURTEISIE.
LAURENTIUS DE LEICESTRE.
WILLELMUS DE BELETUNE.
ROGERUS DE LA HIDE.
WILLELMUS DE HEREFORD,
    SELLATOR.
JOHANNES DE WINTON,
    SELLATOR.
GILBERTUS TINCTOR.
HEREBERTUS DE LEICESTRIA.
WALTERUS DE LICHEFELD.
JOHANNES MILES.
ROBERTUS BARUN.
HENRICUS DE CESTRIA.
REGINALDUS
    THE LETHERKERSUERE.
RICARDUS PASSAUANT.
OSBERTUS DE EXCESTRE.
WALTERUS WHITTAWER.

THE GUILD MERCHANT

Nicolaus de Bristoll.
Willelmus de Srobesburgia.
Gillefintan.
Thomas de Oxonia.
Robertus Nigel.
Robertus Halberd.
Dawe de Cestria.
Adam le custurer.
Willelmus Sailard.
Simon de Reuni.
Radulphus de Langeford.
Gilbertus de Nortune.
Johannes Gule.
Math. de Leicestre.
Willelmus de Karlel.
Willelmus
    pistor archiepiscopi.
Rogerus de Lichefeld.
Willelmus de London.
Willelmus de Gaweie.
Willelmus filius Johannis
    tanur.
Rogerus de Derebi.
Laurencius de Winton.
Dauid parmentarius.
Robertus filius Willielmi
    baliste.
Johannes de Cestria.
Edmundus Coruiser.
Ricardus Balle.
Thomas de Winburne.

Willelmus de Srobesburi.
Rogerus de Henley.
Adam de Wincheleseh.
Gilbertus Mutun.
Randulphus de Nas.
Tebaldus de Drohedath.
Robertus clericus de merc.
Martinus de Farleh.
Alanus de Srobesburia.
Johannes de Dunwich.
Willelmus crispus.
Johannes loksmith
    filius Simonis.
Simon le cureer.
Willelmus tailur.
Willelmus turner
    de Srobesburia.
Osbertus turnur
    de Srobesburia.
Hobekin the ledere.
Osbertus de Midia.
Willelmus de Dunstaple.
Ricardus de Lichefeld.
Osbertus de Kilmainam
    pulleter.
Willelmus de Dunstable.
Robertus Urry.
Willelmus Bulling.
Willelmus Capefurre.
Willelmus Peuerel.
Rogerus de Warewik.

Hugo de Cowpland.
Johannes Trubuil.
Ricardus filius Rogeri.
Galfridus filius Gilberti
    de Alretune.
Rogerus de Croftune.
Ricardus de Gretenofere.
Willelmus de Daltune.
Liolf mercenarius
    de Endeglene.
Warinus Ferthing
    de Karlel.
Robertus Rot
    de Kirkudbricht.
Patricius de Wurkintune.
Willelmus de Wurkintune.
Willelmus filius Turstein.
Leonardus Rauins.
Ricardus Malger.
Thomas Rand
    de Gernemuta.
Thomas Scrogmus.
Stephanus de Wintonia.
Dauid map Rob.
Ywein.
Gregorius de Hingam.
Michael de Dumfres.
Ricardus Swan
    de Dunwico.
Barth. filius Boti
    de Dunwiko.

Ricardus de Karlel.
Willelmus niger
    de Chepstowe.
Thomas Ulf.
Hammundus de Larie.
Henricus de Glouernia.
Wilekin de Wincestria.
Hugo Bos.
Henricus Scoticus.
Hugo Lancequir.
Ricardus de Kildare
    filius Hugonis.
Nicolaus palmerus
    qui fuit cum—
Mainerus de Portu.
Johannes de Pardeu.
Gidau de Mundmiseme.
Walterus de Burd.
Adam Lardmer.
Henricus Albus.
Odo de Couintre.
Rogerus le wilde.
Jacobus de Bleodun.
Jordanus Bernard.
Ricardus de Leicestria.
Radulfus axbernere.
Rogerus Blund
    de Drokeda.
Ricardus de Exonia.
Ricardus vaginator
    de Kouingtre.

Ricardus del Nas.
Willelmus Saluage.
Hugo de London.
Petrus de Hen.
Alanus filius Mauricii.
Gilbertus pictor.
Jacobus tailiator
　　　filius Herui.
Johannes Hod.
Laurencius Sumor
　　　de Cestria.
Dauid Whitegos.
Radulfus faber.
Germain faber.
Ricardus Francigena.
Hugo Gos.
Reginaldus Rutur.
Gilbertus Walensis.
Radulfus, frater
　　　Gilberti, sacerdotis.
Petrus Barker de Hare.
Willielmus Hurry.
Hugo de Kilmainan
　　　petente.
Rogerus de Redelond.
Thomas Walensis.
Henricus Curtes.
Johannes de Botune
　　　de Kardiul.
Johannes Ailward
　　　de Bristoll.

Ricardus de Glassan.
Ricardus filius Normanni.
Ricardus Maloisel.
Thomas albus de Trum.
Reginaldus de Hugeleuilæ.
Johannes Ballard.
Johannes de Brabant.
Johannes de Loueine.
Johannes Malmatin.
Willelmus de Oxenford.
Willelmus Walur.
Adam Rig.
Dauid Grim.
Willelmus de Bristoll.
Ricardus Stamer.
Robertus de Bikintun.
Johannes le fustere.
Walterus de Hampton.
Ricardus le lokismith
　　　de Tickehille.
Alanus le Pestur.
Robert de Drokeda.
Radulfus Blundel.
Hugo pistor.
Eduardus tannator.
Walterus Despenser.
Ernaldus de Kermein.
Willelmus Scurrein.
Walterus palmerus
　　　de Dameswich.
Reginaldus de Piro.

Thomas de London.
Dauid Rufus de Swerdes.
Radulfus filius Seberne.
Rogerus le cercler.
Willelmus clericus
 de Galweie.
Johannes le corduaner.
Johannes de Sellingford.
Alexander de Glouernia.
Hugo le limbernere.
Ricardus Cocus
 de Cornwale.
Willelmus Norrensis
 de Heddune.
Robertus Flandrensis
 frater Johannis
 sacerdotis.
Clarambaldus de Amiens.
Ricardus de Greimemese.
Robertus de Warewich.
Gunnig forestarius.
Ricardus de Northfolk.
Robertus de Tiuertune.
Adam le chalimer.
Willielmus Palmerus
 piscator.
Andreas Colmuth.
Dauid lebas.
Robert Le mathu.
Johannes Wlbete.
Walterus Coc falconarius.
Robertus filius Boidini.
Rogerus Brian.
Alanus filius Stephani
 de Eborac.
Dawe piscator.
Robert de Wluesee.

The admission of 224 members into the Guild Merchant of Dublin in a single year is evidence of the flourishing condition of the Guild at this early date. The new members appear to have been recruited chiefly from England, Scotland and Wales. Continental countries contributed their quota as is evidenced by such names as " Ricardus Francigena," " Ricardus filius Normanni," " Reginaldus de Hugelevile," " Johannes de Brabant," " Johannes de Loueine," " Clarambaldus de Amiens." Irish names are conspicuous by their absence. The name " Gillefintan " is Irish, but names such as " Willelmus de Trum," " Tebaldus de Drohedath," " Osbertus de Midia,"

THE GUILD MERCHANT

"Ricardus del Nas," which appear in the list, are doubtless those of colonists who had settled in the places named. The Guild was predominantly English in composition, with a sprinkling of Welsh and Scotch and other foreigners. Irishmen were excluded. A few of the names may be those of Danish inhabitants of Dublin.

The roll is valuable in illustrating the extraordinary blend of races in the civic community of mediaeval Dublin. The old Town of the Hurdle Ford seems to have acted as a magnet in drawing all these strangers to itself.

The Guild Merchant of Dublin was recruited from many occupations. Amongst the members admitted in the year 1226 were "Oliuerus de Nichol, aurifaber," "Phillipus the ropere," "Willelmus de Hereford, sellator," "Gilbertus tinctor," "Johannes miles," "Reginaldus the letherkersuere," "Adam le custurer," "Willelmus pistor archiepiscopi," "Dauid parmentarius," "Edmundus Coruiser," "Johannes loksmith filius Simonis," "Simon le cureer," "Willelmus tailur," "Willelmus turnur de Srobesburia," "Hobekin the ledere," "Osbertus de Kilmainam pulleter," "Radulfus axbernere," "Ricardus vaginator de Kouingtre," "Gilbertus pictor," "Radulfus faber," "Hugo de Kilmainan petente," "Johannes le fustere," "Eduardus tannator," "Willelmus clericus de Galweie," "Rogerus le cercler," "Johannes le corduaner," "Hugo le limbernere," "Gunnig forestarius," "Adam le chalimer" "Willielmus Palmerus piscator," "Walterus Coc falconarius." None of the new members is described as a merchant or dealer. The majority of the names in the

Craftsmen in Guild Merchant.

list is followed by no occupational description. It may be the case that all of these members belonged to the class of dealers in wares as distinct from those who manufactured goods for sale.

The thirty-seventh and thirty-eigth membranes, relating to the years A.D. 1256 and 1257, shew that sixty-five members were enrolled in the Guild Merchant in the former year and one hundred and forty in the year 1257. As showing the extraordinary variety of trades represented by the members of the Guild the following occupations, none of which appears in the earlier list, may be mentioned:—" Ricard le chapman," " Walterus le tiffere de Couintre," " Wilhelmus de Preston, lorimarius," " Johannes albus de Atherde (Ardee) scissor," " Robertus de Nouo castro Zonarius," " Adam le Koppere de Cestria," " Wilhelmus Seuere de Bristoll junior," " Johannes le Honte de Cestria," " Thomas le Hopere de villa Palmeri," " Symon Bi the watere de Wikinglo," " Johannes el Winplere," " Ricardus de Cestria, sutor," " Alexander le loger," " Petrus scriptor," " Nicholaus de London, pelliparius," " Rogerus de Clondulkan comin." " Robertus spiciarus de Couintre," " Herbertus, frater Agnetis, vinetar de Cestria," " Johannes le draper de Glouernia," " Willielmus cyrothecarius de Cestria," " Ricardus le maliere de Kardigan," " Unfridus de la Velde, carnifex," " Marcus le gabler de Rothomago," " Jacobus de Durham, Marinarius," " Willielmus le seler de Rothomago."

More than fifty different occupations were represented by those admitted to the Guild Merchant of Dublin in the three years A.D. 1226, 1256 and 1257. This list is

THE GUILD MERCHANT

by no means exhaustive of the crafts represented in the Guild as a whole. The inclusion of craftsmen in the Guild Merchant was, according to Gross, a feature common to the merchant guilds of the twelfth, thirteenth and fourteenth centuries. Every man who bought or sold goods was to a certain extent a merchant or dealer. The craftsman purchased the raw material, which he worked up and sold as a finished product. The tanner bought raw hides and bark, and sold leather. The cordwainer or shoemaker bought leather from the tanner or dealer in merchandise, and sold the shoes which he made. The weaver bought the yarn, which he sold as cloth.

The Guild Merchant was the Parent Guild.

The Guild Merchant was the parent guild from which the craft guilds sprang. According as the population of the mediaeval town increased it became necessary to have a larger body of craftsmen to cater for the needs of the citizens. More bakers were needed to make their daily bread; more spinners and weavers and tailors to clothe them; more tanners and shoemakers to provide them with footgear; more masons and carpenters to house them. As the craftsmen grew in numbers, the necessity for regulating the details of their craft and for securing the welfare of the workers led to their organisation into separate craft guilds. The craftsmen, although now organised in their own guilds, continued for a time to retain the membership of the Guild Merchant. Gradually the craftsmen disappeared from the Guild Merchant and confined themselves to their own fraternities. Ultimately the Guild Merchant became restricted to the merchants and dealers. This seems to have been the course of development in Dublin. Prince John granted to the citizens the right to have all reasonable guilds as the burgesses of Bristol had. The Guild Merchant is the only guild in Dublin of which there are records during the thirteenth and fourteenth centuries. It is not until the fifteenth century that the craftsmen appear organised in their own guilds.

The citizens of Dublin, in addition to the privilege of having a Guild Merchant for the organisation of their trade, enjoyed other trading privileges from which non-citizens were excluded. Thus the charter of Prince John of the year 1192 provided that no foreign merchant should buy within the city corn, hides, or wool, from a foreigner, but only from the citizens; that no foreign merchant should have a wine tavern unless on ship-board; that no foreigner should sell cloth in the city by retail; and that no foreign merchant should tarry in the city, with his wares for sale, beyond forty days.

The corn, hide and wool trades were the staple trades of the city. The prohibition in the charter against a foreigner purchasing these goods from any but a citizen secured to the men of Dublin the profits arising from the trade in these commodities. The charter also secured to them the profits of the retail trade in wine and cloth. The prohibition against foreigners remaining more than forty days aimed at preventing strangers, who were exempt from the ordinary burthens of the citizens, enjoying for a lengthy period the advantage of the important Dublin market. Foreign merchants were, however, liable

THE GUILD MERCHANT 13

to the payment of tolls and customs upon their goods, a burthen from which members of the Guild Merchant, in fact, all the citizens, were exempt. The term "foreigners" included not only those from other countries but even traders from other cities and towns in Ireland.

The municipal records of Dublin, with the notable exception of the Roll of names before referred to, contain no reference to the Merchant Guild or other Guild until the fifteenth century, although a Guild Hall is mentioned. The "Liber Albus" contains a record of a grant made in the year 1282 to one Robert Willeby, citizen, of permission to build upon the stone wall of the Guildhall of Dublin.* From the same source it appears that the Guildhall was situated in Winetavern Street.† A grant made in the year 1311 is to the effect that "The Mayor and commonalty of Dublin grant to Robert de Bristol, their fellow citizen, all their tenement, where their old Guildhall stood, in the Taverners' street in the city, with two marcs of yearly rent from two cellars under it, and with the garden in the rere towards the east." It was doubtless in the Guild Hall that the members of the Guild Merchant met for the transaction of Guild business.

Valuable records of the Guild Merchant, consisting of a charter of Queen Elizabeth dated 1577 and books of proceedings dating from the year 1438, were in the possession of the Governors of the Merchant Taylors' School, Dublin, until the year 1908 when they were lodged for greater safety in the Public Record Office, Dublin. These records perished in the year 1922 when the Four Courts were destroyed. A transcript made from these

* C. A. R. D. Vol. I, 106. † Ibid. p. 109.

records by William Monck Mason is included in the Egerton MSS., British Museum, and has been availed of by Gross in his history of the Gild Merchant. Another transcript is included amongst the Gilbert MSS. in the possession of the Dublin Corporation which collection is housed in the Charlemont Mall Library. The latter MSS. has been chiefly used for this account of the Guild Merchant.

In the year 1451 Henry VI. by charter granted liberty to certain persons to found and establish anew a certain fraternity or guild of the art of merchants of Dublin already established in that city. The text of the Charter which is in Latin appears in the Gilbert transcript. Permission was granted to found and establish anew to the praise and honour of the Holy Trinity a certain fraternity or guild of the art of merchants of the city of Dublin already established in the chapel of the Holy Trinity in the Cathedral Church of the Holy Trinity in Dublin. Such guild was to have perpetual succession and consist of both men and women. Power was given to the brothers of the fraternity to choose from amongst themselves annually two masters and two wardens for the regulation, government, and supervision of the fraternity or guild, and for the custody of the lands, tenements, revenues, goods and chattels, which the said fraternity then held or sbould thereafter acquire. The right to have a common seal and to plead and be impleaded in all Courts was likewise granted. In other words, the guild was incorporated. The privilege was granted to the masters, wardens and brethren in perpetuity that

Grant of Charter by Henry VI.

no stranger should buy within the city or suburbs or franchises of Dublin any merchandise by retail or wholesale unless from the merchants of the city. If any stranger should thereafter be found guilty and be convicted before the Masters and Wardens of the guild of buying goods contrary to the terms of the charter, power was given to the Masters and Wardens to consign him under their common seal to the prison of the city, there to be detained until released by their authority.

Liberty was granted to the Guild to hold lands and other property to the value of forty pounds a year. The fraternity or guild was further empowered to found a chantry. This chantry was to consist of four priests who should celebrate Divine service daily for the welfare of the King, the Lord Deputy, the founders of the Guild and the brethren and sisters of the Guild during life, and after death for the repose of their souls and the souls of all the faithful departed. Power was given to the brothers and sisters of the guild to depose and remove the said chaplains as, and when, occasion arose, and to appoint other suitable chaplains in their place. The term " chantry " implies that the service, or portion of it, was sung.

This charter brings into prominence the fact that the Guild of Merchants, like the craft guilds, as will subsequently appear, was under religious patronage. Divine service was to be celebrated each day by the chaplains, who were officers of the guild. It is worthy of note that the sisters of the Guild were empowered to take part in the election and removal of the chaplains.

By virtue of this important charter the merchants of Dublin, in other words the members of the guild, were secured in the enjoyment of the profits arising from the sale of merchandise, to the exclusion of non-citizens. This charter strikes the keynote of the whole guild system, namely, exclusiveness.

That there was already in existence a Guild of the merchants of Dublin under the patronage of the Holy Trinity is evidenced by this charter of the year 1451. Apart from the Roll of Names already referred to, the record of the proceedings of the Guild dates back to the year 1438. The bye laws of this year refer back to the time of Henry V. (A.D. 1413-1422). They refer to the liberties of the Guild as being "alowyt by owr king that nowe ys, henri the fyfte."

Henry VI.'s charter informs us where the religious observances of the Guild were to be carried on. The municipal records of Dublin afford information as to where the secular work of the Guild was conducted. In the Assembly Roll for the period A.D. 1447-1461, the oldest Roll extant, appears a record of a grant made in the year 1451, the year of Henry's charter, to the Guild of the Holy Trinity, Dublin. An upper apartment in the Tholsel was granted by the Common Council or Assembly of Dublin to the Guild for the purpose of deliberations and meetings, at an annual rent of three shillings and eight pence silver, which apartment the Guild covenanted to keep "stiff and strong." The right of the civic authorities to enter and occupy the chamber was reserved. The Tholsel was situated in Skinner's Row,* which formed part of the present Christchurch Place.

Meeting Place of Guild.

---

* Gilbert: History of Dublin, Vol. I. ch. v., p. 161.

THE GUILD MERCHANT

The charter of Henry VI. and the bye laws of the Guild provide abundant material with regard to the constitution and working of the Guild in the fifteenth and sixteenth centuries. They illustrate the system of communal trading that obtained during that period. The control exercised by the Guild authorities over the conduct of trade by the brethren, and over the general conduct of their servants and apprentices, is clearly exemplified. The information thus afforded is supplemented and confirmed by the municipal records of Dublin.

According to Henry VI's. charter the fraternity or Guild of Merchants was to consist of two Masters, two Wardens and an unlimited number of brethren and sisters. The Masters and Wardens were to be elected annually by the members. It is not clear from the charter whether the sisters were entitled to vote at the election equally with their male brethren. The right to choose these officers was vested in the *fratres*, a term which might be held to include both the brethren and the sisters, as both men and women composed the *fraternitas* or guild. Support for this wider interpretation of the term is afforded by the fact that both the brothers and sisters of the fraternity were empowered to appoint and remove the chaplains of the guild. The Masters and Wardens, according to the charter, were to be appointed for the regulation, government and supervision of the fraternity or guild, and to keep custody of the lands and tenements, revenues, services, possessions, goods and chattels of the guild.

One of the earliest ordinances of the guild on record, made at an Assembly of the Masters, Wardens and brethren on May Day A.D. 1438, indicates a tendency on the part of the fraternity or guild to become a close corporation, confined exclusively to merchants. It is to the effect that no brother of the Brotherhood of the Holy Trinity Guild should adhere to any other Brotherhood of the city of Dublin, except the Brotherhoods of Saint Anne and St. George, in any way which should be hurtful to the said Guild. The Brotherhood of Saint Anne was a purely religious guild. That of Saint George was not associated with any particular art or craft.

Quarterly meetings of the Guild Merchant were held after Michaelmas, Christmas, Easter and Midsummer. The nature of the business to be transacted at these meetings is indicated by two bye laws made in the year 1452. It was provided that a "grette quarter semble" should be held every quarter, "and that hyt be holdine allwaye the mondaye before the grete quarter semble of the sayde cytty, except the mondaye semble next after Michaelmas, the which shall be after for reyssonable cawssis and in that Semble yt be laffull to them to make brethirn and all othe lawis, reules and statuts yt is nedefull to them for ye profitte of the sayde yelde." The "grete quarter Sembles" of the city were held on the fourth Friday after Michaelmas, Christmas, Easter, and the 24th day of June respectively. No reason is assigned in the bye law for fixing the dates of the Guild meetings immediately before those of the Common Council. It is suggested, however, that the reason was to enable the Guild Merchant to influence civic legislation in the interests of the merchants through their representatives on the Common Council. At the Michaelmas Assembly of the

Guild Meetings.

THE GUILD MERCHANT 19

Council the Mayor and Bailiffs for the succeeding year were chosen. This election affected the choice of Guild officers as will hereafter appear. Besides the quarterly assemblies of the Guild Merchant, the Masters and Wardens had power to summon other assemblies at their discretion, " and in those sembles to examyne and enquere apon all mattirs done within themselfys and to correcte and execute theme accordynge to there rulys and stattutis." By a subsequent bye law of the year 1573 it was directed that the quarterly assemblies should be held between the hours of eight and nine in the forenoon.

One of the purposes for which the " grete quarter sembles " were held was the admission of new brethren. Such admission could only take place " in pleyne Semble " and with the assent of all the brethren. If any brother had a grievance against a prospective member, the latter was not to be admitted until he had made sufficient amends to the said brother (Bye law of the year 1438).

The " Vellum Book of Bye Laws " of the Guild Merchant, transcripts from which appear in the Gilbert MS referred to, opens with " A law to be read in the Quarter Assemblys: that noe brother talke in Assembly time to the disturbance of the assembly nor speak to any matter whilst another brother is speaking." Then follows the law in detail. A fine of twelve pence was directed to be imposed upon any brother who should so offend. If the fine were not immediately paid, the culprit was to be expelled the house and not admitted again until he should have paid the fine.

The bye laws of the year 1438 include the following: " All so what so ewer brothere answere nought to dwe

Somes, he schall lese l. li. wax as offt tymes as he makyth the default, But yff he hawe a Reysonable excuse." *

In the year 1452 it was ordained " that all the brethirn may be sworne to kepe all cownsayll of all matters that bene meuit (moved) in the sembles and in specyall of bargaynes that bene boght and solde upon payne of x. li."

Every brother attending the four quarter assemblies was required by a law of the year 1573 to wear a " gowne " under penalty of forfeiting six shillings and eight pence.

Guild Juries. Juries were impanelled from amongst the members to inquire into abuses affecting the Guild. Failure to attend before the Masters and Wardens when summoned to attend on such a jury rendered the members liable to fines. An example of an Inquest or inquiry held by a Guild jury in the year 1597 appears in the second book of Proceedings of the Guild Merchant, and is here given as it appears in the Gilbert MS: " The verdict of the said XII men and what they have found as hereafter ffolowth the XVIII of January *anno* 1597 according the artickles given them in charge. The first four they ignore—to the 5th they find that a brother Patrick Dixon keepeth one fford as an apprentice who is no freeholder's son." To the 6th, 7th, 8th and 9th " They ffind nothing in effeckte." To the 10th " They ffind that Perce Welshe suid Mychell Hamlin a brother of this yeld before Mr. Mayer without lyssens of the Masters and Wardings according the lawe in that behalf." To the 11th, 12th, 13th, 14th and 15th, " They saye nothing to eny gret efeckte." To the 16th " That the parties under written hath and doth intollerablye

* Gilbert MS. 78 p. 73.

THE GUILD MERCHANT

intrude upon the corporation of this yeld." "All the contents aforesaid aperith under severall of the said XII men's hands upon the ffyle of bylls for this yere."

It is regrettable that the charges in the cases in which the jury found "nothing in effeckte" are not stated. However the verdicts brought in in the other cases illustrate the nature of the Inquests or inquiries held by the Guild jury.

In one of the cases above cited a member of the Guild was found guilty of having sued another brother before the Mayor of the city without licence from the Masters and Wardens. Such conduct was contrary to the spirit of the fraternity and the letter of the law as is evidenced by this ordinance of the year 1438:* "All so yff there hap eny Waryaunce or dyscorde, wyche God defend, betwoix brethern of the sayd yeld, that than non of them shall sew othir at lawe. But fyrst he that felyth hym self grewid shall cum and complayn to the Mastirs of ye sayd yeld for the tym beynge, the wyche shall call the Brethered togeddere & make acorde betweix the personnes thus beyng at debate; and he that wyll not obey ye rewlle of the Brethered shall be put out of ye yeyld, and the Bretherred to mayntene ye othyr Brothyr gaynste hym in hys Ryght; and if anny strange man have a quarrell agayne eny brother of the yeld, yat than ye bretherhed shall maynten the Bretherhed & harre Brothyr in hys ryght; and whoo so Breke this Reule to fall in ye payne of X. li."

Settlement of Disputes between Brethren.

* Gilbert MS. p. 30.

Admission to the Guild Merchant of Dublin in the fifteenth century showed a tendency to become confined to those following the art of merchandise. Apprenticeship to the art for a number of years was becoming a necessary preliminary to its practice. The powerful Guild of the Merchants began to impose restrictions upon the carrying on of trade by the general body of citizens.

Exclusion of Non-Merchants.

In the year 1452 the ordinance went forth, " that no maner man shall hawe no maner off marchandys that comyth to ye cettie off Dublin that is boght by ye byers of ye sayd citei but he that hawe ben a prentese with a marchaunt of the sayd Citei at marchaunt craft & that he be Brether off ye sayd yeld After forme of marchandise."

It was further ordained at the same Assembly " that no maner man dwellyng within the syttye of Dublinge use no facultye of marchaundyse within the fraunchis of this cyttye bot he that hawe bene a prentyse with a marchaunte at marchaunddyssis, by the wych he is made freeman of the sayde syttie, laste than he sholde be plegyt (pleaded) by the assemble of the sayde bretherede & make a fyne, & ye proffyte thereof goo too the sayde yelde."

In spite of the declared policy of the Guild to restrict membership to merchants alone, persons of other occupations continued to find their way into the Guild Merchant. A bye law of the year 1553 makes bitter complaint " that tayllors, bowchers, shomakers and men of occupacion whych by there sayde occupacion myghte get and win there lywing ownestlye according there voccacion, as allsoo dywers othirs that neuer wan the sayde

THE GUILD MERCHANT

brothred by byrthe, marryache or prenteship, according the olde auncient lawes, usagis and customs" had been admitted to membership with the connivance of "the Masters and Elders of the sayde howse" and that the evil had grown to such an extent that "the lywinge and trade of marchaundyse all most is lost." It was provided accordingly that for the future no one should be admitted under a fine of forty pounds "unless [he] win the same by byrthe, maryage or prenteshipe."

This bye law is important in that it brings to light the fact that according to the ancient laws, usages and customs of the Guild Merchant, membership was won by birth, marriage or apprenticeship. The sons of brethren were eligible for membership by right of birth. By marrying the daughter of a member the husband became entitled to admission to the Guild by right of marriage. Those who had served an apprenticeship to a brother of the guild became entitled to admission by right of servitude or apprenticeship. The civic franchise or freedom of the city was also obtained by the rights of birth, marriage, and servitude. In admitting these rights to freedom the Guild Merchant modelled itself upon the great corporation of the city. What was a virtue in the case of the latter became a vice in the case of the former. Persons who had no connection with the commerce of Dublin were admitted to the Guild by right of birth and by right of marriage.

It was further provided in the year 1573 that no member of any other corporation of the city should be admitted as a Brother of the Guild until he had sworn to give over the liberties of such other corporation. The craft guilds are frequently referred to as "corporations."

In the same year a law was made which enacted that before any person be admitted to the Brotherhood he should serve seven years as an apprentice, then three years as a journeyman, then occupy two years for himself before

Apprentices.

he be made a stapler (that is, a Merchant of the Staple, an institution which will be referred to later). Seven years was a long period to fix as the duration of apprenticeship to a merchant brother. Such a regulation effectually limited the number of new members. It is interesting to note that the young man who had spent these long years learning the art of merchandise had to practise the art for a period of three years before becoming a Guild brother.

The taking of apprentices by the brethren, and the general conduct and demeanour of the apprentices, were matters which occupied a good deal of attention on the part of the Guild Merchant. The lot of the apprentice in the fifteenth and sixteenth centuries was not a free and easy one like that of his fellow to-day. Not alone was he under the strict supervision and control of his master while at his work at the stall, in the shop, or in the counting house, but when he sallied forth in the evening, or on a holiday morning, jealous eyes watched to see that he dressed and comported himself as an apprentice ought, wise heads shook if his amusements were aught but simple and harmless, and busy tongues carried the tale of any excess or licence to the ears of the Masters and Wardens. Woe betide the apprentice who fell beneath their displeasure!

According to the rules of the Guild Merchant, the

THE GUILD MERCHANT 25

initiation of an apprentice was a formal act to be carried out with due solemnity. A certain looseness of practice had grown up amongst the brethren which was considered detrimental to the welfare of the Guild. The preamble to a bye law of the year 1573 recites that " whereas contrary to the orders of this house, the Brethren of the same doe take unto their apprentiship their apprentices without their presentation before the Masters and Wardens the next quarter assembly then next following the taking such apprentices, whereby there is not onely such number of apprentices amongst the Company as the same is thought marvelous to the principall estates of this realme, but also this worshipfull Company is had in great derision for that so many Irish natives and others of simple birth are allowed apprentices contrary to the statutes of this realme provided in that behalfe which procureth the Government to threaten our liberties, as we doubt they will deale therein unless present reformation be used and whereas alsoe contrary to a lawe of this Guild which is that none shall be admitted to this Company but by triall of inquest as is wether he or they should be thought worthy of admittance." It was, therefore, directed that fines should be imposed upon any brethren who should be guilty of a breach of the Guild laws in this respect.

Native Irishmen were to be excluded from Guild membership in accordance with " the statutes of this realme provided in that behalfe." This was, unfortunately, a characteristic of the Guild Merchant and of the craft guilds of Dublin. The bye laws of the Guild merely reflect the policy of the central government as exemplified in the statute law and that of the civic government as shown by the ordinances of the Common Council. In the year 1454 the Common Council of Dublin had decreed " that no maner of man dwellyng within the said cite take no Iryssh prentises ne Iryssh servantes fro this day forward uppon the payn of XLs. as ofte as hit may be founde."*

That an apprentice should practise his trade for his own benefit has always been regarded by masters and journeymen as a serious breach of discipline, and contrary to old-established custom. Certain persons appear to have gained admission to the art of merchandise in the sixteenth century by becoming enrolled as apprentices and to have started then to trade on their own account, but in their Masters' names. An ordinance was accordingly made in the year 1573 to prevent illicit trading by apprentices " they being made such to enable them to trade in a covert way." Perhaps with the same object in view the guildsmen also decreed that no apprentice should be made by any merchant beyond what he needed under a penalty of forty pounds.

The following bye law, one of the many confirmed or enacted in the year 1573, throws a vivid light upon the position of the apprentice in the sixteenth century. It runs as follows :—

" Whereas divers prentizes and servants of the brethern have wasted their masters' goodes sum by pilfringe and stellinge sum by playinge at unlawfull games sum ryotously and in excesse of aparrail to the greate hurte of their masters and slander of this Company for remedeye whereof yt is ordeyned and for a lawe made in this assembly that frome hence forthe yff eny prentize or servante of eny brother off this company do pilfer or steale waste spende or play

* C. A. R. D. Vol. I. p. 281.

above the value of XIId yr (Irish) of his Masters goodes ether that he haunte taverns or live viciouslye or beget anny woman with child that prentize so offendinge in any of the premises shalbe broghte by his Master to the tolsell before the Masters & Wardens of this company and they findinge that he hathe offended in eny of the premises shall se him striped naked and also se him punished with whippinge with greene birchen roddes so much as his faulte shalbe thoghte by them to hawe desarwed whiche punishment shalbe done by two or fowre men disgized and in the presence of twelve or more othir prentizes who maye by souche example be admonished And if eny brother of this Company do conseale the faults of his servants so as this lawe be not put in execution that brother so offending uppon due proffe therreof made shall forfeit XX.s. yr (Irish) *tociens quociens* the one half to the presenter and thother half to the treazory of this yelde: And further yt is ordeyned that no brother of this yelde shall suffer his prentize to weare any appareil except yt be olde appareil of his Masters but suche as becomethe a prentize that is to say a coate of clothe decentely made without gardinge cuttinge or sylke to be wroght thereon or put thereto in anny wyse also a doublet of sm thinge so hit be not of sylke meete for a prentize wherin no silke in any wyse is to be worne also a shurte of this cowntrey clothe wth a decente band theirrto of the leike clothe and the ruff thearof to be one yard longe & the same not to be wroghte with sylke or other thing in eny wyse is to be worne, also a payre of hose whiche shall not be made of any more clothe than towe yardes being yarde broade or so muche of any othir clothe to the like quantitie and the breche of the same hose shall not be bolsterede out with ether wool heyre or eny other thinge but shalbe made with one lyininge wch shalbe close to the tieghe nether shall the same hose be cut or draven oute with any thinge or stiched wth any sylke but shalbe made playne in all respects."

The " servants " referred to in the foregoing bye law were the journeymen. A law of the Merchant Taylors' Company of London, dated 1578, makes mention of " every servant or journeyman free of the city, and a brother of this mystery."* The law of the Dublin Guild Merchant above quoted does not state what punishment was to be inflicted upon the journeyman or servant guilty of evil conduct. Perhaps he, too, was whipped like the apprentice.

At an assembly held on 13th January, 1588, it was decreed that from thenceforth no brother of the Guild should procure, detain, maintain or keep by any manner of means the servant or apprentice of any brother of the House. The penalty upon conviction before the Masters and Wardens was forfeiture of £10 to the Guild and £10 to the complainant.

The revenue of the Guild Merchant was derived from fines paid by the brethren upon admission to the Guild, amercements or pecuniary penalties imposed *Revenue of* upon members guilty of breach of the bye *Guild.* laws, quarterage—a fixed payment made every quarter by the brethren for the sustentation of the Guild and being its chief source of regular income, cesses or levies made for special purposes, and finally from the common stock or property of the Guild.

* Ashley : Economic History, p. 114.

Reference to this common stock is made in an old bye law of the year 1452, which runs :—

"Memorandum that it ys accordyd by authorytye of this assemble and from henceforwarde the newe Mastirs shall resewe the olde stok, be hit mony othir cheffware othir hidis to labowr hit to the awaille of the yelde, and that theye delywir the sayde stoke with the encrese to the newe mastirs, and soo from yere to yere to accompte therefor." This stock appears to have been distinct from the common purchases of goods made by the Guild on behalf of the brethren which will be dealt with in a later section.

The fine payable upon admission to the Guild is mentioned in a bye law of the year 1452, which states : "All soo whate man prayethe to be brother of the sayde yelde in forme of marchaundyses that he be noght admytted bot by fyne, as ye masters wardynes & he may accorde to paye yerlye, besyde that VIII.d." According to this law the fines paid yearly by the brethren were of variable amounts and were fixed by agreement between the guild authorities and the brethren individually.

When cesses or special levies were imposed upon the brethren, due regard was paid to the equitable distribution of the burden. According to a bye law entitled "A lawe for cessing brethren according to their abilities" it was provided that three or four "indifferent" men of the Guild be chosen as "commoners" by the Masters, Wardens and Brethren, as accustomed, to impose cess upon every brother of the Guild according to his ability.

Power was given to the Masters and Wardens by a bye

* Wares.

law of the year 1452 to distrain for all manner of fines, amercements and quarterage. A law of the year 1485 further provided that the Masters and Wardens were not to permit a brother whose quarterage was in arrear to share in the common purchases made by the Guild.

The bye laws of the Guild were enforced by various sanctions. Fines of varying degree were imposed for the majority of offences. A brother who disturbed a meeting of the brethren and failed to pay the fine of twelve pence immediately was expelled from the meeting, *Enforcement* and not readmitted until he had paid the *of Bye Laws.* fine, according to a bye law already quoted. Apprentices and, possibly, journeymen were flogged for misdemeanours. At a later period stocks were ordered to be purchased for the punishment of apprentices. Expulsion from the Guild was the penalty imposed by a bye law of the year 1573 upon brethren who failed to pay for merchandise received. Henry VI.'s charter gave power to the Master and Wardens to commit to the city prison any foreigner buying goods in retail or in gross from any but the merchants of Dublin. The Masters and Wardens had power under the bye laws to commit brethren to prison for certain breaches of the Guild laws. Exclusion from the right of sharing in guild purchases above mentioned was another effectual sanction. These sanctions are well illustrated by a bye law of the year 1575, which provided that if any brother struck another he should sustain fourteen days' imprisonment and be fined at the discretion of the Masters and Wardens; and if any quarrel happened between any of the brethren upon which blood should be spilt, the brother so offending should be dismissed from the brotherhood.

Dr. Gross, in his history of " The Gild Merchant,"* states: " The Gild was the department of town administration whose duty was to maintain and regulate the trade monopoly." This definition does not fit in accurately with the facts of the case so far as the Guild Merchant of Dublin is concerned. Most modern governments administer national affairs through the medium of departments. The division into departments of justice, of industry and commerce, of education and others, is familiar to all acquainted with the working of national governments. Each department is supreme in its own sphere, and has the power of the whole government behind it. The sphere of each department is carefully delimited by the national government. Keeping within those limits, the department governs or administers. Furthermore, the department is the creation of the central government. From the analogy with national government it can be shown that Gross's definition of the Guild Merchant does not apply. So far was the Guild Merchant from being a branch or department of the municipal government of Dublin that the civic authorities levied cess upon the Guild and borrowed money from it, to recover which, the Guild on one occasion threatened an action against the Common Council.† The Guild Merchant of Dublin was, in fact, co-eval with, distinct from, and subordinate to, the civic government. Subject to these limitations, the latter part of the definition,

side note: The Function of the Guild Merchant.

---

* The Gild Merchant, Vol. I. p. 43.
† Ibid, Vol. II. p. 78.

namely, that the duty of the Guild was " to maintain and regulate the trade monopoly," applies. In a later section the relations of the Guild Merchant with the civic government of Dublin will be described.

"To maintain and regulate the trade monopoly" was the *raison d'être* of the Dublin Guild Merchant. A very valuable and jealously guarded monopoly was that of the trade of Dublin possessed by the Merchant Guild collectively to the profit of its individual members. The key-note of the Guild laws is exclusiveness. The bye laws concentrate upon the one object, the preservation for the guild members exclusively of their privileged trading position.

The Guild Merchant was not a mere association of traders, like a modern Chamber of Commerce. The Guild was a great trading corporation, buying and selling goods on a large scale. It dealt not in bales of cloth, barrels of wine, and hundred-weights of salt and iron, but by the ship load. It bought for

System of Common Purchase.

its members collectively on a large scale, and apportioned the purchase amongst them according to their requirements. The selling price for the goods was fixed by the Guild. Beyond this price the guildsmen could not charge, save at the risk of incurring the penalty of a fine. It was a system which had great advantages, the chief of which was that the members obtained their wares at a much lower price than if each had to bargain individually for the goods he needed. The smaller traders were enabled to obtain their wares on the same terms as the wealthier merchants, an advantage from which they are debarred in these days of competitive trading. Furthermore, the system led to an equitable distribution of the purchased goods amongst all the brethren who wished to partake of them, thereby preventing engrossing or "cornering" on the part of one or more wealthy brethren.

The common purchases of goods which were made in Dublin during this period were effected through the medium of the "buyers for the city." In the Assembly Rolls of the City of Dublin appears a record of the appointment of "buyers for the city" made at a meeting of the Assembly or Common Council at Michaelmas in the year 1452.*

At the Michaelmas Assembly in the year 1453, John Waryng and Thomas Savage, merchant, were appointed "buyers for the city on behalf of the jurees," and John Synnagh and William Byrne, merchants, "buyers for the city on behalf of the commons." In a city bye law of the year 1454 mention is made of the "byeris for the tyme beyng." In the year 1455, Thomas Newbery, John White, John Tankard and Thomas Savage were appointed buyers for the city. Buyers for the city continued to be appointed throughout the fifteenth century.

The description of the buyers as "buyers for the city," and the fact that during the fifteenth century they were appointed annually at the Michaelmas meeting of the City Assembly, would suggest that these purchases were made by the city on behalf of the citizens generally. The records of the Guild Merchant, however, afford conclusive proof that these purchases were made by the Guild Merchant on behalf of the brethren who retailed the goods purchased

* C. A. R. D. Vol. I., p. 276.

amongst the citizens generally. This was done with the sanction and assent of the civic authorities.

The following ordinances made at a "holle Semble" of the Guild Merchant in the year 1452 bear upon this point: "In primis, that no maner man shall hawe no maner off marchandys that comyth to ye cittie off Dublin that is boght by ye byers of ye sayd citei but he that hawe ben a prentese with a marchaunt of the sayd citei at marchaunt craft & that he be Brether off ye sayd yeld After forme of marchandis."

"All soo that II mastirs of the yelde be alway II of ye IIII byers & the II wardens be all waye twoo delyweres, trewly to delywir and dewydid untoo all the brethyrin, as it shall be apoyntid by the sayde mastirs & byers, to ewery man after his degree."

"All soo anny maner off bargayne that is boght by the sayde mastirs & byers that than the mastirs & wardens shall doo somon all ye brethirhed that be marchaunts to the sayde hall & witt there what ewrye man will holde of the sayde bargayne. And yt be noght all holden at that tyme, that than the sayde mastirs, byers & wardens shall set the owerplus of the sayde bargayne apon all ye brethred that bin marchaunts, ewery man after his degree. And yff the sayde bargayne be lasse than his holdyne by the sayde brethirhede that bene marchaunts, that than the sayde mastyrs, byers & wardens schall mesore & devyde truely to ewery of theme after harr degree."

In the oath administered to the Masters of the Guild in the fifteenth century the following passage occurs:—*
"Allso whate bargayne ye makith for the cyttye ye shall

* Gilbert MS. 78.

trewlye make rewlacion to the brethirne of the sayde yelde, & trewly mynstir after the rewlis of the same brotherede."

In the year 1573 it was decreed by the Guild Merchant that brethren receiving goods bought by the Guild should pay for the same within ten days.

Fixing of Prices.
The Guild authorities fixed the price at which the brethren were to sell the merchandise which formed the subject of these common purchases. In the year 1438 it was ordered by the Guild Merchant that " Salt, yren & Collis and suche othyr merchandyse shall be sold by all the brethren of ye sayde yeld at on prise, as hit shall be notteffyd to ye Brethern by byll from ye mastirs of ye sayd yeld, apon ye payne off XX. li."

In the year 1452 the Guild decreed that " as soone as anny bargayne ys delywerid that than the mastirs & wardyns shall appoyncte a semble & call the brethirne toogythire and set a reyssonable pryse & apon all marchaundysses, and all the brethirne shall keepe that pryce and syll thereafter, apon the payne of X. li."

The common purchases made by the buyers were as a rule confined to certain staple commodities. Those usually mentioned in the Guild records are salt, iron, coal, wine, pitch and resin. A bye law* of the year 1483, however, indicates a much wider field. It reads: " Allsoo hit is ordyned by the assemble that all manner of marchaundis that comithe with allyants as well merceri as groceri balry habbirdashe and all manner of warris to be bought by the byers and to be delywerid among the bretherne by the Wardens wth the oversight of the Master as salt yerne wyne

* Gilbert MS. 78 p. 41.

colls pitche and rossyne and souche othir manner of marchaundisis affor ussyt and whoo soo brek this lawe to fall in the content of X. li. and lossing his bretherede for ewir."

The Guildsmen, indeed the citizens generally, were forbidden to anticipate the city buyers in purchasing any of these goods brought to the city for sale. Nor could they offer a higher price than the buyers offered. Even if the buyers refused the bargain offered, the brethren were not permitted to make individual purchases without the assent of the buyers.

With regard to the regulation of dealing in these commodities, the Common Council of Dublin and the Guild Merchant worked in harmony. At an Assembly held at Michaelmas in the year 1454, the Common Council decreed:* " that no maner of man dwellynge in the said cite shulde not intermitte ne by salte, ire, pych, rosyne, collys, ne no portage that commyth within the fraunches of the saide cite in no shippis but onely the byeris for the time beyng uppon the payne of c. s. by actorite of this presente semble wso do the contrary."

Two years previously the Guild Merchant had made a bye law as follows: " Allsoo that no brothir of the sayde yelde by noo marchaundyssys, that is too say, salt, wyne, yerne & collys that commys to be solde too the Syttye, tyll the IIII byers hawe forsaken yt & that he hawe lewe of the IIII byers, apon peyne of XX. li."

These bye laws must have been frequently infringed, for the Guild Merchant found it necessary to impose drastic penalties in the year 1485. A bye law of this year

* C.A.R.D. Vol. I. p. 283.

reads: "Allsoo hit is ordeyned that no marchaunte of the Cittye by noo maner yorn, salt, colls, wyne, pytche, ne rossyne that bene poynted hythire to ye cittie wythe owte consente, assent or lewe of the IIII byers; and yff he doo, too paye to the yelde c. s. & too be putt out of the yelde & the bargayne to be dystribute among thebretherred. And yff hyt maye be fownde that enny man graunte othir profyre anny penny to annye forrene marchaunte more than the IIII byers proferythe without lewe of the sayde IIII byers he to fall in ye forsayde payne."

The purchase of wine is specially dealt with in a bye law of the year 1533, which throws a vivid light upon the system of common purchase, namely: "That noo brothir of the sayde trynyte yelde, ne othir inhabytante of the Cyttye of Dublin shall bye anny winnis within the stremmis and lybertys graunted to the sayde cyttye, But onely mastir mayor and the mastirs and byers of the sayde yelde for the tyme being, and when annye winnis shall com, after a comenaunce* had and a pryce drywin betwyxe the mastirs and biers aforsayde and the marchaunts of the winnis, and thereuppon the wardins of the sayde yelde send to the brethirne of the same to knowe whate ewery brothir will holde, then after relacion made by the wardyns to the mastirs and byers aforsayde whate the bretherine will holde, yf the Mastirs and byers persewe there bye that that wyne maye not be holdin & thereupon refuse and gywe ower the bargayne, Yet all this wythstanding, no brother ne inhabytante aforesayde shall interprise ne presume to bye the winnis soo refused, ne anny parsell thereof, wythowte

Purchase of Wine.

* Agreement.

especyall lycense of the master and byers aforesayde; and in kase anny of the sayde bretherine hawe lycense, as aforesayd, to by the wines so refused and thereuppon bye them, then all suche bretherine shall hawe that porsyon of winnis that then was contendid to holde at the wardings desyre uppon the sendinge of mastir mayor and the mastyrs and byers, as aforsayde to the same pryse as they shall be boughte and allsoo that anny mastir of the Cyttye, yff he will, maye hawe a hoggyssed or a bott of wine for his owne drinkine to the sayde price, and whatsooewer brothir or brethir attempte to infreing or breke this sayde lawe in anny poynte, as oftin timis as he or theye soo doo, that same brothir or brethirne shall forfeyte X. li. the oone holfe to the mayore and baillyffis for the time being, the othir halfe to the trynnyte yelde."

A bye law of the year 1573* lends an interesting human touch to the Guild records. It prohibited merchants from privately tasting and marking wines bought for the community, so that they might know which to choose when the wines were delivered by the Wardens.

The brethren were required by a bye law of the same date to pay for their share of the common purchase within ten days. Should a member fail to pay, the Masters and Wardens, in order to preserve the credit and good name of the Guild, paid for the purchase. The defaulting member was expelled for one year and only re-admitted to the fraternity on paying a fine equal to four times the value of the merchandise received.

The profits of trading in the commodities mentioned were confined exclusively to the brethren of the Guild. The

† Gilbert MS.

THE GUILD MERCHANT 39

members were strictly forbidden to buy or sell goods on behalf of and for the profit of non-Guildsmen, whether of the country or foreign. "The Reule & ordynance of the Trenite yeld of Dyvlyng ordeynit & made *Profits of* by a holde semble" in the year 1438 *Trading* contains the following provision: "All so *Confined to* no Brothyr of ye sayd yeild schall by ne *Guildsmen.* salt ne yrne ne collis to use or awaylle of no man of the Contrey ne of ye Cittei but by hyt to his owne awaylle & use, and aftyre he hawe Cellerrit hyt, hyt schall be lewfull to hym to syll hit out of his cellerre by wyght, yrne, salte & collis, & in none other maner, apon payne of X. li."

In the year 1452 the Guild decrees that "noo marchaunte being brothir of the sayde yelde by no maner of marchaundyssys inwarde ne outwarde to delivir to noe man of the country as the bargayne is bought apon payne of XX.s." And further "that no brother of the sayde yelde ne none of there membe be attorne for no maner of man ne wooman to flaundyrs ne to none othir plase, no to bye none of there goodys in collor and let to hawe the profyte thereof, bot hyt be for a brother of the sayde yelde or a freeman of the syttye of Dublin that wolde sene for stoff of his howssolde, apon the peyne of V. li."

The monopoly enjoyed by the members of the Guild Merchant did not extend to victuals or foodstuffs the trade in which was open to all the citizens. This important department of trade was expressly excluded from the grant to the Guild made by the charter of Queen Elizabeth.

A later ordinance of the Guild forbade members to aid or abet foreigners in carrying on trade in Dublin with aliens under pain of dismissal from the fraternity.* This law reads: "Allsoo hit is ordined by semble that no man that is resident of the citty of Dewling shall supporte nether mayntene no Lumbarde, byrtton, ne Spaynnarde, nethir ne auliant to be alegere to engrose the markete of no maner ware, ne bye ne sill wyt no alliant; but when ye comithe a ship with anny ware that then lawfulle the mastir and byers chosin for to by there goodys after harr discrecion, and to be delywerid among the brethirne by the wardyns with the owersight of the master; and when the ship is delywerid, the alient to resewe his payment, and so to depart with the same shyp othir with som othir shyp by soche days as the mastir will award; and who contra this lawe to lose XL. li. and to be put owt of the brethred forewir."

A further bye law was enacted by the Guild in the year 1516: "that no Lorde, gentyleman, Abbaye, freman ne forrine, excepte only bretherine of the yelde, shall not be serwid of salte, yerne, collis, wine ne othir warris at the keye ne at the kran by watter mesure or kran weyght in, noo wyse; and that no mastir, byere, ne wardine yewe lysins to the contrairie hereof, upon payne of XX.s, as often as any of them offend, withowt grace; and that none of the bretherne yew anny parte of his complement to anny othir not beinge a brothir, ne take up in his holding to gywe any othir (by) colore or otherwise, upon payne of XIII.s. IIII.d. as often as he offendithe, withowte grace, & half of the sayde pennalty to the finder of the sayde pennaltis & the othir halfe to the Balliffis, and no mercye to be yewin."

Notwithstanding the Charter of Henry VI., which

* Gilbert MS. under date 1573.

THE GUILD MERCHANT 41

forbade strangers to buy goods in Dublin from any but merchants of the city dwelling therein, and the various Guild bye laws restricting the art of merchandise to the members of the Guild, a considerable amount of illicit trading was carried on to the detriment of *Illicit Trading.* the Guildsmen, as appears from the preamble to a Guild law of the time of Edward VI., namely: "Memorandum, Where as dywerse and many straungers as well forrens as aleans, being the kings subjects and othirwyse, doo dalye (resorte) unto this ye kyngs mayestyes Cyttye of Dublin and there demurr and hawe there abood and dwelling, wch dothe from tyme to tyme dayly by and syll by retaylle and parcells at there will & plesure all kinde of marchaundyssis in lyke maner and sorte as those that be made fremen of the sayde Cyttye dothe contrary to the lybertyes and auncient usagis of the sayde syttie, unto the grete lossis, domages & impow(er)ysshing of the mastirs, wardyngs and brethirne of the sayde trynyte yelde being established by auctoritie of parliament & auctorryssed by the same to make and establyshe all suche ordynaunces as they shall thinke mete frome time to tyme for the rulle & gowernaunce of the sayde yelde and fraternytie of the same and of all othir the inhabytaunts and fremen of the sayde syttye, and lyke to ensuing to there utter dekaye, unlesse the same be the sown be redressyt; for remedye whereof the 1111th frydaye next after the feast of sayncte myghell the Archangyll, being the XXth day of octobir in king Edwarde the VIth by the grace of God king of England, fraunce and Erland, defendor of the faythe, at semble then holdine in the tollsell of the sayde syttye of Dublin, It is ordyned, enacted and establyssed by the Mastirs, Wardyngs and bretherne of the sayde yelde, being awctorrysed, as aforsayde, that from henseforthe no manner of person ne persons, what so ewer he or they bee, be he or they subjects unto the Kyngs mayestye or othirwyse, being no freman made within the sayde sytty by the lawis and lybertys of the same, shall by or syll by retaylle or parcells anny manner of kinde of merchaundyssis or warris to or with anny straungers, forren or alien, be he or they the kings mayeste is subjects or othir wyse within the sayde syttye, lyberties or fraunches of the same, only to or wythe the fremen of the sayde Cytty so made, as is aforsayde, upon payne of forfayture of ewrye thing soo to be solde or bought contrarye to the tennor, porporte and trewe mennyng of this present ordinance; the one halfe thereof to the seysere and takere, and the othir halfe to the thersurere of the sayde cyttye for the time being to thuse and behoffe of the mayor, ballyffs and syttysins of the same; and that the syller and retayller, as oftine as he or theye shall offend contrary to the tennor and trewe mennyng of this present ordynnance, shall forfaite X. li, to be satysfyed & delywerid unto the thesurer of the behowffe of the sayde cyttye for the tyme being, unto the use and behowffe of the Mayor, ballyffs and syttysins of the same; and that the mayor, ballywis for the tyme being shall cawse ewery suche syller and retayller to be imprysoned in the comen gyll of the sayde cyttye, there to remayne tyll suche time as he the sayde syller & retayller doo satysfye and paye unto the sayde treasurer for the time being the sayd X. li. prowydid alwaye that this ordynance shall not take effecte tyll suche a tyme as it be openly red in

THE GUILD MERCHANT 43

the markete place in a market daye in the sayd cyttie."

In this bye law the Masters, Wardens and Brethren of the Trinity Guild asserted a right to make ordinances not only " for the rulle & gowernaunce of the sayde yelde and fraternytie of the same," but also " of all othir the inhabytaunts and fremen of the sayde syttye." A great number of the Guild laws did, in fact, affect the general body of freemen and inhabitants. In this case a moiety of the goods forfeited and the whole of the pecuniary fine went, not to the profit of the Guild, but to the benefit of the civic exchequer. The law being of general effect, was published in the market place.

In the year 1577, Queen Elizabeth granted a Charter to the Guild Merchant confirming the Letters Patent of Henry VI. and formally incorporating the *Charter of* fraternity. By this Charter it was granted *Elizabeth.* that the members of the fraternity or guild should have sole power and authority to buy and sell in gross or by retail all kinds of merchandise, all manner of victuals only excepted, brought into the city, suburb, liberties or franchises of the said city, either by sea or land. And that no foreigner, merchant, stranger or other person whatsoever, not a member of the fraternity or guild, should buy or sell, or offer for sale any merchandise, save as excepted, in gross or by retail within the said city, liberties or franchises, or within the circuit, ambit, suburb, or precinct of the Cathedral Church of Saint Patrick of Dublin or near Dublin, or within the place or places commonly called " the Bishoppes glebe," or within the circuit, ambit or precinct of the Cathedral Church of the Holy Trinity within the said city of Dublin, commonly called "Christes Churche," or within the ambit or precinct of St. Sepulcre or the Abbey of the Blessed Virgin Mary or the Abbey called "Thomas Courte" unless from or to a merchant of the said Guild under pain of forfeiture of the merchandise bought or sold or offered for sale. Foreigners and merchant strangers were further required to bring all their merchandise, victuals only excepted, to the place called "le common hall" of the said city or to such other convenient place or places within the said city, suburb, franchises or liberties as might be assigned for the purpose by the Masters and Wardens under penalty of forfeiture of all merchandise deposited elsewhere. In "le common hall," or other place assigned by the Guild authorities, foreigners, merchant strangers, and other persons, not admitted to Guild membership, were to sell their wares. Goods so deposited for sale were not to be removed for a period of forty days without the special licence in writing of the Masters and Wardens under penalty of forfeiture. Power was given to the Masters and Wardens to inspect and examine all places within the aforesaid limits in order to see that these regulations were not contravened. Any goods bought or sold contrary to the Charter, or deposited in an unauthorised place, were to be seized and converted to the use of the fraternity.

The Common Hall. Mention of this "Common Hall" is made in the Dublin municipal records prior to the date of Queen Elizabeth's Charter. At the meeting of the Assembly held after Christmas in the year 1556, the following laws, amongst others, were made: "The keaper of the commen haull shall suffer no forreyne to enter the haull for cheaping or

THE GUILD MERCHANT 45

bieng of waris, saving souche as be awners of the waris; and if the keper do the contrarie, then he to forfaict for every time VI.s. VIII.d., halfe to the Shiryves and informer or spier, and halfe to the treasorie."

"The clerc of the commen haull of this cittie shall make a boke of all suche waris as shalbe brought to the said haull, and of the names of them that shall bye the said waris, upon payne of forfaictur of XX nobles sterling to the tresorie and losse of his office if he be founde faultie therein, and that he shall keape watche hymselfe with a mastyve dogge nightlie, and shall have for his paynes II.d. of every poundes worth of waris there solde, and shall have of every pack (of) waris that shalbe taken forth the said haull unsold I.d. out of the pounde, and of fardels and souche outher lyke after the rate aforsaide."

"No pewtrer bringing any pewter to be solde out of England or elsewhere, being no freman of this cittie, shall sell any their pewtyr tyll the same be brought into the commen hawle, ther to be solde onelie in gros to fremen of this cittie, upon payne of forfaictur of all suche waris as the said forreyne pewtrer shall be founde selling contrarie to this ordre, thone halfe to the spier and fynder, and thother halfe to the treasorie."

In the year 1586, nine years after the date of Queen Elizabeth's Charter, the Guild Merchant enacted a bye law in amplification of the details of the Charter and of the civic ordinance of the year 1556. It directed that every stranger bringing merchandise to the city to be sold should bring the same to the Common Hall or Common Cellar, and that the merchant stranger should be taken by the Wardens or Clerks before the Masters and Wardens of the

Guild, to depose whether he brought any more goods than the quantity placed in the Common Cellar. The Clerks were to keep a book having an account of every man's goods. They were not to permit any goods to be sold to any persons but brethren of the Guild, nor even to them without licence from one of the Masters and Wardens. The Clerks were to take notice of what every brother bought, to the end that none of those goods should be sold to any but a brother of the house, nor be retailed in any of those places but by way of distribution amongst the brethren. Four or six brethren were to watch the landing of wares coming to the river, to the end that they be brought to the places appointed.

The Guild Merchant and the Guild of the Staple. The records of the Guild Merchant and the civic records contain a number of references to the Staplers or merchants authorised to deal in Staple wares, namely, wool, hides and sheep-skins. In the "White Book" of Dublin are recorded the Ordinances of the Staple of England, Ireland and Wales issued by Edward II. at Kenilworth on 1st May, 1326, and which the King commanded the Mayor of Dublin to cause to be proclaimed, published and observed in that city and throughout his bailiwick. Under these ordinances aliens were permitted to purchase wool, hides, skins and other merchandise in Ireland at Dublin, Drogheda and Cork only. Merchants of Ireland desiring to convey wool, hides or skins from the Staples to sell elsewhere were not to remove them from the Staples until they had been, during fifteen days, on sale there. Wool, hides and skins were not to be exported unless from the Staple towns.

THE GUILD MERCHANT

Merchants were to be governed by the Law Merchant in all affairs connected with merchandise, transacted at the places of the Staple. Wool merchants were to be empowered to appoint Mayors of the Staple.

A number of other Irish towns were from time to time raised to the dignity of Staple towns. Dublin remained for centuries a Staple. The ordinances of the Staple of England, Ireland and Wales aimed at controlling the export trade in Staple commodities and facilitating the collection of revenue. The regulation of trade at each of the Staple towns in Ireland was carried out by the Guild of the Staple of which the chief officers were the Mayor and two Constables.

In the year 1526 the following reference to the Staple occurs in the records of the Guild Merchant:—

" And, it is concludid by holle fraternyte of the Trinite Yelde here assembled the mondaye nexte after Relyke Sowndaye, the XVIIIth yere of the Reynge of our sowerayne Lorde Kinge Henrie the VIIIth, that no man free ne forron shall lade or ship anny maner woll, hidis othir stapill warre, sawing onely marchaunts of the stapill, and theye so lading to make ther entre thereof befor the mair of the stapull for the tyme being, upon peyne of X. li. *tocyens quociens*; & that no marchaunts of the stapill sell anny stapill ware to anny man sawing to a staplere within the land, apon the same payne, prowidid that no Staplere by this lawe be restrayned to sell hidis to straungers for mony or ware, as hathe bene ussed in timis past."

The institution of the Staple at Dublin conduced to the better supplying of the citizens with important commodities which had to be imported from abroad. At an assembly of the Guild Merchant in the year 1544 it was agreed that no Stapler of Dublin should sell hides to any persons save those who brought the value of the said hides in iron, wine, salt or grain, or in any other merchandise from France, Flanders, Spain, Britain or elsewhere. Merchants bringing the wares above-written were empowered to buy the value of one quarter of said wares in hides above the quantity of the said wares sold by them to any Stapler. The penalty for breaking this statute was £40, whereof one half was to go to the Mayor of the Staple and the Masters of the Guild, and the other half to the City and to the finder of the offender.

According to a Guild law of the year 1573, before any person should be admitted to the Brotherhood he was required to serve seven years as an apprentice, then three years as a journeyman, then occupy two years for himself before he be made a Stapler.

The Staplers, accordingly, were no ordinary merchants. Dr. Gross says:* " The staplers seem to have constituted a higher branch of the Society of Merchants, probably consisting of its wealthier members." They seem, in fact, to have formed a Guild within a Guild. In the same year as the above-mentioned qualification for becoming a Stapler was prescribed by the Guild Merchant, it was ordained that the Mayor of the Staple should be elected yearly by the " Company of Staplers " in the Quarter Assembly holden next after the feast of St. Michael, and that the person so elected should be certified to the Court of Chancery " accordinge thaunciente usadge of this

* Gross: The Gild Merchant, vol. 1, p. 147.

THE GUILD MERCHANT

cittie." The record proceeds: "This lawe is thoghte metye to be enrolled amonge the lawes and ordenans of the Staple then to be amongeste the lawes of the bretherede."

In Gilbert's Calendar of the Ancient Records of Dublin the name of Walter Kelly appears as Mayor of the Staple and one of the "Keepers of keys of treasury" for the year 1530-1531 and again for the year 1531-1532. At the Michaelmas meeting of the City Assembly in the year 1532, Thomas Barbe was appointed Mayor of the Staple. He had been Mayor of the city in the year 1530. In the year 1533, Nicholas Gaydon became Mayor of the Staple. He had been Mayor of Dublin in the preceding year. Robert Shillyngford, Mayor of Dublin in 1534, became Mayor of the Staple two years later.

In the year 1558 the following bye-law was enacted by the Common Council of Dublin, namely: "That the Maior of this cyttie shall henceforth, after his Maioraltie ended, be, the yere following, elected master of the Trynitie Gild, and the yere after that Maior of the Staple, and the yere then folowing, tresorer, without that just cause to the contrary be moved in the tyme of the eleccion."

An interesting institution with which the Guild Merchant was closely associated was that of the Master Porters.

The Guild Merchant and the Master Porters. From about the middle of the fifteenth century Porters for the city were chosen each year at the Michaelmas Assembly of the Common Council. In the year 1457, Richard Tory, Simon Lardagh, Thomas Gerrot, John Gerrot and Richard Blewe were appointed "Portowrys." In the year 1463 four Porters were appointed, the number including three of the foregoing. Four years later three appointments were made, amongst them being John Gerrot and Richard Blewe. Generally, four Porters were appointed. Re-appointment of one or more of the Porters for a number of years was common. As an illustration of the close connection that existed between the Common Council, the Guild Merchant and the Porters, it may be mentioned that the Porters of one year were sometimes "Buyers for the City" another year. Three of the five Porters appointed in the year 1457 were Buyers for the year 1459.

The Guild Merchant made a number of bye-laws dealing with the Porters. From these it appears that each of the Master Porters had under him a number of ordinary Porters or bearers. The duties of the Porters were to weigh and measure corn, coals, salt or any other merchandise offered for measurement and to transport these goods from place to place in the City. The Guild Merchant regulated the distribution of work amongst the Master Porters, fixed the rates for the measurement and carriage of coals, salt, grain, and other merchandise. The Masters and Wardens of the Guild were empowered to punish porters or bearers refusing to obey the Master Porter under whom they were placed. A number of undated bye-laws of the Guild dealing with these matters appear in the early part of Gilbert's copy of the Guild Records.

* Gilbert MS. A.D., 1573.

CHAPTER II.

THE CRAFT GUILDS.

CHAPTER II.

The Craft Guilds.

BY the end of the fifteenth century the craftsmen of Dublin had arrived at a certain degree of organisation. The followers of different crafts had become organised into distinct bodies capable of corporate action and taking part in their corporate capacity in the life of the city. One of the most interesting records of mediaeval Dublin is that of the law regulating the pageant that was held in the city on Corpus Christi Day—a pageant that for sheer picturesqueness can scarcely have been excelled in any town in Europe. To this pageant the Guild Merchant and the various bodies of craftsmen contributed, each in the allotted manner.

The Pageant of Corpus Christi Day.

The "Chain Book" of Dublin, so called because it was chained for the use of the citizens in the Tholsell, or Assembly Hall, contains a record of the pageant as follows:*

"The pagentis of Corpus Christi day, made by an olde law and confermed by a semble befor Thomas Collier, Maire of the Citte of Divelin, and Juries, Baliffes and commones, the IIIIth Friday next after midsomer, the XIII yere of the reign of King Henri the VIIIth (1498):

*C. A. R. D., Vol. I., p. 239.

"Glovers: Adam and Eve, with an angill followyng berryng a swerde. Peyn XL.s.

"Corvisers: Caym and Abell, with an auter and the ofference. Peyn XL.s.

"Maryners, Vyntners, Shipcarpynderis, and Samountakers: Noe, with his shipp, apparalid acordyng. Peyn XL.s.

"Wevers: Abraham (and) Ysack, with ther auter and a lambe and ther offerance. Peyn XL.s.

"Smythis, Shermen, Bakers, Sclateris, Cokis and Masonys: Pharo, with his hoste. Peyn XL.s.

"Skynners, House-Carpynders, and Tanners, and Browders: for the body of the camell, and Oure Lady and hir chile well aperelid, with Joseph to lede the camell, and Moyses with the children of Israell, and the Portors to berr the camell. Peyn XL.s. and Steyners and Peyntors to peynte the hede of the camell. (Peyn) XL.s.

"(Goldsmy)this: The three Kynges of Collynn, ridyng worshupfully, with the offerance, with a sterr afor them. Peyn XL.s.

"(Hoopers): The shep(er)dis, with an Angill syngyng *Gloria in excelsis Deo.* Peyn XL.s.

"Corpus Christi yild: Criste in his Passionn, with three Maries, and angilis berring serges of wex in ther hands. (Peyn). XL.s.

"Taylors: Pilate, with his fellaship, and his lady and his knyghtes, well beseyne. Peyn, XL.s.

"Barbors: An(nas) and Caiphas, well araied acordyng. (Peyn) XL.s.

"Courteours: Arthure, with (his) knightes. Peyn, XL.s.

THE CRAFT GUILDS

"Fisshers: The Twelve Apostelis. Peyn, XL.s.
"Marchauntes: The Prophetis. Peyn, XL.s.
"Bouchers: tormentours, with ther garmentis well and clenly peynted. (Peyn), XL.s.
"The Maire of the Bulring and bachelers of the same: The Nine Worthies ridying worshupfully, with ther followers accordyng. Peyn, XL.s.
"The Hagardmen and the husbandmen to berr the dragoun and to repaire the dragoun a Seint Georges day and Corpus Christi day. Peyn, XL.s.'

The pageant of Corpus Christi day must have been one of the great events of the year; for those taking part in it, probably the greatest. It is easy to imagine the rivalry that must have existed between the different bodies of craftsmen, vieing with one another to have the most successful representation. The pageant consisted, not of a series of *tableaux vivants*, but of a succession of mysteries or miracle plays performed in the open on movable stages which were transported from street to street.* The actors had for audience all Dublin, every man, woman and child, as well stranger as denizen, striving to be present—a large and appreciative, though doubtless a highly critical audience.

Twenty-eight occupations are mentioned in the regulations for the pageant. The law dealing with the pageant was already "an olde law" when confirmed by the Assembly in the year 1498. This law affords interesting evidence of the degree of organisation of industry in Dublin in the fifteenth century.

* See interesting account of the Religious Customs of Dublin Guilds by Rev. Myles V. Ronan, M.R.I.A., in *Irish Ecclesiastical Record*, September, 1925.

THE GUILDS OF DUBLIN

None of the records which have survived of the craft guilds dates back as early as those of the Guild Merchant. It is difficult to state when many of the craft guilds of Dublin first took shape. The charter granted by Prince John in the year 1192 contemplated and authorised the establishment of craft guilds. Under that charter the citizens of Dublin were granted the right of having all their reasonable guilds as the burgesses of Bristol had.

In the year 1835 the Commissioners appointed to inquire into the state of municipal corporations in Ireland, inquired *inter alia* into the origin and then existing state of the Dublin Guilds. In a supplement to their Report on the City of Dublin they deal with the Guild Merchant and then state: " The following are the charters of the remaining guilds, as far as we have been able to discover:—

Guilds	Charters
Smiths	Hen. II 14 Edw. Car. II.
Barber-Surgeons	25 Hen. VI. Eliz.
Bakers	4 Edw. IV. Eliz.
Cooks	22 Hen. VII. 7 Eliz. 1 Jac. I. 4 Jac. II.
Tanners	17 Edw. I. 4 Jac. II. 7 Will. III.

THE CRAFT GUILDS

Guilds	Charters
Tallow Chandlers	{ Edw. III. { 26 Car. II.
Glovers and Skinners	{ Edw. I. { 4 Jac. II. { 1 Anne.
Weavers	{ Hen. II. { 4 Jac. II.
Carpenters &c.	{ 23 Hen. enrolled { Rot. Pat. { 27 Eliz. m. 9
Shoemakers	{ 5 Edw. IV. { Henry VIII. { 4 Jac. II.

Guilds of an origin later than the sixteenth century have been omitted from the above list. The Commissioners do not state whether the charters were produced to them, nor what evidence was adduced. Only in the case of the Carpenters' guild is a reference to the enrolment of the charters given.

Craft Guilds in Municipal Records. The Dublin municipal records afford evidence as to the existence of a number of craft guilds in the fifteenth and sixteenth centuries. In the following pages are given details of the earliest references to individual guilds as they appear in the municipal records.

A bye-law of the year 1454 points to the existence of a general organisation of the crafts. It ordained that apprentices should not be admitted to the freedom of the city until they were equipped with arms, and that the persons so equipped should appear " at two tymes in the yere befor the wardyns of the Trinite Yelde for the merchandis, and for all other prentises the maisteris of every (craft). The word " craft " is supplied by Gilbert in the Calendar. Another civic law of the year 1461* decreed that no " fisher," butcher nor baker should be " fre in ther crafte withowt that thay pay custum therfor, except them that hath boght hyt."

Further mention of the butchers is made in a civic law of the year 1484 which leaves no doubt as to their being then organised in a guild of their own. This law reads : " That it is ordyned bi auctorite of this semble that the bouchers of the saide cite shall ordeyn betwix them a keper of the flesshambles of the same, to locke and steke the dorres and wyndouus of the saide shambles, and so kepe them fast at all tymes but when the said bouchers selleth ther flesshe in the same. And giff *Butchers.* the saide durres and wyndowes may be founde opyn anny tyme without the said bouchers be theryn occupied, that then it be lawfull to the Maire and Bailliffes of the said cite for the tyme beyng to take of the maisteres and wardynes of the said bouchers for the tyme beyng VI. s. VIII. d. as ofte tymes as the said dorres and wyndouus bethe opyn, except as it is abow said, halfe therof to the court of the said cite and the other halfe therof to the tresory."

From this date a long period elapses before any mention of the guild organisation is made in the municipal records. In the year 1555 the City Council enacted that, inasmuch

* C. A. R. D., Vol. I., p. 311.

THE CRAFT GUILDS

as foreigners were found to be working at various arts in the houses of free citizens to the injury of freemen of the same faculties, it should be lawful for the Masters and wardens of the said arts or faculties to enter such houses and take the said foreigners "to be justified according to the lawes of the said facultie or art approved by the court of the cittie."

Goldsmiths. Two years later the Common Council gave an undertaking to the corporation of goldsmiths whose charter had been accidentally burnt that, if they should bring the true copy of the enrolment of their charter before the Mayor and Sheriffs they should have the exemplification or confirmation thereof under the common seal of the city. From "auncient writinges exhibitit by them" it appeared that the goldsmiths had been from "auncient tyme incorporate by the progenitors of our said soveraigne lady" (Queen Mary).

Barber-Surgeons. The first mention of the guild of the barber-surgeons in the municipal records appears in a law of the year 1557 which decrees that "no forrayne surgeon shall exercise that facultie within the fraunches of this cittie without licence of the master and wardens of the barbors and surgeons, soe longe as ther shalbe hable surgeons of cittizens, without it be that the surgeon of eny bande of the kinge's armey doo cure eny of his fellowes that is hurt in the cittie."

Like the goldsmiths of Dublin, the skinners had the misfortune to have had their charter burned. The Common Council at their quarterly meeting held after Christmas in the year 1577 "agreed that the skynners of this cittie, for that ther charter of corporacion is burnt and lost by chaunce, that yf thenrolment therof may appere, they shall have an exemplificacion therof under the cittie seale; yf not, they shall have a graunt therof by the cittie." The date of incorporation of the skinners' guild is not stated.

Skinners.

In the year 1558 the Common Council granted to the saddlers a charter establishing a "corporacion" similar to that of the goldsmiths.

Saddlers.

A lease of Isold's Tower for a term of forty-one years, at a rent of twenty shillings Irish, was granted by the Common Council in the year 1558 to "the master, wardens, and corporacion of the bakers."

Bakers.

The Bowiers and Flaichers, or makers of bows and arrows, are the next craft of whose organisation mention is made in the civic records. In the year 1559 the Common Council decreed "that no forren bowier ne flaicher shall wurk ne sell any bowes, shaftes, or arrowes tyll they agree with the company of the said occupacion being freemen of this cittie of Dublin."*

Bowiers and Flaichers.

The "companye of glovers" is first mentioned in a bye law of the year 1562 wherein the Common Council made important regulations for the welfare of this craft.

Glovers.

At the meeting of the Assembly held on the fourth Friday after Easter in the year 1563 the following order

* C. A. R. D., Vol. II., p. 8.

THE CRAFT GUILDS 61

was made: "Yt is also agreed that the gardeners of this cittie of Dublin shall have a grant of a corporacion, souch as shall be thought goode by the devise of Mr. Maior, recordor and aldermen." This is the only mention of the gardeners in the municipal records. It is possible that the "haggardmen" of whom frequent mention is made in the records were the recipients of this charter. In the law dealing with the pageant of Corpus Christi day the following occurs: "The Hagardmen and the husbandmen to berr the dragoun and to repaire the dragoun a Seint Georges day and Corpus Christi day." That the "haggardmen" were still an important body at the time when the Assembly decided to make the grant of a "corporacion" to the gardeners is evidenced by a civic law of the year 1558-9 which ordained "that every haggardman within the fraunches of this cittie shall pay for the reparacion of the dragon that have been don before this tyme, eighteen pence; and from hensforth every of them to paie yearly, for the maintenance of the said dragon and bearing thereof on Saint Georges daye and Corpus Christi daye, twelve pence to the tresorer for the tyme being."

Gardeners.

The crafts of the carpenters, masons, joiners and slaters, were all united in a single fraternity or guild. According to the municipal records of the year 1564 this guild under the name of the "corporacion of the carpendars, massons, juyneres, and heliers" were to be granted a lease of the upper room of the house called "the Taylors haule, in the Wintavern Strett."

Four Crafts in one Guild.

Cooks.

Smiths.

The Cooks who have given their name to a Dublin street are first mentioned in an ordinance of the year 1565 which forbade any person "beying of the corporacion of the quokes" to sell "any fleshe or fishe rawe, unboyled, baken or rosted" at their houses, stalls or windows.

It is not until the year 1579 that we find any mention in the municipal records of the guild organisation of what were probably two of the oldest crafts in Dublin, the smiths and the shoemakers. The goldsmiths having complained to the Common Council that they were charged with an undue share of the cesses which they bore with the blacksmiths, it was ordered that the Mayor should summon the Masters and Wardens of the smiths and the goldsmiths "and what order he take therin by the poste assembly, the same to stande and be enrolled to contynue."

The goldsmiths were represented separately from the smiths in the pageant of Corpus Christi day. The former body had been incorporated, according to evidence submitted by them to the Common Council, by the progenitors of Queen Mary. In confirming their charter in the year 1557 the Common Council gave power to the goldsmiths to choose annually one master and two wardens for the government of their "fellowshippe or brotherhede" according to the custom of other fraternities in the city. The mention of the Masters and wardens of the smiths and goldsmiths in the ordinance of the year 1579 would seem to indicate the existence of separate fraternities. It is curious, therefore, to find towards the end of the sixteenth century one common guild referred to. In the

THE CRAFT GUILDS 63

year 1593 the Common Council orders: "That the masters, wardens and corporacion of smiths and goldsmiths shall have a lese for tearme of thre skore and one yeares, begyning at Easter last past, uppon Gormonds Gate, otherwyse cauled Ormond's Gate, with the appurtenances, payeing therefore yearly to this cittie foure shillings, sterling, current mony of England, they covering the same with lede, and doing such other thinges as shalbe incerted in theire lese." At a later period two distinct guilds reappear, the smiths' guild under the name of the "Guild of St. Loy" and the goldsmiths' guild under the name of the "Guild of All Saints."

The "company of shomakers" make their first appearance in the civic records in connection with a suit instituted against them on behalf of the city. In the year 1579 Patrick Dowdall, formerly Treasurer of the city, was allowed credit in his account for disbursements made in connection with the said suit. This guild, however, dates back to the year 1427 when a charter was granted by Henry VI. authorising the establishment of a guild of shoemakers in Dublin.

Shoemakers.

The "master and company of weyvers" are mentioned for the first time in the municipal records of the year 1580. Complaint had been made by the said body "that dyvers free cittezens of this cittie putteth ther worck to forrens to be wrought and don by them contrary to a lawe and order hertofore made." It was ordered, accordingly, by the Assembly that the said law and order should be put in force, and that "no such forreners shalbe permitted

Weavers.

to entrude uppon the said master and companys occupacion, but shalbe forbidden and restrayned therof, upon the said master and companys chardges, so farr forth as ther chartor doth warrant." The craft of weaving was probably one of the earliest to be organised in Dublin. The "company of weyvers" was doubtless a long time in existence before the date of this record. In the Municipal Corporation's Report of the year 1835 the weavers are stated to have had a charter from Henry II. to whom is also ascribed the first charter of the smiths.

Tallow Chandlers. Amongst the acts and ordinances made at the Easter meeting of the Common Council in the year 1583 was one for the granting of a charter to the company of tallow-chandlers.

The company of skinners, first mentioned in the year 1577, appears to have fallen upon evil days when the following municipal ordinance was made in the year 1593 namely: "Where (as) the company of skynners hath bene of ould tyme accustomed to bere in all sesses with the company of glovers, the one halfe of theire chardge, who nowe are decayed and not of abyllytie, therefor, and forasmoche as theire trade is decayed, and that theire abyllyties is far under the abyllyties of those that in former tymes used theire occupacion: it is agreed, by the aucthorytie aforsaid, that the said skynners shall from henceforth bere with the glovers in all sesses as members of that company in state of theire abyllyties."

In the same year the municipal records contain the following further reference to the bakers, a craft which occupied much of the attention of the City Fathers:

THE CRAFT GUILDS

"Whereas it is complayned by the comons that the company of bakers, or some of them, taking the chardge of mylls aboute this cittie, worketh not onely therby the hyndrance of the cittezens, in letting them from theire steven or course for grynding theire corn as hath bene accustomed, but also the same company of bakers, to make theire owne gayne, do forbere baking brede for the cittezens for the space of eight or ten daies, in which tyme theire corn being grounde do perish in meale, with other lick iniuryes: for remedy wherof, it is agreed and ordered, by the aucthorytie of this assemblie, that the auncyent usadges of stevening every cittezen as his corn cometh into the mylls be contynued, uppon payne of grevous ponishment, to be executed by Mr. Mayor for the tyme being, as well uppon the masters, owners of the mylls, as uppon ther substytutes serving under them; and lickwyse it is ordered that, uppon complaynt of eny cittezen grevid by the abuse of the bakers in the causes above specyfyed, and proved before Mr. Mayor for tyme being, that ponishment be executed therin, as to hym shall seme convenient."

Complaint against Bakers.

The various crafts mentioned are the only crafts appearing in the municipal records down to the year 1600 A.D. as having a guild organisation. This organisation is styled variously "fraternity," "brotherhood," "fellowship," "occupacion," "company," or "corporacion."

The term "guild" is not yet used as a common designation for these bodies. Twenty-one different crafts are mentioned in the Calendar of the Ancient Records of Dublin as having a guild organisation before the end

F

of the sixteenth century. These twenty-one crafts were embraced in seventeen guilds. The barbers and surgeons formed one guild. The four crafts of carpenters, masons, joiners and heliers (slaters) were grouped in a single guild. The bowiers and flaichers are reckoned here as one craft.

Twenty-one Crafts in Guild Organisation.

The constitution and powers of the craft guilds are set forth in the charters and grants made to the guilds. At the head of each guild was a master chosen annually from amongst themselves by the members. With the master were associated the wardens, generally two in number, who were likewise elected annually. The members of the guild who were known collectively as the "brethren" included women in some, if not in all, cases. For convenience in managing the affairs and property of the guild, a committee which included the master and wardens and certain of the senior members appears to have been appointed. But it is not until a period later than that at present under review that this governing body definitely emerges under the title of the "Council of the House." The members of each craft guild formed an exclusive body. No one outside its ranks was allowed to practise the craft with which the guild was associated.

Constitution and Powers of the Guilds.

In the year 1427 Henry VI. granted a charter establishing a guild of shoemakers in Dublin under the title of "The Fraternity or Guild of the Blessed Mary." Power was given to the brethren to choose annually from amongst themselves two masters who should be of the art of shoe-

THE CRAFT GUILDS 67

makers for the rule and government of the fraternity or guild. The masters were to have custody of all lands, revenues, possessions, goods, and chattels which might be acquired by or granted to the guild. The right to have a common seal, one of the marks of their corporate entity, was given. The brethren were further empowered to establish to the praise of God and in honour of the Blessed Virgin Mary a chantry consisting of one or more chaplains who should celebrate divine service every day perpetually in the chapel of the Blessed Mary in the Church of Saint Michael in the High Street for the welfare and souls of the king, the justiciaries or governors, the brethren and sisters of the guild and their successors and benefactors. The guild was empowered to hold lands of the clear yearly value of £10, notwithstanding the Statute of Mortmain. This charter was subsequently confirmed in a Parliament held at Trim on the Monday next after the Feast of St. Lawrence, 5 Edward IV. An exemplification of the charter was granted by Henry VIII. in the eighth year of his reign at the request of Michael Harris and Thomas Walsh masters of the art of shoemakers.*

Records dealing with the Tailors' Guild and the Guild of the Goldsmiths afford further information regarding the guild system in Dublin at an early date. Under a charter enrolled on the Exchequer Roll of 33 Elizabeth and granted, according to Dr. Berry, by Henry V. in the year 1419 power was given to John Talbote and others to found a guild of the art of tailors in Dublin, to be known as the "Fraternity or Guild of St. John the Baptist."

---
* A transcript of the exemplification by Henry VIII. appears in Monck Mason's *Collections for a History of Dublin* in the "Gilbert Library," Dublin —De Rebus Eblanae, Vol. III., Part I

The members of the guild were empowered to choose from amongst themselves annually a master and two wardens who were of the art of tailors of the city and suburbs for the government of the guild. The master, wardens and brethren were to assemble at convenient times for the regulation of guild affairs. The master and wardens were authorised to inquire into all offences connected with the art, and to punish offenders by fine or imprisonment within the prison of Dublin. Persons so committed could be released only on a warrant signed by the master and wardens. With regard to internal disputes the master and wardens had cognisance of all disputes between tailor and tailor and between masters and their servants and apprentices.*

A grant made to the guild of the goldsmiths in the year 1557 followed on similar lines. In that year the goldsmiths whose charter was " by mysfortuen burned " petitioned the Common Council of Dublin for confirmation of their privileges. In support of their petition they produced evidence showing that they had been from "aunceint tyme incorporate by the progenitors of our soveraigne ladye (Queen Mary), and indowed with privyledges as is accustomable used in cases of like fraternities erected." The Common Council, in response to their petition, " graunt and agree that John Hanne, John Latton, Terrence Bryne and Adam Colman, goldsmithes of this cittie and fre cittizens of the same, shall use and exercise within the franchise of this cittie the arte or facultie of goldsmyth as bretherne of that arte

Confirmation of Goldsmiths' Charter.

* See Appendix to Municipal Corporation Report, 1835.

THE CRAFT GUILDS

or scyence: and that theye shall yerelie chose of theymself, and souche outher as they shall admytt and receve into their fellowshippe or brotherhede, a master and two wardens, as in outher fraternities of this cittie is usid: and that the said master and wardens, with the rest of the fraternytie, shall assemble theymsilves together, and make and establishe orders and lawes for the good and reasonable use of the said facultie, and for the peasible conversacion of the bretherne therof: and that none shall within this cittie or franchise therof use or exercyse the said arte or facultie of goldsmythe onelesse he be therunto receyved, admytted and allowed by the master and wardens for the tyme beinge, uppon paine to be ponyshed as outher usurpour uppon eny franchise or libertye within this cittie may by the point of the same charters be corrected and ponysshed: and the sayde master and wardens shall have the correcion, ordre and ponysshement of all suche of the said facultie as shalbe founde within this cittie or franchise to violate or breake their good orders, or outherwise to offende in eny thinge touching the said facultie or arte, in such and like manner as outher masters and wardens in this cittie may."

This grant from the Common Council of Dublin was in effect only a confirmation of rights and privileges hitherto enjoyed by the goldsmiths of the city. In making the grant an important proviso was inserted, namely, that the Mayor of Dublin for the time being should have the oversight and correction of their orders and doings as often he should think expedient. This condition enabled the Common Council to intervene at any time should the

Authority of the Mayor.

conduct of the guildsmen or the regulations of the craft appear prejudicial to the welfare of the general body of citizens.

With regard to the admission of members it was further provided that none should be admitted to the fraternity "without he be of English name and blode, of honest conversacion, and also fre cittysyn of this cittie." The grant provided that none of the faculty or art of goldsmith should be admitted or received into the franchise of the city (whereby he become a free citizen) unless he be first admitted and received to use the said faculty by the master and wardens for the time being.

Irishmen Excluded.

Important conditions with regard to apprenticeship are contained in the charter granted to the tailors above referred to. It was provided that apprentices, before being bound, should be brought before the master, wardens and clerk of the guild, and if found to be of free condition, of the English nation, and of good conversation, to be received as apprentices, and their indentures enrolled before the master and wardens within a year. The term of apprenticeship was fixed at seven years. Upon the expiration of that term, it was provided that the apprentice should be brought by his own master and by the master and wardens of the guild, to the guild-hall of Dublin, and there be received to the freedom of the city, in the presence of the Mayor and Bailiffs. Power was given to arrest, upon a certificate under the common seal of the guild, apprentices who should run away from their masters during their term, wherever the said apprentices should

Apprentices.

THE CRAFT GUILDS 71

be found, either within or without the liberties of Dublin.

A certain standard of craftsmanship was required on the part of those who sought admission to the guild. The charter provided that no one should exercise the art of tailoring within the city or suburbs unless judged sufficiently skilful by the master and wardens. The imposition of a test of their skill upon would-be-members of a guild was a common feature of the guild system in Ireland as in other countries. To gain admission to the Goldsmiths' guild in Dublin, a candidate had to serve seven years' apprenticeship and execute a piece of work of silver called his "masterpiece" which should be approved of by the wardens of the guild.

The Masterpiece.

The craft guilds, like the Guild Merchant, had a religious aspect. The latter was under the patronage of the Holy Trinity. The craft guilds were under the patronage of the Blessed Virgin or some Saint. On the day dedicated to the Patron the members of the guild met together in the chapel appropriated to their use for the celebration of Divine service. Attendance was obligatory on the part of the members. Some of the guilds maintained chantries in certain of the city churches. In other words, they appointed one or more chaplains whose duty it was to celebrate Mass daily for the spiritual and temporal welfare of the members of the guild and for the founders and benefactors of the guild, and after their death to pray for their souls. The chaplains received a yearly salary, and on feast days food and drink. Sometimes pious brethren

Religious Worship.

or citizens devised property for the support of the guild chaplain.

A grant of this nature is recorded in the case of the shoemakers' guild. In the Monck Mason Collection* entitled "*De Rebus Eblanae*" is a transcript of an old deed of the year 1434 which reads as follows: "An Indenture made between John Waryng and Juliana Lorying executors of the Will of Jeoffry Parker, Nicholas White, Chaplain, and others of the one part John Tath and James Palmer church wardens of the Church or Chapel of St. Michael in High Street of the other and Thomas Keatyng and Walter Mulghan Master of the Guild St. Mary of the said City of another part Witnesseth that said N. W. and others were enfeoffed in 2 messuages and a garden on the North side of Castle Street parish of St. Werburgh to intent that said wardens of said guild shall receive all rents and profits from same for ever for supporting one chaplain or more at the altar of St. Mary's Chapel in St. Michael's Church aforesaid according to last Will of said Geoffry Parker—and that the said masters shall keep said houses stiff and staunch for ever. If they shall fail to keep or supply said chapel with a chaplain for divine service for one day every year for ever or to keep such said houses in repair it may be lawful for the Church Wardens of St. Michael to recover and hold for ever said messuages to use of said chaplain—6 September 12 H. 6."

The records of the Guild of St. Mary Magdalen or Guild of the Barber-Surgeons of Dublin preserved in the library of Trinity College, Dublin, throw light upon

* Municipal Library, Charleville Mall, Dublin.

THE CRAFT GUILDS 73

the duties of the brethren as members of the guild. The oldest record book of this guild, a volume bound in oak and leather, opens with the Oath taken by the Master, wardens and brethren of the Guild. According to a note following the Oath it was transcribed in the year 1535 by Barnabas Kelly at the request of Thomas Grace the Master and Henry Filch, the preceding Master, according to their royal charter. The writing is in a beautiful hand and is in striking contrast with the other entries in the book which can be deciphered only with great difficulty. The opening words in the book read:—

Duties of Brethren.

"Heer foloweth the othe of the master and wardines also bretherne of Mary Magdalen is yelde callid the fraternite of the Barbor crafte of the citie of Dublin from tyme that ther charter was purchased that every of them have gywen at the time of ther creacon and ingresse into the said yelde."

According to this Oath the person taking it promised

(1) To honour God and St. Mary Magdalen on the days and at the times appointed according to the statutes and customs of the guild.

(2) To observe and keep the statutes, laudable customs, and laws of the guild, with all diligence and with the help of his goods.

(3) To humble himself "with honestie and goode manners," and so to be obedient to the master and wardens and their successors.

(4) Notwithstanding that he should "change the copi of the Barbors crafte," to bear all manner of charges as if he had continued using the "Barbors" craft during life

(5) To attend in person at any place to which he should be summoned to appear by the Master and Wardens.

(6) To desire no man's help or counsel in resisting the Master and Wardens of the guild.

(7) To give no counsel to any one in rebelling against the Master and Wardens.

(8) Should any discord or strife arise between him and the Master and Wardens or between him and another brother to "abide the sayng of foure of the bretherne within the said yelde."

(9) To pay his quarterage and all duties, mulcts, penalties, and fines imposed upon him by the Master and Wardens or to deliver a pledge to the value thereof.
"an I do not so"

(10) To take such correction within the prison or ward of the New Gate of Dublin as the Master and Wardens may command, and to remain therein until released by their order.

(11) Should he "cum owt presumptuusly of the saide warde" to pay twenty shillings Irish to the Master and Wardens to the behoof of the guild and to return within the New Gate until released.

(12) Should he rebel and disobey the master and wardens of the guild and persevere in rebellion for the space of one month, to suffer himself to be expelled from the guild without further grace and so to confess himself guilty, and

(13) Not to use either secretly or openly the barber's craft within the city of Dublin.

(14) To close the door and windows of his shop, and

THE CRAFT GUILDS 75

(15) Not to use his craft otherwise than the tenor of the charter should permit.

(16) "All the premissis and all articles within the boke or (which) may depende of them to kepe and observe."

This guild is described in the opening note as " the fraternite of the Barbor crafte of the citie of Dublin." It was not until the year 1577 that the surgeons were formally incorporated with the barbers. Prior to this date, however, members of the fraternity had been practising the art of surgery. The municipal records of the year 1557 make mention of " the master and wardens of the barbors and surgeons."

A by-law of this guild dated 1569* shows how the guild protected the interests of the individual member from infringement by his fellow members. The law reads: *Memorandum* " that it is enacted by the Mr. and Wardings of St. Marie Magdalens yild and by the consent and assent of all the brethren of the same the Xth daie of June in anno 1569 patrick bicton being mr. Patrick Coulle Rolland mery wardings that what so ever brother doth entysce or pcure eny customer from anny other brother or call in to his shop enny person or persons so knowing him to be customer to eny of the reste of the brethern to forfyet and paye for every suche faulte comited VIs VIIId. Also it is enacted by the said Mr. brethren and wardings that no brother shall not intrude nor take enny cure out of anny other brothers hands except he gyw him licence in payn of forfiture as above wrytten."

The actual, everyday life of the craft guilds of Dublin

---

* Original Record Book of Guild of Barber-Surgeons in Library of Trinity College, Dublin.

down to the close of the sixteenth century can be best learned from a study of the working of one particular guild. The guild of the tailors specially lends itself to that study. The records of no other guild contain such a mass of vivid and illuminating detail. The guild of the tailors is worthy of a special chapter.

CHAPTER III.

A TUDOR ACCOUNT BOOK.

CHAPTER III.

A Tudor Account Book.

ONE of the earliest crafts in Dublin to be organised under the guild system was that of the tailors who received a charter in the seventh year of his reign from King Henry V. Under this charter John Talbot and others were empowered to found a guild of the art of tailors of the city of Dublin, to be named the "Fraternity or Guild of St. John the Baptist."

The members of the guild were empowered to choose from amongst themselves annually a master and two wardens for the government of the guild. Power was given to the brethren to make by-laws for the regulation of the guild. The master and wardens were authorised to inquire into and punish all offences connected with the art of tailoring by fine or imprisonment. They were given cognizance of all disputes between tailor and tailor and their apprentices and servants. The charter ordained that apprentices before being bound should be brought before the Master, Wardens and clerk of the guild, and if found to be of free condition, of the English nation, and of good conversation, to be received as apprentices, and their indentures enrolled. The term of apprenticeship was fixed at seven years, at the expiration of which time the master was required to bring his apprentice to the guild hall of Dublin, there to be received into the freedom of the city, in the presence of the mayor and bailiffs. It was further provided that no one should exercise the art of tailoring within the city or suburbs unless judged sufficiently skilful by the master and wardens and admitted to the freedom of the city. Under this charter the art of tailoring in Dublin was organised and controlled for a considerable period.

Important records of the Tailors' Guild, consisting of Charters, Minutes of Proceedings and Books of Account,

Destruction of Records. survived down to the year 1922, when they perished in the destruction of the Four Courts. They had been previously in the custody of the Governors of the Merchant Taylors' School, who placed them for greater safety in the Public Record Office. Their good intention was unhappily frustrated. Fortunately, however, the utter destruction of the whole of these valuable records was counterbalanced to some extent as Sir John Gilbert had had a transcript of the Books of Account made in the year 1867. This transcript is in the Gilbert Collection at the Public Library, Charleville Mall, Dublin. The oldest Book of Account covered the period from 1550 to 1606, and consisted of the accounts of their receipts and expenditure by successive Masters of the Guild.

From the Masters' Accounts it appears that as early as the sixteenth century the Tailors' Guild was possessed

Property and Income. of substantial property from which a good portion of the annual income was derived. The property mentioned in the accounts of the sixteenth century consisted of the lands of Baskin in the county of Dublin, a house and land in Wicklow, a shop and garden in High Street, a house

A TUDOR ACCOUNT BOOK

in Oxmantown and garden in Frap Lane, and the Tailors' Hall which was situated in Winetavern Street according to the Municipal Records of the year 1564.

The following entries appear in the Master's Account for the year 1552:—

"Recd from Maystras Maude for the garden rent in the hold yere . . . . V s."

"Recd of John Spenfell for the schope rent in the holde yere . . . . V. s."

"Recd of George Buke for the holdeyerys rente of the Baskyng . . . XXXIII. s. IIII. d."

"Recd of Edwarde Harbart for the house rente in Oxmanton for the holde yere V. s."

In connection with their lands at Baskin in the county Dublin the Guild enjoyed the right of "heriot." This was an incident of the feudal tenure of land under which the lord was entitled on a change in the tenancy to claim the best beast, be it horse or ox. A local jury was summoned to approve of the selection made.

In the year 1566 the following entries occur, namely:—

"Payd to Jamys hood for goynge to ballrodrey to sewe for our herthell . . . II. s. VIII. d."

"Payd for grase to our herthell for 11 dayes & nyghtts . . . . VIII. d."

"Payd for the bringen of hyr home . . IIII. d."

"Payd more to Jamys hood that he gaive to the XII men in balrodrey that paste upon our harthell . . VII. d."

"Payd for bryngen of the harthell out of balgreffen . . . . II. s."

The Master's Accounts for the year 1575 include an item of forty shillings sterling received "of James fforster for the price of the harthiell that came from the baskin."

In addition to the rents and other dues received from the tenants of the guild, income was derived from the fines paid by brethren on admission to the fraternity and by apprentices on admission to the craft. Regular payments known as "quarterage" were made by the brethren by reason of their guild membership. Breaches of the Guild bye-laws were punished by the imposition of fines which went to fill the common chest. The use of guild property, such as torches, brought in a substantial return.

Fines Paid by Brethren.

The amount received for quarterage varied greatly. In the year 1559 the sum of three pounds and twelve pence was " recd of the bretherhode for the foure quartter days " while in the year 1576 the sum of twelve shillings only was received " of the brethren for the fower quarteradges."

The Account of James Hoode, Master of the brotherhood of the Tailors for the year ending at midsummer 1561, contains the following entries:—

" Receyved of John Kene in pte payment of his fyne for an incombe as a brother . . . VIII white testors."

" Recd of Henry Small for his incombe as a journeyman II white groats."

" Recd of Rowland Toole in pte of paymente of his fyne as a brother the VIIth of November } XX. s. st. viz. browne backs rest in testors."

" Recd of Wm. Wycke in pte of payment of his fyne for his incombe XXXII white testors."

A TUDOR ACCOUNT BOOK

"Rd. of Jeffrey Mysell the thurde of October for his incombe as a prentice VI test II grotes III ob."

"Recd of James Walshe for his incombe as a prentice . . . . VI testors."

Fines of a different nature are recorded in the following entries:—

Amercements. "Recd of Iwan Rishe for hys furste payment of hys ffyne for the adwariens that was betwyxte hym and me . . . XIII. s. IIII. d. as mone goes." (Account for the year 6 Edw. VI.)

"Recevit for a fyne of Thomas Kardif for beying absent from evensong on Saint Jhon mydripis day . . I. d."

"Itm recevit of Hughe Ameas for beyng absent of Saint John mydripis day V. d."

"Itm recevit of Cornell Seynge for being absent a Saint Jhons mydripis day for pese of evensong Id. as m⁰ g^s."

"Item recevit of Edwarde harbart for beinge absent from the begynyng of mattens Id. as m⁰ g^s."

Guild Chaplain. The items relating to fines for absence from religious worship are taken from the Master's Account for the year 1 & 2 Mary (A.D. 1554). The entries show that the observance of the Patron's feast day was a duty strictly enjoined upon the brethren. Three of these four entries make specific reference to St. John's Day. Attendance at religious services on other days seems to have been voluntary. The tailors' guild, like other Dublin guilds, maintained a chaplain or at least contributed to his maintenance. The salary mentioned in the guild records was so small that the chaplain could not have existed on it. It is probable that one of the parish clergy performed the duties of guild chaplain in addition to other parochial duties.

A number of entries relate to expenditure in connection with the guild chaplain. Eighteen pence was "pait to the preste a saint Johnys ewyn & day Mydrype." The Master's Account for the year 1 & 2 Mary opens with:— "Itm furst laid out to the preastis & clerkis at St. Jhon mydripis ewen ... VIII. d. irish." Later in the account for the said year the Master took credit for 13s. 4d. "paied to Sr. Jhon Callan your preast for the mydsomr qrtr." and 6d. "paied for drynke to the prestes & clerkis on mydsomer ewen." In the year 1556 occurs the following entry "paied to the preste for his hole wadgs for one hole yere ... III.s. IIII.d." The amount stated, three shillings and four pence, seems incorrect in view of other payments mentioned.

The following entries appear in the Account for the year 1557:—

"Paid for drinke to the priests and clerks after dyrige ... III.s. III.d."

"Paid to Sr. John Kelly for reading the Roll ... VI.d."

"Paid to the pson for his light at dryige & at masse ... XII.d."

The second entry is interesting embodying as it does the name of the priest or parson with the Elizabethan title "Sir" prefixed. "Sr Jhon Callan, your preast" was the chaplain three years previously.

The small salary or wage mentioned in the records may have been supplemented by offerings made by the brethren at Mass. The receipts for the year 1558 include the following:—" Receved at masse the Sondaye after S. Jhon ys daye of our pte of the offren XXI. d. irish" and " Item Recd of our pte of the offren S. mydrype ys daye at Masse . . . IX. d." The other part of the offering may have gone to the priest.

The items of expenditure in this year include the following:—Payed for V. copps that ys on the standartts in S. John ys churche . . . XV. d. Payd for mending St. John ys noose . . . IIII. d. ob.

The auditor's note on the Account of James Hoode for the year 1561 states *inter alia* that the said Master " must satisfie the priest for his hole yeres wages for that we have allowed him the hole yeres quarterage of all the brethern for that purpose wch. amontithe to that some and some what more."

The Master's Account for the year 1573 records that he " payd to James Quaytrod one of the proctors of St Johnsis Church for one whole yeres stipend due towards the fynding of a preeste to serve within the same church . . . XX. s. st."

Deceased Brethren. When a member of the guild died the bells of the church wherein the brethren met were tolled. A general commemoration service for deceased brethren and sisters was held from time to time and was known as " ringing the mynd." The " Month's Mind " is a term still in popular use.

The sum of twelve pence was paid " for ryngyng of Nicholas lyman ys knell in o^r churche " in the year 1553. In the Master's Account for the year 1 & 2 Philip &

Mary he takes credit for having "payed to the Clerke for ringing the mind .. VI. d." A similar sum was paid in the year 1557 as well as three pence "Paid for drinke to the Ringers." In the year 1560 the Master "payd for rengen of the mynd for brethren & systrys ... VI. d." It may have been on the same occasion that he "paid to III children of the quere (choir) ... III. d."

A number of payments were made out of the guild funds for the burial of deceased members and wives of members. The following items appear in the Master's Account for the year 1575:—"Itm for buryinge of fowre of the pore people ... VI. s." (The preceding entry refers to "oᵣ pore people."

"Itm for burying of patrick modier ... II. s."

"Itm for the buriall of Richard Kene is wyff ... XII. d."

"Itm paid for the buriall of sorrey neill ... XVIII. d."

One item in the Accounts deals with the expense of the wake of a deceased person, doubtless a member. It is recorded in the year 1576 as follows:—"Itm for bread & drink of ye wache women when denise dyed ... XII. d."

The charity of the guild seems to have extended beyond their own members, as in the same Account is recorded the entry:—"Itm paid for the pore man at the pore house called Willm is buriall & knell ... XX. d."

Charity towards the living as well as charity towards the dead was practised by the guild. A number of charitable payments were made in the year 1575, the Account for which year opens on the disbursement side with "Itm paid for the chardge of the sek people of Allhallouse ... XIII. s. III.d." A marginal note states "This was the time of the great plague." The next entry reads:—"Itm to o^r pore people at sondry times ... VIII. s." and is followed by "Itm to barnabe greshena at sondry tymes in waye of almes agreid ... VI. s." A later entry records the payment to Thomas Hay of "money in waye of almes by assent of the house" to the value of four shillings. In the year 1588 two shillings was paid "to the pore people."

Guild Charity.

A curious custom prevailed in the Tailors' Guild, namely, that of hiring out torches at burials. The Master's Account for the year 1559 contains the following items:—

Funeral Torches.

"Recevd of peter forde for the waste of the torches to the byryall of Jhon bratton ... XIII. s. IX. d."

"Recd for the waste of the torches to the buryall of Capten Wyllms ... X.s."

"Recd for the waste of the torches to the buryall of Edwarde Stappull ... XV.s."

"Recd for the waste of the torches to morrys Russell ys buryall ... III.s."

It would seem contrary to the spirit of the fraternity for the guild to make these substantial charges at the burial of members. The persons named above may have been non-guildsmen, and were perhaps important citizens at whose obsequies the guild hired out their torches. "Capten Wyllms" is unlikely to have been a tailor.

In the same account which includes the receipts for the "waste of the torches" appear a number of entries dealing with their manufacture. These entries read as follows:—

"Payd for VIII. stone of Rossen . . . XXX.VI.s."
"Payd for XXXV. *li.* of yarne . . XVII.s. VI.d."
"Payd for wynden of the yarne . . . IX.d."
"Payd for a lood of wood . . . XVIII.d."
"Payd for A lood of trowes . . . VI.d."
"Payd for the caryage of the Rossen . . . IV.d. ob."
"Payd for werdegrece . . . III.s."
"Payd for gresse . . . X.d. ob."
"Payd for the charges that was at the maken of them . . V.s. VI.d."
"Payd for the maken of them . . . V.s."
"Payd for the spykes to the same . . . III ob."
"Payd for the cordys . . . VI.d."
"a Racke to hang them . . . IIII.d. ob."

Social Life. The social life of the guild is illustrated by a number of items in the Masters' Accounts. The most frequently recurring items are those dealing with the annual banquet held on the feast of St. John the Baptist, the Patron Saint of the Guild, on the 24th day of June. The Accounts for the year 1553 include the following:—

"Itm moore payd for a p^c of whete agaynste mydsomer to make cakes . . . III.s. VI.d. as m^o g^s."
"Itm moore ffor whyte wyne & clare wyne att mydsomer . . . II.s. XI.d. as m^o g^s."
"Im moore for ale att mydsomer drynkyng . . . VI.s. VIII.d. as m^o g."
"Itm in seke the same tyme . . . II.s. XI.d. as m g."

On the same occasion the floor was strewn with rushes

at an expenditure of four pence halfpenny as money goes. The following item of expenditure was incurred probably at the same time, namely:—

"Itm moore for VI. yardes & a di. ffor a carpett to the hall borde ... XIX.s. VI.d. as mº gˢ."

A visit to the lands of the guild at Basken on 16th July 1576 seems to have been the occasion of a great festivity. The Account for that year shews the payment of the following items:—

"16th July 1576 for VI. quarts of claret wyne at IIII.d. p. qrt. II.s. and for one potle of seck XII.d. ... III.s."

"Itm for bred & drinke yt was carried to the basken the same daye ... II.s."

"Itm for the company's supper the same night ... VIII.s."

"Itm for III. qrts. claret wyne & a quart of seck that same night to supper ... XVIII.d."

A general meeting of the guild was held once a quarter. These meetings were held in the morning as was customary at the time. In the case of the Tailors' Guild they appear to have been occasions of festivity. The Master's Account for the year 1575 records the following item:—
' For oʳ breckfaste the foure quarter Dayes ... VIII.s."

The sisters of the guild appear to have been separately entertained. In the year 1595 the master took credit for two shillings and six pence expended *isters*. "for the entertaint. of the women the second quarter daie." Two years later appears "Itm for pottell of wyne to the women ... XVIII.d."

The Master's Accounts for the sixteenth century open and close on a musical note. The first and only item in the Accounts for the year 4 Edward VI. is the following:—
" Payd to the mynstralis the daye of Richard taverneres brekeffaste . . . XII.d."

In the account for the year 1600 A.D. occurs:—" Itm to the musicons the day the maior was sworne . . . IIII.s."

The Guild and City Pageants.

The Guild of St John the Baptist, like the other city guilds, took part in the annual pageant on the feast of Corpus Christi. According to the regulations for this pageant made in the year 1498 the tailors were to represent "Pilate, with his fellaship, and his lady and his knyghtes, well beseyne." The records of the guild for the year 1554 contain the following items, namely:—

" Itm paid to Steven Casse for playnge pilote a Corpus Criste day . . . II irishe."

" Itm payd for his Dynner and his Ladies . . . XII.d. irishe."

" Itm paied for gloves and trayels* to pilote . . . IX.d. irishe."

Two years later Steven Casse was again employed and paid two shillings " for plainge on corpus cristy daie."

The guild appears to have taken part also in the Pageant of St. George's Day or at least to have borne their share of the expense. In the Calendar of the Ancient Records of Dublin the following particulars of the Pageant are given:—

* trayels : the trains of the gowns of Pilate and his wife.

"The Pageant of St. George's day to be ordered and kept as hereafter followeth:

"The Mayor of the yeare before to finde the Emperour and Empress with their followers, well apparelled, that is to say, the Emperor, with two Doctors, and the Empress, with two knights, and two maydens to beare the traynes of their gownes, well apparelled, and (the Guild of) St. George to pay their wages.

"Item: Mr. Mayor for the time being to find St. George a-horseback, and the wardens to pay three shillings and four pence for his wages that day. And the Bailives for the time being to find four horses, with men upon them, well apparelled, to beare the pole-axe, the standard, and the Emperor and St. George's sword.

"Item: The elder master of the yeald to find a mayd well aparelled to lead the dragon; and the Clerk of the Market to find a good line for the dragon.

"Item: The elder warden to find St. George, with four trumpettors, and St. George's (Guild) to pay their wages.

"Item: the yonger warden to finde the king of Dele and the queene of Dele, and two knightes to lead the queene of Dele, with two maydens to beare the trayne of her goune, all wholy in black apparell, and to have St. George's chappell well hanged and apparelled to every purpose with cushins . . . russhes and other necessaries belonging for said St George's day."

This account of St George's Pageant throws light upon a number of entries in the old Account Books of the Tailors' Guild. Thus in the Account for the year 1 & 2 Philip & Mary the following entries occur:—

"Payd to themperour . . . II.s."

"Payd for gloves for themperor & empres . . . IX.d."
"Do ther breckfast & dinner . . . XVIII.d."
"Do paynting the emperors hed . . . XVIII.d."
"Itm payed to the Cutler for scowrynge of the sword . . . VI.d. irishe."

In the year 1567 the Master entered in his Account the following items:—

"Payd to the payntor for tremynge of the paganette for the Empore & for the crowen for the Emprace . . . II.s. st."

"Payd for drinke to hym . . . II.d. st."

"Payd for the empror's glowes and for the emprace . . . VIII.d. st."

"Payd for the tremynge of thempror's sword . . . VI.d. st."

"Payd for themprace ys breckfaste and Denner . . . II."

The most important aspect of the Tailors' Guild was not religious or social, but industrial. The purpose of the guild was to regulate and control the craft of tailoring in Dublin. Very valuable material bearing upon this important matter must have been contained in the Books of Proceedings of the Guild destroyed in the Four Courts. Useful, but meagre, details are however contained in the transcript of the Masters' Accounts.

Control of Craft.

These entries show that the authorities of the guild were constantly engaged in preventing encroachments upon their craft by foreigners or non-guildsmen, and punishing breaches of the bye-laws on the part of members. Under the Charter of Henry V. the Master and Wardens

A TUDOR ACCOUNT BOOK

had power to inquire into all offences connected with the art of tailoring, and to punish offenders by fine or by imprisonment within the prison of Dublin. In the Masters' Accounts occur numerous payments which were made in connection with the arrest of persons guilty of offences connected with the art. The guild employed standing counsel to advise on the question of their rights and to assist in the prosecution of those rights.

It appears from the Accounts that the guild of tailors exercised jurisdiction over hosiers working in Dublin and over the sale of hosiery by them. In the Master's Account for the year 1575 six pence is recorded as having been received "from a man from the countrey for his quarteradge of lycens to sell hose in the marketts of Dublin." A similar amount was paid by the Master to one Nycholas Sedgrave "fore aresting one that sould short hoses." The Account for the year 1587 contains the following items:—"Pd for aresting VIII. payer of stockings ... III.d." and "Pd for aresting II payer of stockings that were to be sold in the markett .. III.d." The association of the tailors' guild with the hosiers' craft can be better appreciated when it is remembered that down to Elizabethan times hose were made of stuff, cut and fashioned to the limbs in the same way as garments of cloth.

Jurisdiction over Hosiers.

A considerable part of the Master's Account for the year 1553 is taken up with payments in respect of proceedings against a certain hosier. What the hosier did is not stated. The interests of the guild must, however, have been seriously involved, as the matter went before the Mayor of Dublin, the Recorder, the Archbishop of Dublin, Baron Bathe, Justice Luttrell and Justice Howth, arbitrators or "wards men" un-named, and the Lord Chancellor respectively, but in what order it is not clear.

The following entries appear in the Master's Account:

"Itm more James Cune ffor wrytyng of the articles agaynste the hosyer . . . VI.d."

"Itm to the Sarjente ffor bryngyng of the sayd hosier II afor m^r mere . . . VI.d."

"Itm more to Stanton ffor restyng of the sayd hosier . . . VI.d."

"Itm moore for intryng a playnte agaynste the said hosyer . . . VI.d."

"Itm moore to Mr. Stanyhurst & to Mr Recorder in his chamber aboute the hosyer ys matt^r in brede and ale . . . XII.d."

"Itm to Sweteman of the newegate ffor puttyng a payre of bollts apon the hosyer . . . III.d."

"Itm to the sumnor & intryng of his name in the spirituall Courte . . . VI.d."

"Itm moore for a susspencion agaynste hym . . . XII.d."

"Itm moore the daye that Edwarde harbrt george bucke and I was in Crychur & Iwo Kyle afore m^r barron bathe & m^r Staynyhurst in ale and wyne . . . IX.d."

"Itm moore the same daye that I entryd hym in the spyrytuall cowrte for James hode ys brekeffast and myne own . . . VI.d."

"Itm moore the daye that the hosier was recd in the morro in ale & blesir to the wards men that was betwxte hym & us . . . III.d."

"Itm to one that wente wth the adwarde that was betwxte us and the hosyer to lasmole to my lorde Chansler . . . XII.d."

"Itm moore payde the daye that edward harbrt and I was before my lorde of Dublin in crichurche & the hosyer Justice luttrell & Justice howth wth bothe the officials then p^rsent when they had doone spelowyed in wyne . . . XI.d."

It is probably the same hosier who is mentioned in the Accounts the following year when four pence was charged "for entrynge of the accon against thomas hosier in the tolsele" and twelve pence "for buying sam is Diner & myne the furste quart. day after mydsomer."

In the year 1574 three pence was "payd for arestyng the taillor that wrought at St Mary abbaie." A number of tailors were arrested in the following year, including the Lord Deputy's tailor. The following entries are of interest, namely:—

Arrest of Tailors.

"Itm paid for aresting the L. Deputie's taillor . . . III.d."

"Itm paid for aresting James fforster & Cornelius dermote is servaunts for working with captaine Morres . . . XII.d."

"Itm paid for the chardge of such of the compagney as gaive attendaunce upon the M^r to arrest the erle of essex is taillor . . . VIII.d. st."

"Itm to the officers for goyng for the said taillor . . . VI.d."

"Itm for arestyng of hym . . . III.d. st."

"Itm paid for aresting forests man that wrought wth the said taillor ... III.d. st."

It is probable that the tailors who were arrested were non-guildsmen who carried on their trade without having obtained the sanction of the guild, conduct which would immediately call for the interference of the guild authorities. It is to be noted that the arrest of the Earl of Essex's tailor was carried out directly by the Master assisted by certain of the company or guild. In the year 1576 four pence was paid "To the constables of Oxmonton for the apprehending of bryan tailor."

A jury was summoned in the year 1578 to hold an inquisition with regard to one who worked at Castlebragg, doubtless an unlicensed non-guildsman. The entries relating to this event are as follows:—

"Recevid of hym that wrought at Castlebragg" .. (blank).

"Itm to XII. men that past uppon ye man at Castlebragg" ... (blank).

A clear case of the arrest of non-guildsmen for working at the tailoring craft occurred in the year 1587. The Master's entry reads:—

"Paid to one that brought me word that forryn taylors wrought in St Thomas Street ... VI. d. and for arestinge them to John Whit VI.d. ... XII.d."

Prosecution by Guild. Some years previously the guild had prosecuted certain foreigners at Blackrock. The reason is not stated, but it was, doubtless, for infringing the guild's monopoly. The Master's Account for the year 1576 contains the entries relating thereto, namely :—" Itm disburrsed uppon ye company yt went with me to Black Rock to prosecute agaynst ye forrens."

" Itm to the XII. men yt past uppon patrick Lennon at ye said Rock . . . VI.d."

" Itm to our Lerned Counsell to prosecute agaynst francis Arnold and Richard Benett (ye forrens) before ye L.Chauncellor."

Another prosecution was instituted in the year 1580, the Account for which year includes the following payment, namely:—" Itm the chardges of the Company that went wth me to the Court at Cabraghe to psecute against patrick ball . . . VI.d."

In the year 1588 the Guild again invoked the jurisdiction of the Court. In that year the Master " paid to a woman that came to beare witness to ye countie courte that davye wrought with the Dean of St Patricks man . . . VI.d."

It is a noteworthy fact that in a number of instances recorded in the Masters' Accounts persons who had infringed the rights of the guild were not dealt with by the Master's tribunal, but the jurisdiction of a higher Court was invoked Why this was so is not clear. The Accounts, unfortunately, throw no light upon the special circumstances of the cases. Under Henry V.'s charter the Master and wardens had power to inquire into all offences connected with the art of tailoring and to commit offenders to prison.

The tailors of Dublin, through their guild organisation, bore a share of the burden of defending the city and the English Pale. In the year 1575 six shillings were expended " for keeping or guarding the gate of the cittie." The Account for the year 1585 includes the following entries:—

"Itm to soldiors going to the forces £3 4s." and "It to ye soldiors that went withe ye shypp . . . XX.s." Two years later the guild equipped one Bryan Whit for a warlike expedition. The entries read:—

Defence of City.

"Paid to Bryan Whit going to a journey . . . V.s."
"more for a shape to his sworde . . . IIII.d."
"An for a ramer heade to hys caliver . . . VI.d."

The following entries occur in the Master's Account for the year 1566, namely:—

"Payd to the barbers and weweres to help ther chargs to the jorney into the northe . . . VIII.s."

"Payd to the barbers and weweres towards the second sesse to the northe the second jorney . . . IIII.s."

"For the thyrd sesse to the northe . . . III.s. Iryshe." The "jorney into the northe" was, it is suggested, a warlike expedition organised by the government or by the civic authorities in defence of the Pale. According to the State Papers for the year that district was in a disturbed, if not precarious, condition. In a letter written by Sir Nicholas Bagenall to the Earl of Leicester the writer stated that he never knew the country "so out of order" and that robbery, stealing and killing, took place throughout the English Pale. Lord Deputy Sydney in a letter to the Earl of Leicester dated 1st March 1566 dealt with the alarming power exercised by Shane O'Neill. According to the Lord Deputy O'Neill was able to burn and spoil to Dublin gates and go away unfought.

In this year the Tailors Guild merely contributed to the expenses of the weavers and barbers of their "jorney into the northe." Some years earlier the tailors themselves

A TUDOR ACCOUNT BOOK

bore their turn. The Master's Account for the year 1557 includes the following item, namely:

"Paid for VIII. yards of white fustian to o^r men that went to the northe . . . XII.s."

The tailors guild further contributed to a loan to the Lord Deputy. In the year 1566, when Shane O'Neill was a source of such anxiety to the government, the tailors "payd over plus to the ses mony lent to the lord Deputy III. li: VI.s.: II.d." In the year 1580 the Accounts show the repayment of a similar loan. One of the items reads:—"Recevid of Mr Nicholas duffe nowe mayor for the last lone mony lent to the late L.Justice wch was lent out of the box . . . XL.s. VIII.d."

The guild box must have been well lined about this time, as the Accounts show the guild undertaking the building of a new hall. The Accounts *Tailors' Hall.* for the years 1583 and 1584 contain a large number of items dealing with payments for material and wages. The hall was built chiefly of wood, although some stone was used in its construction, and had a slated roof. The expenditure amounted to about £89: of which £58 was spent on the purchase of material, £2 on carriage, and £29 on wages. One of the entries records the payment of one shilling for the carriage of some timber to Back Lane, where a substantial brick and stone building, known as "the Tailors' Hall" at present exists.

The relations between the guilds of Dublin and the Common Council or governing body of the city were as a rule of a harmonious nature. An exception to this rule appears to have occurred in the year 1575, when, for some reason not stated, the Master and Wardens of the Guild of Tailors were committed to prison   In the Master's Account for this year the following entries occur:—

Master and Wardens committed to Prison.

"Itm paid the keper of the newe hall for his fees of the Mr being Mr Maior put to ward . . . VI.d."

"Itm bestowid for my chardge & wardings chardges there remaining VI. dayes the some of XXVIII.s. I.d. st."

"Itm paid the gealor for both the wardings at there entrey XII.d."

"Itm more for the said Mr & wardings fees there remayninge a wick at VI.d. st. a pec (apiece) XVIII.d."

In the Account for the following year occurs this entry:—

"Itm more my chardges in ye sd hall (ye newe hall) ye night yt all ye Mrs of companyes was comytted there by Mr Mayor . . . IX.d."

Again at the close of the century the Master of the guild was in trouble. An entry dated 1600 reads:— "Pd for my chardges & ffees to the marshall att III. sewall tymes I was comitted . . . XXXIII.s. X.d."

CHAPTER IV.

THE COMMON COUNCIL AND THE GUILDS.

CHAPTER IV.

The Common Council and the Guilds.

THE Mayor, Bailiffs and citizens of Dublin were a corporation by prescriptive right. The Guild Merchant and the Craft Guilds were also corporations, but lesser corporations, strictly subordinate to the great corporation of the city. The Master of the Guild corresponded to the Mayor, the Wardens to the Bailiffs, while the Common Council through which the municipal corporation acted had its counterpart in the Council of the House, the ruling body of the Guild. Like the corporation of the city, the Guild had corporate property and administered its own finances. The Guild made by-laws within its own sphere. Its by-laws were enforced by sanctions as were the laws of the city. The Master and Wardens acted in a magisterial capacity as did the Mayor and Bailiffs. The former imposed fines upon or sentenced to imprisonment offenders against the ordinances of the Guild as the Mayor and Bailiffs did in the case of offences against the civic by-laws. In short, the whole organisation of the Guild was modelled upon that of the corporation of the city.

Over all the Guilds and over every detail of Guild administration the Corporation of Dublin, through the Common Council, exercised an over-riding authority. Between the guildsmen and the citizens generally the Common Council held the scales of justice evenly. Membership of the Guild conferred a privileged position upon the guildsman. The keynote of the Guild system was exclusiveness. To practise any craft in Dublin it was necessary to belong to the Guild associated with that craft. This exclusiveness was much more strictly preserved by the Guilds than it is by modern trade unions. The result of this exclusiveness was that the guildsmen exercised a complete monopoly over the industry with which they were associated. This monopoly frequently tempted them to abuse their position. To increase their gain they resorted to various devices. They limited the number of craftsmen in their own branch of industry. They raised prices, sometimes to an exorbitant extent. Inferior materials were used. Work was scamped. These abuses were by no means permanent features of the Guild system, but, human nature being what it is, they recurred from time to time. The general body of the citizens suffered by such abuses. In such cases as these the Common Council intervened for the protection of the citizens, and always successfully. Should the guildsmen prove obdurate in any of these malpractices the Common Council threatened to throw open the industry to non-guildsmen. Such a threat usually resulted in immediate compliance upon the part of the guildsmen. Disputes between crafts as to their respective spheres of industry were submitted to and settled by the Common Council.

From a very early period the Common Council had regulated the wages of workmen and the prices of goods. In the "Chain Book" of Dublin appear the following rates of wages, assigned by Gilbert to the fourteenth century :

COMMON COUNCIL AND THE GUILDS

For weaving cloth thirty ells in length of one colour—sixteen pence.

Fixing of Wages and Prices.

For weaving fine red cloth—three farthings per ell.

For fulling cloth thirty ells in length—three shillings; if more than thirty ells—at the proportionate rate per ell.

For each fuller, per day—two pence.
For dyeing thirty ells of cloth—three pence per ell.
For carding a stone weight of wool—one penny.
Porters: for carrying, so far as the city market, a wey of salt—three pence; a wey of iron—three half-pence.

In the year 1469, owing to the corvisers selling "a paire of shoes derrer by one penny than ever they didde," it was ordered by the Common Council that the price should be no greater than of old and that a penalty of six shillings and eight pence should be imposed upon any craftsman charging more.

Meat prices were fixed in the following year by the Council which decreed as follows: "It is ordined in this semble that the bouchers of the saide citte shall sell a quarter of ther best kyddes for one penny farthing, and of the secunde a quarter for one penny; and in likewise of ther lomes; and a quarter of ther best veles for five pence and the (second) for four pence. And the biers to pay ther silver upon ther flesshe bordes. And if the saide bouchers will not suffre the biers too take with them what thei haith boght, then thei to compleyn to the Maire for the tyme beyng, and he to pay the overpluse, and he to deliver to the biers what thei have boght, and the bouchers to pay VI.s. and VIII.d. as ofte as thei doith the contrary;

halfe therof to the tresory and the other halfe to the courte, withoute any grace."

The members of the Butchers' Guild seem to have availed of their monopoly to charge excessive prices to the citizens, a practice which resulted in the civic authorities calling in butchers from the country to supply the citizens.

Country Butchers Called In. Owing to their continuance in extorting high prices the Common Council made the following ordinance in the year 1552: "Wher of long great scarsitie and derthe of fleche have her within this honorable cittie contynniud by meanes that the bouchers of the sam ar so suffred to have ther owen voluntarie and wylfull mynds, as well in silling ther fleche at ther wyll and pleysur, as also in making promese to Master Mer to retayll the sam at certayn reysonable prises, (and all to have the bouchers of the contrie banishite and exilid forthe of the cittie) whiche they hawing so ther mynds do not onlie reise ther said wictaills to unreysonable and highe prices, (to far beyonde mesur and honestie), butt also with Master Mer have violated and broken ther said order, by whiche ther doing have not onlie hynderit the commens of this said cittie (by meanes of ther said highe and great prices), butt also it redouns to ther owen dishonestie and sham in regressing fro the said order taken with the said Master Mer. And for that the said Master Mere, with the Aldermen and comens, persewing ther shamfull and ungodlie disseving of the por and innocent people, have, with ther consent and by auctoritie of this present assemble, orderid and for a lawe mad, that it shalbe lawfull for all bouchers of the countre and others to repayr to this cittie with all kynde of fleche and other wictaills two dayes in the wike, that is to say, Twisday and Saterday, and the sam to syll in gros as by quarteris, halffe, and holde, at their wyll and pleysur, and to pas and repas to and fro the said cittie with ther said fleche, without any let, molestacion or disturbaunce of any person or persons of the said cittie, and that thys said lawe shall stande and be putt in execucion untill suche tym as the sam be broken by a assemble; and also that the said bouchers, or others so repayring, to syll ther said fleche under the towr next Seynt Owen is chyrche."

In the following year, a butcher was appointed to act as assessor to the Mayor in fixing the price of meat, " the said boucher to be a controller upon all bouchers to kepe a reysonable assis (assize) as the price of catell gothe, and he to remayn in the shamblis all the day to cause them syll according Master Mer is assis, and to cut ther fleche according as it may be sold with reysonable gaynes."

Rates of Wages. A general ordinance fixing rates of wages was made by the Common Council at their Michaelmas meeting in the year 1555 in the following terms: "It is ordeyned, by auctoritie aforsaid, that a maister mason, maister carpender, and so the maister of every occupacion, shall have by the daie, when he haith no meate nor drinke, fyftene pens, the jorneyman, XII.d., the prentice X.d.; and when he haithe meate and drinke, the maister shall have by the daie VI.d., the jorneyman IIII.d., the prentice III.d.; every laborerer shall have by the daye, without meate and drinke, VII.d., *ob.*, and with meate and drinke, III.d.,; and if any within the franches of this cittie do take more than is here ordred, he shall forfait (halfe of) the some he taketh, and the gyver shall forfeit as mouche, halfe to the accusor or informer, and halfe to the treasure of this cittie." These rates of wages mark a considerable advance upon the two pence per day earned by the fullers as recorded in the " Chain Book."

Towards the end of the sixteenth century the Common Council found it necessary to intervene owing to the high prices charged in different crafts. The subjects of complaint this time were candles, shoes, and bread. The records of the Council read as follows:—

"Whereas the company of tallowchallners are complayned on for exceeding the pryce of III.d. the pound of candles, contrary to the effect of theire *Excessive* chartor: it is agreed and ordered, by the *Prices* aucthorytie of this assembly, that from *Charged.* henceforth the said company of tallowchallners shall sell and utter candles at III.d. sterling, the pound, and not excede that pryce, uppon payne to forfeyt theire chartor; and uppon complaynt of eny cittezen agaynst them, or eny of them, the Mayor to see the former lawes and this order executed agaynst the offendors." *

"Whereas complaint is exhibited against the shoemakers of this cittie for the exceading prices they sell shoes at (heydes being soe cheape): it is therfore ordered, by the aucthority aforsaid, that proclamacion be presentlie sett forth by Mr. Maior for cauling in the contry shoemakers every markett day, as hertofore hath ben accostomed."†

"Whereas complaint is made that the company of bakers in this cittie and subburbs exacteth from the citizens

* Michaelmas Assembly, A.D. 1598. † Christmas Assembly, A.D. 1598.

XII.d., sterling, for baking a peck of corne, contrarie to the accustomed usadge, without eny just cause or occasion to move the same, for which they have desarvid ponishment, theire fault wherin we refer to Mr. Maior to be delt with as becometh; and therfor yt is ordered, by the aucthority aforsaid, that from henceforth none shall pay above VIII.d. sterling, for every peckes baking; and yf eny baker shall take more, he shall receave twentie daies imprysonment, uppon profe of his offence herein."*

It is interesting to note that the sanctions were different in all three cases, although the fault committed was the same. The tallowchandlers were threatened with the forfeiture of their charter. In the case of the shoemakers their craft was to be thrown open to the country shoemakers. Imprisonment was to be the lot of the avaricious bakers.

Common Council Raises Price.

On the other hand, the Common Council sometimes raised prices when occasion called for it. At the same meeting at which the bakers were threatened with imprisonment for their exactions, the butchers were suffered to increase the price of tallow. The preamble to the by-law reads: "Forasmoche as at this present the scarsyty and derth of beofes, farr beyonde that which hath bene accustomed, for which respect, and for other consyderacions moved in this assembly, the company of boucher shall have for every stone of tallow, during the derth of beofes, II.s. II.d. sterling, notwithstanding by former ordynances they ought to have but onelie II.s."

* Assembly Meeting, 4th Friday after 24th June 1599.

Several ordinances were made by the Common Council of Dublin for the purpose of enforcing good workmanship upon the part of the guild brethren. Thus a bye law of the year 1469 recites that whereas the corvisers charged more for shoes than ever they did, and "the leddre wors barket then hit was of olde time, wherefor that ther be men ychose to serche ther ledre, that is to say, Walter White and Robert Nevell, to serche ther ledder that hitt be wal barket; and giffe hit be not well barket that then hit be forfet unto the workys of the citte."

Good Workmanship and Material.

In the year 1571 the Council appointed two assay masters to examine all leather offered for sale. In the words of the by-law they were " to veiwe searche and judge wheather the saide lether offred to sale be sufficientlie tanned, and fyndinge the same sufficientlie tanned, to signe and seale every hyde soe to be solde with a seale appointed for the same purpose, the saide sayemasters takinge for every hyde soe sealed and allowed *ob** Irishe." The penalty for infraction of this law was forfeiture of the sum of six shillings and eight pence, and imprisonment according to the Mayor's discretion. Shoemakers of the city buying leather in the country of country tanners were required to bring the same before the " sayemasters " to be assayed and sealed before being converted into boots and shoes. The first assay masters appointed under this law were " Richard Broocke, currier and Johne Williams, shoemaker."

Bound up with the question of good workmanship and,

* Obolus, one half-penny.

indeed, almost inseparable from it, was that of the use of good material. Upon the use of the latter the Common Council was equally insistent. In the year 1574 it is ordered " That the shomakers of this cittie shall make shoes of goode stuffe, well tanned and curryed, to shoue the cittizens."

From the earliest times the City Fathers had sought to protect the interests of the citizens by penalising the use of inferior or faulty material. Amongst the " Laws and Usages of the City of Dublin " appearing in the " Chain Book " is one dealing with the penalties to be imposed upon bakers for selling faulty bread. This law is recorded in Gilbert's " Calendar " as follows: " Fines on bakers for faulty bread: for the first offense—fifteen pence; for the second—thirty pence; for the third offence, they shall stand in the pillory and swear to leave the city for a year and a day. If they seek afterwards to return, they must renounce their trade, if they have not sanction from the Mayor and commonalty. Under penalty of half a marc, bakers must put their stamps and names on their bread. For the misdeeds of his servants every master-baker shall answer by life and limb, if he have not property."

Amongst other " Laws and Usages " recorded by Gilbert are the following: " No woman-brewer shall brew with straw, under penalty of twenty shillings." And " The fine on any woman-brewer for inferior ale is fifteen pence for the first offence, two and sixpence for the second, and for the third, suspension from her occupation for a year and a day."

The Common Council in the year 1558 ordered " That no baker shall make breade, to be eatten by man, of corne that is not sounde, uppon paynes conteyned in thauncient lawes for evyll brewing."

In part consideration for the monopoly enjoyed by the guildsmen the duty was imposed upon them of keeping the citizens well supplied with the particular commodities in which they dealt. Thus by a law of the year 1567 the butchers were required to "store the cittie with fleische upon the Thursday wyckely." Upon their failure to do so the Mayor was authorised to call in the "forreyne bowchers." And in the year 1599 a decree of the Council orders that "the tallowe challners and theire successors shall from henceforthe furnishe this cittie at all times with good store of candells of all sortes, and shall not exceede the pryse of III.d. sterling the pound, and that of good stuffe."

City to be Kept well Stocked.

It is clear from the by-laws quoted that the Common Council of Dublin watched with a strict eye the doings of the guildsmen. The primary object of the Council was to secure the welfare of the general body of citizens. With this object in view they regulated wages, fixed prices, enforced good workmanship and punished the use of faulty or fraudulent material. The guilds, in short, were made to subserve the interests of the citizens. Through the medium of the guilds the Common Council secured that the city should be well stocked with provisions and the various commodities which were in daily use.

The following by-law, made in the year 1569, shows how the Council intervened to prevent undue limitation of the members of a particular craft to the detriment of the citizens. It reads: " Wheareas certeine abussis is thoughte

COMMON COUNCIL AND THE GUILDS 113

by the assemble to be in the fre masons of this cittie, beinge feawe in nomber, not permittinge others masons that be good craftsmen to occupie or labor in this cittie without exactinge and payinge (as it is affirmed) halfe ther daylie wages to the saide free masons; for advoidinge of which abbuse, it is agreid by this assemblie that suche forren masons, beinge goode craftsmen, as will come to Mr. Maior and Mr. Recordor, shalbe by them licensed and permitted to worke in this cittie, and within the fraunches of the same till the next assemblie for proffe of ther workmanshipe and goode demeanor, and beinge founde then to be good workmen, and of honeste conversacion, shalbe admitted free unto fraunches of this cittie, puttinge ther billes up to the assemblie, and that the said free masons, nor the master or wardens of ther corporacion, shal not vex, areste, or sue the saide forren masons in the meanetime."

Limitation of Craftsmen by Guilds.

While the masons were prevented from unduly limiting their numbers to the detriment of the citizens, the Common Council intervened on behalf of another body of craftsmen, lest by too great an increase in their numbers the members of that craft should suffer. This intervention occurred on behalf of the tallow chandlers in the year 1572. A by-law of this year reads: "It is agreid, by thauctoritie of the saide assemblie, that Mr. Maior of this cittie for the tyme beinge, and his successors, with thadvice of syxe of his breatherne, the aldermen, shall nominate, assigne and appointe the number of talloo chaunlers in this cittie for his yeare,

And by Common Council.

J

and that none outher persone nor persons then souche as shall soo be appointed shall wourcke or make any candels for sale within the fraunches of this cittie, upon payne of forfiture of the candels so made to be solde, thone haulfe therof to the seiser, and thother haulfe to the cittie wourckes."

Welfare of Guilds Promoted.

While the Common Council imposed many restrictions upon the members of the guilds in the interests of the citizens generally, they promoted the welfare of the guilds in many ways. Some of the guilds, as, for example, the saddlers, owed their existence to the Council. Others, such as the goldsmiths, had their privileges confirmed. At a later period the various guilds were given a voice in the Council Chamber itself by being granted the privilege of returning members to the Council.

In order to secure to the tanners and glovers the raw material for their crafts the Council in the year 1534 prohibited the butchers of Dublin from selling sheep fells or skins to any but the glovers and tanners of the city " prowydit that the tanners and glovers pay well and trewly for the fells unto the boucher att the days appoyntyd and lymytyd twix them."

In the year 1558 the butchers were forbidden to cut trills out of hides to the damage of the tanners. This by-law reads: " Wheare the bouchers of this cittie and ther servaunts dothe contynuallie cut trills out of every hyde, to the greate hyndrance of the tanners of the said cittie, and greate disfyguring of the hides that cometh to the merchaunt: for remedy and eschewing wherof, it is ordeyned and establsshed, by thauctoritie of this present

COMMON COUNCIL AND THE GUILDS

assemble, that every person and persons hensforth may laufully seise and take as a forfaicture all and every suche tryle as shalbe founde to be solde within the franches of the said cittie, and that the bowcher that shall be found to cut eny such trills shall forfaict III.s. IIII.d. *tociens quociens*, thone haulf to the fynder, and thother haulfe to Mr. Maior and Shyryves."

The glovers of Dublin were protected in their home market by a decree of the Common Council assigned by Gilbert to the year 1562. This decree reads: "Forasmouche as by the gready desyre of some wilfull persons in this cyttye whiche have no respecte to a commen or publicque weale, but are hollye sett upon ther pryvatt gayne without regarde howe or in what sort theye make the same, the companye of glovers within this cittye have susteyned and dalye do susteine intollerable detryment of the uttere decaye of the same companye yf due remedie be not provyded to meet with the insaciable covetise of the said persons, as by the greavouse complaynt of the sayd companye of glovers made unto this assemblye doethe at full appeare: It is therfore for redresse of the said disordres and for the better mayntenance and furtherance of the sayde companye ordeyned and establisshed by thauctoritie of this assemblye, that noo cittisin or inhabitant of this cyttye outher then of the sayd companye of glovers shall from thensfurthe buy to be sold agayne within the franches of this cyttye any wurke made by glovers of the cuntreye, or by the glovers of any cyttye or towne of this realme out of this cyttye of Dublin, as gloves, purses, whit tawe and suche like wurke apperteyninge to thoccupacion of glover upon payne of forfeicture of the wurke so bought contrarye to this ordinance, halfe to the treasorye of this cyttye and halfe to the companye of glovers aforsayd."

By the same ordinance the butchers of the city were forbidden to sell sheepfells to any persons but those belonging to the company of glovers. Country butchers bringing " mottons " to be sold in Dublin were ordered to bring the sheepfell with the " mottons " and sell the same to the company of glovers and to none else under penalty of forfeiting double the value of the sheepfell not so brought.

This law gave to the master and wardens of the guild of glovers authority to take, seize and levy the penalties and forfeitures prescribed for the breach of its provisions, the master and wardens accounting quarterly to the Treasurer of the city for one half of the said penalties and forfeitures. In order that the law might be better known and observed it was to be proclaimed once every quarter in open market in the city.

Two by-laws made in the year 1555 reveal the anxious care bestowed by the Common Council on the welfare of the guildsmen. The first law was directed against foreigners working in Dublin in competition with the city craftsmen and reads: " Forasmoche as forreins doo at this present exercise tharts of soundrie occupacions in this cittie in the howses of frèe citizens, and elsewhere, to the greate injurye of fremen of the same faculties: It is ordered, by auctoritie of this assemble, that if any forreyne do from hensforth so use any art or facultie within the fraunches of this cittie, it shalbe lauffull for the master and wardens of the same art or facultie, or any of them, takinge with hym or them one of thofficers of the cittie to enter into

COMMON COUNCIL AND THE GUILDS

every suche place wheare any forreyne or forreynes shalbe knowen to worke, be it fremans house or other, and shall tak the said forreyne or forreyns to be justified according to the lawes of the said facultie or art approved by the court of the cittie."

The second by-law extended the ban to work done by strangers outside of the city and sent to Dublin for sale. " Forasmoche as taylors, smythes, shomakers, and outher men of occupacion within this cittie," it recites, " do at this tyme sufficientlie furnyshe the cittie with all things of their occupacions and faculties, and that merchaunts and outhers of this cittie, rather myndyng their private gayne then the comen wealth, doo dailie bringe into this cittie readie made hosen, dowblets, trusses, gerkens, boots, shoes and other suche things to be solde, to the greate hyndraunce of those that be of ocupacion in this cittie : It is ordeyned, by auctoritie aforsaid, that from hensforth no merchaunt or outher shall bringe into this cittie to be solde eny thinge readie made belonging to any facultie within the cittie, and whiche the men of that facultie do make and wurke, saving that in the market daie and during the tyme of market it shalbe laufull for smythes and shomakers of the countrey to bringe in things of their facultie, as they have used, yeving theirin a cheaper price than the citizen doeth, and that the master of the same faculties in this cittie shall have the viewe and correction of whatesomever the same forreins shall so (carrie) to be sold. And if any merchaunt or other do hensforthe offende contrarie to this ordenaunce, it is ordeyned, by the auctoritie aforesaide, that all that he shall

Ready-made Goods not to be Imported.

soo bye to be solde shalbe forfaict, halfe to the seisor or accuser, and haulfe to the treasure of the cittie."

In the year 1557 " forrayne " surgeons were prohibited from practising in Dublin without licence from the master and wardens of the barbers and surgeons, so long as there were " hable surgeons of cittizens."

The employment of foreign weavers to the detriment of the Dublin weavers was prohibited by a law of the year 1580 which recites: " Where(as) the master and company of weyvers complayned that dyvers free cittezens of this cittie putteth ther worck to forrens to be wrought and don by them, contrary to a lawe and order hertofore made and established by assembly for that purpose: it is therfore agreed, by the aucthorite afforsaid, that Mr. Mayor shall execut the penaltie of the said lawe and order uppon such fre cittezens of this cittie as so putteth ther worck henceforward to forreners, and that no such forreners shalbe permitted to entrude uppon the said master and companys occupacion, but shalbe forbidden and restrayned therof, upon the said master and companys chardges, so farr forth as ther chartor doth warrant."

Intrusion of Foreigners Forbidden.

One very sound reason for protecting the guildsmen in their monopoly is stated in the following by-law made at a meeting of the Common Council held after Christmas in the year 1577: " Where(as) John Forde, Clement Fraunces, William Kelly, and Thomas Troddane, haberdashers of this cittie, have complayned upon certayne of the merchantes of this cittie for putting a worck and mantayning of forrens to usurpp uppon ther facultie and

COMMON COUNCIL AND THE GUILDS 119

sciens, to ther greate hendrance, as they alleged: it is therefore condescended, graunted and agreed, by thauethoritie afforsaide, that, forasmuch as the forsaide complaynantes are of those that contribut to all chardges of this cittie, that ther be such consideracion had towardes theme as it shall not be lawfull for eny stranger to entrude uppon ther occupacions henceforward, provided they take reisonablie for such worckmanshipp as they worck or herafter shall worck unto eny merchant; otherwise, men to be at liberty; and that frome henceforth no merchant do kepe eny stranger untill fault be founde with the saide complaynantes for ther excessyve takinge."

The authority and control of the Common Council of Dublin over the city guilds is further evidenced by the fact that disputes between guilds as to their respective spheres of industry were submitted to and settled by the Common Council. The following ordinance of the year 1555 affords an interesting illustration:

Disputes between Guilds.

"Forasmoche as the tailors within this cittie do use to furre the garments that they make for men and women, to the greate hyndraunce of the skinners: It is ordeyned, by the auctoritie aforsaid, that no taylor within the franches of this cittie shall furre any garment that they make, nor cause to be furred but by suche of thoccupacion of skynners as may laufullie use the same facultie within the cittie, upon payne, for every default, of treble the value of the hire due for the furring, halfe to the spier or accuser, and halfe to the thesaure of the cittie."

Even the powerful Guild Merchant laid their grievances against the lesser guilds before the Common Council and sought redress from that body. The records of the city for the year 1584 contain the following entry: "The master, wardens and company of the Trinity Guild having complained that the artificers did intrude upon their trade, videlicet, the smiths, by retailing iron by the stone; the taylors traffic to London several times by the year; cutlers and hat dressers bring hats and swords redy trimmed, etc., all tending to the hindraunce and decay of the merchaunts; and inasmuch as the lawes of the citty have layde downe a good and commendable course for such private corporation, and that no merchaunt or citizen should deale in each others faculty or trade, or intrude therin: it was therefore agreed that if any merchaunt or cittizen do so intrude, and the same be proved before the Mayor and Sheryves, the party offending to lose the benefit of his freedome, and never again to be admytted."

From time to time regulations were made by the Common Council dealing with the apprentices of the Guild brethren.

Regulation of Apprentices. The following by-law was made in the year 1496: "Hyt ys ordynyt by the sayd semble that no man ne woman do suffyr ne support no man ys prentes ne serwaunt to ett, drynke, carde, dece, ne non othyr ontryfty play yn ther howsys on the pain of XL.s. *tociens quociens*, and ther boddes to the warde, and ther to abyde ontyll that ther mayster be satysfyd off hys godes, and the fyn to be payt, half to the Mere and Balliffis, and the othyr halff to the fynder."

The taking of apprentices under the age of sixteen years was prohibited by a civic by-law of the year 1551. Three years later it was provided that merchants and craftsmen

COMMON COUNCIL AND THE GUILDS

taking apprentices should enrol their names with the Clerk of the Tholsell. Upon the sealing of the indentures, a fine of six shillings and eight pence in the case of an apprentice to a merchant, and two shillings in the case of other apprentices, was to be paid to the treasury of the city by the father or friends of the apprentice or by his master. This by-law served a double purpose. It provided a new source of revenue for the citizens, and at the same time enabled the civic authorities to regulate the admission of apprentices. Incidentally it may be mentioned that these fines were for a time allotted to the Recorder of Dublin in " augmentacion of his lyving."

At the meeting of the Common Council held after Christmas in the year 1556 it was ordered that the Clerk of the Council should make up the indentures of all apprentices, taking for the writing of every pair only twelve pence, and for the enrolling of the term four pence, provided that the party be at the charge of the parchment for the indentures, if he would have them in parchment.

On completion of his period of apprenticeship the newly-qualified craftsman became entitled to be admitted to the franchise or freedom of the city of Dublin. *Admission to Freedom.* This right to freedom was known as the " right of servitude " or apprenticeship. It was a right of long standing. A statute of the Irish Parliament of the year 1500 recognised its existence in Dublin at that date. A certain looseness of practice had grown up in the sixteenth century whereby craftsmen had been admitted to the freedom of their craft, without being enrolled on the list of civic freemen and, on the other hand, craftsmen had been admitted to the freedom of the city, without the assent of the masters and wardens of their guild. To remedy which it was ordained by the Common Council in the year 1555 that "from hensforth no man shalbe admytted to the franches of any facultie or arte within this cittie before he be made free of this cittie; and that none of any occupacion shalbe admytted free of this cittie without thassent of the master and wardens of his facultie, saving suche whoos fathers have ben free, to whom upon suyt the franches of this cittie maye not be denaied by thauncyent usages therof. And if any shalbe admytted contrarie to this ordeynaunce, the same to be of no force to hym."

That this by-law was no dead letter is shown by a decree of the Common Council made in the year 1590 as follows: "Wheras the master and company of goldsmithes have encurred the penaltie of a lawe in this cittie, in respect of theire admytting of Thadie Tole, coppersmith, to be of theire company, he not being fyrst sworn a freman of this cittie, for which they are to pay X.*li.* as a fyne, nevertheles the boddie of this cittie, having consyderacion of theire fault and unwilling to extend the rygor of the lawe, which justly might be inflycted uppon them, and withall lest theire example should gyve lybertie or be a presydent to other incorporacions to do the lick; it is herby (in respect of theire small abylytie) ordered and agreed, by the aucthorytie of the said assembly, that they shall paye but fyve pounds, which is the halfyndell of the fyne, and of the rest they are herby discharged."

In the following year it was ordered that the by-law should be enforced against the master and wardens of the corporation of weavers for having taken "into theire

COMMON COUNCIL AND THE GUILDS

societie and brotherhod one John Williams, who useth the trade of weyving in this cittie, being never admytted freeman of this cittie."

The acquisition of the freedom of the city entailed certain duties upon the citizens, prominent amongst which was that of taking part in the defence of the city. Military service was not an incident of the feudal system only, it fell to the lot of the ordinary citizen. This duty was brought home to the freeman at the time of his enrolment as is evidenced by a law made by the Common Council in the year 1454, recorded in the Calendar of Ancient Records of Dublin as follows: " Also, hit was ordenyte and stabled in the said semble that no prentise of merchande shulde be admitted unto the fraunches of the said citte till he have a jake bowe, shefe, sallet* and swerde of his owne; and all prentises of othir craftis to have a bowe, arrouys, and a swerde, and at two tymes in the yere befor the wardyns of the Trinite Yelde for the merchandis, and for all other prentises the maisteris of every (craft)."

Defence of City.

Military service within the walls of Dublin had to be rendered freely by the citizens. If required to go to a " hosting " or military expedition beyond the city, payment was made. A civic by-law of the year 1540† states : " Hit ys ordynyd and agreyd by the sayd semble holdyn the day and yere abou writtyn (fourth Friday after 24th June, 1540), that whensoever anny Maister or brother of the Trynite Yeld be appoyntyd to goo to anny ostyng or jornay in his propir person, that he that shall goo, if he be

---

* A light helmet.   † C.A.R.D., Vol I., p. 406.

apoyntyd ahorsebake, shall hawe every day (that he hes owte) toward his costs and charges XVI d. Irish, to be payd unto hym trewly by such persons as shall be apoynted by byll or writtyng to ber to hym. An if he be appoynted to be a fote man, then he to haw toward his charges every day XII.d., Irish, of such as shall be poyntyd to him by bill."

In Gilbert's MS. copy of the records of the Guild of the Holy Trinity it appears that in the year 1597 the expense of setting forth forty men for a general hosting was charged upon the brethren.

The members of this guild were required to keep themselves furnished with a stock of arms in proportion to their wealth. A by-law of the Guild Merchant dated 1573 required that every merchant occupying stock of his own of a value between £60 and £100 should have continually in his house six good even bows with arrows to them furnished and one "calliver furnished." Merchants possessing stock worth £100 and over were required to have double the number mentioned.

In the Record Book of the Guild of Carpenters, Millers, Masons and Heliers in the Municipal Library at Charleville Mall, Dublin, one of the few original guilds records which have survived to the present day, appear a number of entries dealing with civic hostings. One of these records that William Trasse and John Gryffyne were paid 4s. 4d. for hosting money in the year 1536. The former, who may have been of a particularly bellicose temperament, was again selected for duty of this nature and was rewarded with the sum of 7s. 2d. in the year 1539. A shilling a day was the rate of payment made to another member

COMMON COUNCIL AND THE GUILDS

who went to a hosting to "Rathcow" for a period of six days.*

Another duty of the guildsmen was to bear their share in the cesses levied upon them for the support of the civic government and other purposes. The municipal records contain a number of references to these levies. The following by-law was made by the Common Council in the year 1552, namely: "Forasmiche as this honorable cittie have at this present but a littill and small revenus for the advansment of the sam, by meanes wherof suche things as ned to be don ar lefte in oblivion and not set forward, so that miche harme at leynthe might therof growe, if sum remedie be not the sonyr had; for redres wherof, and for setting forthe of this good and godlie purpos, hit is agreid, concludid and ordeyned, by this present assemble, holden the day and yer abowe written, for a tresorie to be had and encresed within this cittie, that every brother of the Trinitie and Merchant Yeld quarterlie to pay fro hensforthe a grote a quarter, to be yerlie lewyed by the wardings of the said gild to the use of the said tresorie."

Cesses Levied on Guilds.

In the year 1576 the Common Council ordered as follows: " That the severall corporacions of and within this cittie shall beare and paye the therde parte of that which the Trenetie Yelde payeth of the (cesse to be) levied for the kepinge of the calledors in Alhallowes, fyndinge of pore seeke people in the same, and otherwise, porters of gates, and others, the som of V markes, sterlinge current of

---

* These and other entries of a similar nature appear in a paper contributed by Dr. Berry to the " Journal of the Royal Society of Antiquaries of Ireland " (Part IV., Vol. XXXV.)

Englond, beinge the therde parte of cc. *li* cest as afforsaid."

The "calledors" are mentioned and the nature of their duties described in a by-law made at the next meeting of the Common Council. This by-law orders "That ther shalbe henceforwarde two callodors and two visitors appoynted to attend frome tyme to tyme, upon those that shalbe infected, within this cittie and suburbs therof, and theme to kepe and burie as occasion shall serve; and the said callodors and visitors to have VI.d. sterling, apese by the daie, and the same to be payde monthlie out and upon the cittie revenues, of the furst that can be receved; and the said callodors and visitors to contynewe in paie so long tyme as it shalbe thought convenient by Mr. Mayor and his bretherin."

The Guild Merchant had been accustomed to bear two-thirds of the cesses levied while the remaining third was borne by the craft guilds. Upon complaint made by the Masters, Wardens and corporation of the Trinity Guild of their inability to continue to bear this proportion, owing to want of trade, a conference of the guild masters and of certain substantial citizens was directed to be summoned in the year 1579 to arrange a more equitable adjustment of the burden. By an Order of the year 1597 the Masters and Wardens were made personally liable for the amount of cess levied upon the brethren and sisters of the guild.

The foregoing account of the relations between the Common Council of Dublin and the guilds evidence the keen interest taken by the Council in the latter bodies. The formation of guilds was promoted and encouraged by the Council. The interests of the guildsmen were fostered

COMMON COUNCIL AND THE GUILDS

in many ways. It was only when the guild brethren were tempted to abuse their privileged position that the Common Council felt called upon to interfere in order to protect that greater interest—the welfare of the general body of citizens. No serious breach in the friendly relations subsisting between the Common Council and the guilds appears to have occurred in Dublin. The secret of these continued friendly relations is to be found in the fact that a very close relation existed between the governing body of Dublin and the merchants and craftsmen. In the towns of mediæval Europe it was the wealthier merchants and master craftsmen who supplied the majority of the members of the civic governments. And Dublin was no exception to the rule.

The constitution of the governing body of Dublin consisted of the Mayor, two Bailiffs or Sheriffs, twenty-four jurés or aldermen, forty-eight demi-jurés and ninety-six councillors. The last two elements were frequently referred to as "The Numbers" or more specifically as "The Forty-eight" and "The Ninety-Six." The *personnel* of the governing body for the year 1600 is set forth in the Calendar of the Ancient Records of Dublin. From an examination of the lists of those admitted to the franchise during the period from A.D. 1575 to 1600 it is possible to discover the avocations of a large number of the members. The published records, unfortunately, do not give the lists of admissions to the franchise prior to the year 1575. Of the Board of Aldermen or jurés none appears in the lists of freemen admitted during this period. But the remark-

Representation of Merchants and Craftsmen on Common Council.

able fact comes to light that, with one exception, the members were ex-mayors or ex-sheriffs. As these offices would be conferred ordinarily upon men of mature years, their admission to the franchise would have taken place in the previous quarter of a century. Of the forty-eight demi-jurés it is possible to identify twenty-six. They include sixteen merchants, two goldsmiths, two tanners, two apothecaries, a miller, a victualler, a shoemaker and a baker. Of the ninety-six councillors it is possible to discover the occupations of no less than forty-six. They include seventeen merchants, six tanners, five shoemakers, three tailors, three bakers, two barbers, a button-maker, a tallow chandler, an apothecary, a smith, a cutler, a carpenter, a pewterer, a butcher, a clerk, and a miller. The classification arrived at is not entirely satisfactory as it is based upon the mere similarity of names. Where the same name appears more than once, as it does in a few cases, the senior freeman has been identified with the Councillor of the same name. Allowing for a margin of error, it may be concluded that the merchants, and consequently the Guild Merchant, had a preponderating voice in the Council of the City, while the various crafts were represented in a varying degree, but in much fewer numbers than the merchants.

Whether the merchants and craftsmen whose names appear in the governing body of Dublin for the year 1600 were elected directly by their guild organisations or chosen by the general body of citizens, it is not possible at present to state. Direct representation of the guild was a feature of the next century. The records of the sixteenth century bearing upon the point are scant. It is probable, however, that during this century, the practice of giving direct

COMMON COUNCIL AND THE GUILDS

representation on the Common Council to the guilds, grew up.

The following by-law of the year 1574 bears directly upon this question of the representation of the Guilds, namely: " That whensoever henceforwarde any place of the nombers of XLVIII and XCVI that shall becum voyde, that the election shalbe made of suche of the corporacions as shalbe thought meate to supplye the same, if none of the Trynitie Yelde shalbe better lycked of by the assemblie to be nominated to that place."

CHAPTER V.

THE GUILD MERCHANT IN THE XVII. CENTURY.

CHAPTER V.

The Guild Merchant in the Seventeenth Century.

THE Guild of the Holy Trinity continued to exercise an active control over the wholesale and retail trade of Dublin throughout the seventeenth century. This control was exercised by the Guild while remaining subordinate to the over-riding authority of the Common Council of Dublin. In other cities and towns the Guild Merchant lost its identity and became merged in the governing body of the town. In Dublin the Guild Merchant was intimately associated with the governing body of the city and, in fact, had a preponderating influence in the Common Council, but it continued to remain a distinct and separate body. During this period the Guild assumed a definitely Protestant complexion, the members attending Divine Service in the Established Church, as by law required, and appointing Protestant Chaplains for their own special Services. The taking of Catholic apprentices by the members was forbidden. The Guild Merchant, however, did not completely exclude Catholic brethren from the fold, many being entered on the books of the Guild as "quarter brothers" as distinct from those who were sworn free of the guild. A certain amount of trade was carried on by Catholic merchants who were in no way connected with the guild. In this and other respects the monopoly enjoyed by the Guild Merchant became gradually weakened.

Another feature of the seventeenth century was the rise to power of an inner body styled the " Council of the House," at the expense of the brethren generally.

The records of the Guild Merchant during the seventeenth century show the active interest which was taken by the guild in the regulation of trade in Dublin. The system of common bargains continued to prevail, the Masters of the guild acting as buyers. Wine was one of the commodities subject to common purchase, and according to the guild by-laws could not be imported by an individual member without license from the masters and wardens being obtained. In the year 1609 Sir John Tyrrell committed a breach of the by-laws by importing a cargo of wine on his own responsibility, an action which was unanimously condemned by the brethren at a meeting held on the 26th day of February in that year. The following entry appears in Gilbert's transcript of the Guild Records. "Whear as Sr. John Tyrrell knight contrary to a lawe in that case provided hath agreed and bargained with one Crafford of the town of Aire in Scotland for his barke in lodinge of french wynes without licence of M^{rs} and Wardens, at £13 11s. each tonn beside all chardges wch are to be alle full at the key, which bargain was callt in Question before the Masters and Wardens the daye aforesaid in an assembly of brethern who in one voyse dothe wysh the Mrs. and Wardens to put the same in execution against the said Sr. John and also that the Mrs. and Wardens shall distribute the wynes amongst the brethern at the rate they were bought by Sr. John Tyrrell."

The system of common purchase was extended to timber in the year 1615. This is the first occasion on which that

GUILD MERCHANT IN XVII. CENTURY

commodity is mentioned as being the subject of a common bargain. At a meeting held on the 5th day of May in that year it was agreed that a ship-load of deal boards, containing three thousand planks, should be purchased by the Guild at the rate of £5 5s. English per hundred, that is, £157 10s. for the cargo.

A Timber Purchase.

The policy of the Guild appears to have wavered about this time with regard to the question of permitting freedom of trade to their members. In the closing years of the sixteenth century the Guild had repealed an ancient law which forbade any brother to trade directly with strangers, by which innovation, it is stated, certain brethren were enabled to buy up commodities which they refused afterwards to dispose of but at excessive prices. Accordingly on the 27th May, 1603, it was ordered that the Masters, Wardens, and buyers should forever thereafter buy and bargain all merchandise coming to the city to the use of the whole brotherhood, to be distributed amongst them according to place or calling.*

Guild Merchant and Free Trading by Members.

Some years later the Guild again experimented with free trade. On the 1st day of April, 1619, a by-law was made declaring that " every free brother of this yeald shall frome hence foorth have licence for three years next insuinge the date herof to buy anny shippe Barque orr boot of wynes, irone orr anny other comodities comeinge to this cittey to be souled (salte onely excepted) he the sayd Brother or brethren soe buying the saide goods paieing for every tunne of wyne orr Irone by theme soe bought five shelings ster.

* Egerton MS. 1765, British Museum Library.

englishe & for evry other comodities by theme bought to paye suche other duties for the same as was formerly reserved beeinge three pence in ye pound. . . . It is ment yt salte shalbe alwayes a comone Bargane."*

Whether this experiment was a success or failure is not stated, nor whether the general licence was renewed, but the system of common bargains continued to prevail during the century. A by-law dated 6th November, 1648, directs "yt ye Masters for ye tyme beinge shalbe booth ye byers and booth ye wardens ye devidors and deliverors of all marchandizes bought or to be bought by ye Masters for ye use of this Guild according ye aunceint custome." In the Gilbert transcript of the Guild by-laws the following note made by the copyist occurs under date 13th October, 1651: "This day two Persons are elected Buyers for this year which is the first time this appointment occurs at least distinct from the Master."

The effectiveness of the control exercised by the Guild Merchant over the trade of Dublin depended upon the loyalty with which the individual members obeyed the Guild bye-laws. Breaches of the bye-laws which involved an infringement of the monopoly enjoyed by the brethren were severely punished. "Colouring" the goods of a stranger, or selling the stranger's goods as the property of a brother, was strictly forbidden, because such conduct tended to break down the Guild's monopoly by allowing strangers to share in the profits made on the sale of commodities. The Guild records of 12th January, 1617, mention the case of one William ffrain, a merchant brother

Colouring Goods.

* Egerton MS.

of the Guild, who was found by a jury to be a great dealer for the Dutchmen, contrary to his oath and to the utter overthrow of many brethren. Being articled before the house, he confessed to have entered twelve hundred hides which were apparently for the use of the Dutchmen. Upon consideration of the case, it was ordered by the Masters, Wardens and brethren that the guilty member should be committed to prison, there to remain until he should pay a fine of twenty pounds English and that he should be dismissed from membership of the Guild.

The policy of the Guild Merchant tended to an equal distribution of trade amongst the brethren. Enterprise on the part of individual members was discouraged, if that enterprise should lead to wealth being accumulated at the expense of the brethren. Thus the principle of the multiple shop was forbidden by the Guild laws.

Certain of the brethren presented a petition in January, 1652, setting forth that there was an ancient law of the house prohibiting any brother from keeping more shops and taverns than one, notwithstanding which several of the brethren kept several shops and taverns to the great prejudice of the Guild. It was ordered accordingly that the said law should be put in execution against whomsoever kept two shops or two taverns.

In January, 1667, the Guild ordained that from thenceforth no brother should set any stall in the street, either before his own house or shop or elsewhere on market or other days for the purpose of exposing to sale any goods or merchandise. This prohibition was rendered necessary, owing to the great abuse committed against the Guild by strangers and others, inhabitants of the city, in keeping stalls in the streets on market days and other days contrary to the ancient custom of the city. Although the by-law prohibited only the brethren from keeping such stalls, it applied with even greater force to strangers and non-members.

Porterage of Merchandise. The carrying trade of Dublin continued to be regulated throughout the seventeenth century by the Guild Merchant. From time to time the number of those engaged in the trade and the charges to be made were fixed by regulation of the Guild. The carrying trade was conducted by a number of Master Porters elected by the Holy Trinity Guild, each Master Porter having under his control a number of men known as "Bearers." In the year 1638 twelve Master Porters were elected. Eleven of these were allowed ten men each, and one was allowed twenty.*

In the year 1650 it was ordered that the Masters and Wardens, calling to their assistance such of the brethren as they should think fit, should consider the laws formerly made touching the porters of the city and should appoint bearing Porters for carrying coals, salt, corn and other merchandize, and settle the rates to be charged for measuring and carrying the said commodities into the several places of the city. The following rates were fixed:—

Rates to be paid to the Measuring Porters by the Seller

For measuring every ton of coals	3d.
For every ton of salt	2d.
For every 20 barrels of any sort of grain ..	4d.

* Egerton MS., No. 1765.

Rates to be paid to the bearing Porters by the buyer

> For every ton of coals or salt landed out of bark or other vessel to be put into a car or cart on the Quay .. .. .. 8d.
>
> For every ton of coals or salt carried out of any bark or vessel on the Quay into any house, yard or cellar on the said Quay .. 12d.
>
> For carrying a ton of said commodities from the places aforesaid into any place in Bridge Street, Cook Street, Winetavern Street or ffishamble St. and to St. John's Lane or the Church of the blessed Trinity 1s. 4d.

Higher rates were fixed for more distant places.

A by-law dated 14th January, 1677, recites that of late years many had taken upon themselves to be Master Porters, not being duly elected and sworn as they ought, and had taken what rates they pleased to the great abuse of His Majesty's subjects. It was accordingly ordered that it be left to the Masters, Wardens and Council of the Guild to elect Master Porters, and that those elected should be sworn before the Lord Mayor and enrolled in the books of the guild. The rates to be taken for measuring and carrying coals, corn, salt and other commodities were to be ascertained by the Masters, Wardens and Council of the Guild. A printed list of the rates so ascertained was directed to be fixed on the gates and public places of the city.

The original records of the Holy Trinity Guild contained the names of those elected as Master Porters down to the year 1731.

THE GUILDS OF DUBLIN

The services of the Guild Merchant were invoked by the Common Council of Dublin in the year 1668 for the purpose of reporting what duties and fees Jonathan Paley should take as tenant of the Old Crane belonging to the city for cranage and wharfage. The following fees were recommended:—

For wines and all other liquor per ton	8d.
For prunes, allom & copperas per puncheon	4d.
Mather the bale and custeele of currants	6d.
For tallow per tun	8d.
For wool ber bag	2d.
For Packs of cloth linnen and woollen	2d.
For Bundles and fardels ditto	1d.
For Large dry fatts	4d.
For Shot per firkin	1d.
For Raisins the cask	1d.
For Figgs	½d.
Fraile fruit per peice	½d.
For sugar the hogshead	2d.
For Tobacco in statute rowle per peice	2d.
For Window glass per crate	1d.
For Large baskets of bottles per basket	2d.
For Butter per cent.	½d.
For Oranges and Lemons per box	1d.
For porterage of every gabbard of the above goods per gabbard	2s. 6d.
For porterage of iron per gabbard	5s.

Out of every ship one bottle of wine
And for all commodities of other goods after the rates of the goods above mentioned.

GUILD MERCHANT IN XVII. CENTURY 141

The strictness with which the Guild Merchant guarded the monopoly of trade enjoyed by its members is exemplified in a number of the records appearing in the Guild books of the seventeenth century.

In the transcript of the guild by-laws in the British Museum Library is given a law dated 15th July, 1611, which enacts that "noe pson or psons of what qualletie or condicon soever he being not ellected admitted or accepted of the said fraternitie or gwield

Protection of Guild Monopoly. shall sett upp or keap eny open shopp, cellar, or standing for the uttering of wares or merchaundize or eny pryvat or close shopp or cellar or standing be it wthin lettise or wthout lettise wthin howse or wthout wthin eny the p^{r}cincts or places heerafter expressed namely . . . . ." (Here follow the names of the places mentioned in the charter of Queen Elizabeth.) Non-members were further forbidden to buy from or sell to any persons who were not members of the Guild under penalty of forfeiture of the sum of £10 for each such offence, one third to go to the informer, "an other third pte to be converted to the meinteinance of the poorer sorte of schollers in the colledg of the holy Trynitie neer Dublin," the remaining one-third to go to the use of the Guild. "Provided always," the by-law continued, "that this acte ordynance or eny thing therin conteyned shall not extend to anie person or persons for bringing or causing to be brought eny victualls to the Citty of Dublin or lybberties therof as they might lawefullie have don before the making therof."

An entry of the next day shows that the Guild authorities

could temper justice with mercy. The entry reads: "Jarvis Sineclare cooke being complained uppon for Retailing of wynes in his howse, he being noe free merchant nor accepted of this yeald which is contrary to the by lawes and charters, whoe appearing before the Mrs and Wardens of this yelde, did desier to be forgiven that fault in regard he was Innocant of the orders in that respect and he wold not offend eny more. It was agreed that he shall be forgiven his faulte and shall paie for a fine Vs. sterl. to the Threasury of this (yelde) and that from hence forth he shall sell noe more wyne within his howse nor this cittie."

A case of unlawful trading between non-members came before the Guild authorities in May, 1648. The records show that whereas John McKneather, Scotch Merchant, having sold unto Daniel Hutchenson 12 tons of iron at £24 per ton without acquainting the Masters and Wardens of the same or having licence from them for the sale thereof, and the said Mr. Hutchenson being no freeman of the Guild the same iron being "forren bought and forren sold" it was lawful seizure to the use of the Guild, and they having submitted themselves to the censure of the Masters and Wardens, alleging that McKneather was a stranger and unacquainted with the privileges of the Guild and that he was upon demurrage with the Master of his ship and required forthwith to pay a great sum of money which could not be paid but by the present sale of the iron, it was ordered that the said censure be remitted upon paying a fine of twenty shillings and the duties of poundage due to the Clerk.*

In November of the same year the following order was

* Gilbert MS., p. 120.

made by the Guild, namely: "It is further ordered and agreed by ye authority aforesaid that wheras sewall and many Intrudors as well freemen of divers corporacions of Smithes, Gold Smithes, Tayllors, Chaundlors, Weavers and Copers as also divers other straungers and forinors doe dailie intrude upon this Guild and doe sett up wynetauerns, cellors, shopps, stalls and doe by and retayle wines and selle all sortes of marchandize contrary to the Chartors, Lyberties and other auncient usages of this Guild. It is therefore ordred and agreed that the Clarke of this house shall take a view of all ye seuerall Intrudors and frome tyme to tyme to make a perfect list of theire names and to returne ye same to ye Masters and Wardens for ye tyme beinge who are to psecute ye said Intrudors according ye lawes of this house made and pvided in that case."

In the second half of the seventeenth century the Guild merchant took drastic steps to maintain the monopoly of the members. The records show that frequent seizures of goods "forren bought and forren sold" were made by the Guild authorities.*

About the year 1663 a controversy arose between the Guild Merchant and the guild of the goldsmiths over the sale of gold rings and other commodities imported by some of the merchants from England. The goldsmiths seized these articles and detained them, alleging that the merchants were not authorised by their charter to sell such wares. On the petition of the aggrieved brethren it was ordered that the Masters and Wardens of the Holy Trinity Guild should attend the Mayor and make application to him to have the petitioners' grievance redressed. The records

* Gilbert MS., p. 134.

do not disclose the decision arrived at by the Mayor. The merchants, however, were clearly in the wrong by encroaching upon the province of the goldsmiths, the precious metals never having been regarded as coming under the heading of merchandise.

Queen Elizabeth's charter of the year 1577 had provided an effective method of controlling dealings by foreigners and other non-members of the Guild Merchant. By that charter it was provided that foreigners and strangers and non-members generally should deposit any wares or merchandise they had for sale in the "Common Hall" or other place assigned for the purpose by the Masters and Wardens. Such goods could be sold only to members of the Guild. This valuable privilege does not appear to have been guarded as carefully as its importance merited. Through lack of funds or mismanagement the Guild Merchant appears to have been deprived for a time of the use of the common cellar. In July 1663, a petition was presented by certain of the brethren shewing that the Guild sustained great prejudice by want of the "Common Cellar," and that it was necessary that the said cellar should be redeemed, so that foreigners might lay their goods therein on the days appointed, whereby the corporation might have the refusal thereof. The petition resulted in an order being made that the sum of £200 should be raised to redeem the cellar.

The Common Hall.

Towards the close of the century the Guild Merchant alienated their *depôt*. The following entries are taken from the Gilbert MS., 4th Aug., 1698: "Ordered that the Common Cellar and Warehouse in Winetavern Street belonging to this corporation be let for the term of three score and one years by way of cant upon Thursday next being the 11th of this instant month at the Guild Hall at 11 o'clock in the forenoon to him that shall bid most for the same."

"11th Augt. 1698—Accordingly the said Common Cellar and Warehouse were put up to be set by cant to the fairest bidder and Mr. John Sharpe bidding most for the same (viz. £33 per annum) it is ordered that the said Mr. Sharpe have a lease of the premises at the above rent for 61 years with a clause of surrender every 7 years of the said term upon giving 6 months notice beforehand."

Notwithstanding the provisions of the Charters and the Guild by-laws a certain amount of illicit trading was carried on in Dublin during the seventeenth century. It is probable that the volume of this traffic went on increasing during this period. From time to time *Compounding* the Guild Merchant made efforts to draw *with* these rival traders within the fold or at *Strangers.* least to bring them under control. By a Guild order dated 13th July, 1646 which recited that many strangers and foreigners, to the great prejudice of the corporation, did set up cellars and shops and retail wine and other commodities, it was directed that the Masters and Wardens should send for such, and having consideration for the misery of the times, might compound with them for their intrusion past and licence them for a certain space, they giving such reasonable composition or acknowledgment for the same grant as the Masters and Wardens should think fit.

L

A year later it was ordered that the Masters and Wardens should call to their assistance such of the brethren as they should think fit to confer with such of the merchants of Christ-Church-yard and others who desired to be brethren of the Guild, to agree upon such fines as they should think fit. The authority given to the Masters and Wardens to negotiate with these merchants was subsequently withdrawn, but the order is useful in indicating the tendency of the time to extend control over all those engaged in the art of merchandise.

The Guild records of the year 1671 present the curious case of a person being admitted to the freedom of the guild without becoming a brother. The entry in the Gilbert MS. is as follows:— "Upon petition of Samuel Clarridge to be admitted unto the freedom of this Guild, or that such rule may be given whereby he may during his life have the liberty of exercising his trade in this city without interruption. And forasmuch as it is known the same Clarridge is not willing to take the oaths administered to every freeman and brother of this Guild but promises to conform to the Laws thereof. It is ordered that upon payment of £5 for the use of the Guild and 10s. per ann. he shall be permitted to exercise his trade during his life as freely as any other brother of this Guild."

An Unsworn Member.

Immediately after this entry the following note occurs in the Gilbert transcript, namely:—" This is the first time mention is made of a person being admitted free of this Guild who is not a brother though such is frequent hereafter."

GUILD MERCHANT IN XVII. CENTURY 147

From this date onwards the records disclose the existence of two classes of members—those who were sworn members of the brotherhood and those who while *Quarter* holding a lower status, were yet permitted *Brothers.* freely to follow the art of merchandise and were known as "Quarter Brothers."

The chief distinction between the two classes would appear to be that the "Quarter Brothers" were ineligible for Guild offices.

The following notice from the Lord Mayor addressed to the Masters of the Holy Trinity Guild appears in the records of the latter body namely:—" Whereas by Act of Michas. Assembly 1675 it was ordered that the Masters of the several corporations of this city should not for the future admit any persons to be Quarter brother or a sworn brother of any corporation in the said City until he be first free of this city. Therefore in pursuance of the said Act you the undernamed are hereby required forthwith to return unto me the names of all such persons who are sworn free brethern of your Corporation as also of such as are admitted Quarter brothers, to the end speedy course may be taken for the prevention of such intrusion. And hereof you are not to fail at your peril.

Dated the 20th Oct. 1675."

It would appear that the institution of "Quarter Brothers" was availed of as a means of permitting Catholic merchants to share in the advantage of Guild membership, without obliging them to take the oaths administered to the free brothers. Samual Clarridge who was exempted in the year 1671 from taking the oaths administered to every freeman and brother of the Guild was, in all probability, a Catholic.

The references to Catholics or "Papists" in the municipal or Guild Merchant records of the seventeenth century are scanty. This is unfortunate, as it is difficult if not impossible now to estimate the extent to which Catholic traders were driven from lawful trading to swell the ranks of illicit traders beyond the pale of the Guild Merchant.

At a meeting of the Common Council of Dublin held after Christmas of the year 1652 the Council orders "that none shalbee admitted unto the assemblies of any of the corporacions of this cittie unlesse hee bee a Protestant, and that noe freeman take any to bee an apprentise but such as are or wilbee and continue in the Protestant religion."*

This ordinance of the Common Council was followed in the year 1662 by an enactment of the Guild Merchant in the following terms:—" It is agreed and for a lawe made by the Masters Wardens and Brethern assembled that noe brother shall hereafter take any apprentice that is a papist under the fine of £100 to be paid by the Master that shall soe offend."†

Some years later Catholic merchants were deprived of the privilege of being Quarter Brothers. On the 14th day of July 1679 at an assembly of the Guild Merchant it was ordered that no person who was a Papist should be admitted in future a Quarter Brother of the Guild: and that such Papists as were then Quarter Brothers not free of the city should be removed out of the protection of the Guild and suppressed from trading.‡

* C.A.R.D., Vol. IV., p. 38.   † Egerton MS., 1765.   ‡ Gilbert MS.

The ban placed upon the Catholic merchant by the civic and guild authorities must have led to a great increase in illicit trading in Dublin with a consequent weakening of the power and authority of the Guild.

Towards the close of the seventeenth century a spirit of tolerance appears to have crept back timidly into the councils of the Guild. In the year 1698 one Tryall Travers, being elected one of the wardens of the Guild for the ensuing year, was called upon to be sworn; but he desiring to be excused from serving by reason he could not take "the little oath" it was ordered that he be excused for ever from serving in the said place upon payment of one guinea fine, which he accordingly paid, but it was declared that such a favour should not be regarded as a "president" for the future. The records do not state that this member was a Papist. They merely show that he had a conscientious objection to taking the necessary oath. The spirit of tolerance shown in this case may well have been extended to others who did not share the religious tenets held by the authorities of the Guild Merchant.

Religious Character of Guild. The religious character of the Guild of the Holy Trinity had completely altered by the middle of the seventeenth century. Originally a purely Catholic body, maintaining a chantry of one or more priests for the celebration of Holy Mass daily, the Guild had become definitely Protestant in character.

The desire of the Guild to break away completely from the old tradition is evidenced by a by-law of the year 1655 the record of which is as follows:—" The peticon of certaine of the Brethren to the Rt. worll. the Mrs.

Wardens &c. Sheweth that the seale aunciently usued by this Corporacon (being a crusifix) is held superstitious. It is therefore desired that a new seale be agreed this quarter assembly wch. shall hereafter be owned as the only seale of this Corporacon. Ordered that a new seale be forth with made where on shall be engraven a ship under sayle with this inscription about it. The Seale of the Merchants Guild of the Citty of Dublin 1655 "* The making of the seal was entrusted to one Joseph Stoker who received thirty shillings therefor.

Except for a period of some years' duration the members of the Guild continued to use the Trinity Chapel in Christ Church Cathedral. Owing to a dispute with the Cathedral authorities the members of the Guild were for a time deprived of the use of their chapel. During this period the Guild was without the services of a Chaplain.

In the year 1645 a suit was instituted by the Cathedral authorities against the Masters, Wardens and Brethren of the Guild Merchant with reference to the repair of the " Tryniti Chapell." By order of the Guild Assembly the Masters and Wardens were authorised to defend the suit out of the issues and profits of the Guild. This suit appears to have dragged on for about three years when the brethren authorised their officers to enter into a friendly settlement with the Cathedral authorities. The record in the Guild books was in the following terms:—

"Wheras on Saterday beinge ye 27th daie of Maie *Anno Dom.* 1648 ye Masters Wardens and brethern of Trinity yeald being assembled together in theire house or Comon Hall in ye Tholsell of Dublin, a peticion was

* Gilbert MS., p. 129.

preferred to them by certaine ye brethern setting forth that tyme beyaunt ye memorie of man they have been possessed of Trinity Chapell within the Cathedrall Church of ye blessed Trinity Dubline for celebrating divine Service therein and to repair of the same at all tymes accustomed and pforme theire accustomed orders and ceremonies therein, and to make use of ye same as a buriall place for ye brethern and sisters of ye said fraternety and had the benefitt and pfitts thereunto belonginge to ye use of the said fraternety, untill of late yeares ye said fraternety were dispossessed of ye same by ye Deane and Chapter of ye said Cathedrall Church, whoe in theire owne wronge possessed them selves of ye said Chapell and ever since receaved the benefit of ye burialls therein, wthout givinge anie accompte to this fraternety for not repairinge ye sd Chapell notwithstandinge they enioyinge the benefitt as afore said. And therefore humblie prayed that ye saide Chapell might be regained unto ye saide Guild whereby they might pforme the ancient customes and ceremonies of theire pdecessors laufully used and accustomed Which petition ye saide Masters and wardens taking into consideracon and for ye prevention of further suite in Law wth. ye said Deane and Chapter and the preservation of ye said Chapell from spoile and ruien It is unanimously consented and assented unto that ye woo[ll]. Sr. Cristofer fforster Kt. Charles fforster alderman and Maurice Pur alderman and Mr. John ffleminge wardens of the same shall forth with conferr and agree with ye said Deane and Chapter of ye said Cathedrall Church not only for ye regayninge of ye saide Chapell but also for and concerninge all differences and controuercies that shall arise concerninge ye same And if the said Deane and Chapter will establish this fraternety in theire possession accordinge ye first ordinacon therof and maie enjoy and receave ye benefitt of ye burialls therin wth. ye priviledges and customes of ancient tyme by theire pdecessors laufully used and accustomed That then this fraternity will undertake to repair and keepe up ye said chapell in all decent & necessary reparations for ever' at the p(ro)per coste and charges of this guild. And it is alsoe ordered that whatsoever the said masters and wardens shall doe or consent to be done in ye regayninge and repairinge ye said chapell as aforesaid the guild shall will and doe ratifie and confirme the same."*

The negotiations with the Dean and Chapter appear to have been successful as on 21st January, 1649, the Guild appointed Robert Parry, Minister of St. Audoen's, as their chaplain during pleasure at the yearly salary of £6 10s. 4d., " he to preach the word of God five times in the year; viz.:—Trinity Eve, and upon the four quarter days in the morning and to perform other duties unto the said Guild as a Chaplain ought to do."

In April 1656 Mr. Seele, " minister of God's word " was chosen chaplain at the yearly salary of 20 nobles. On his resignation it was ordered by the Guild in July 1666 that Mr. John Glandee, Minister of the parish of St. Michael, be appointed to the vacancy. It was ordered that he should receive timely notice to prepare himself to preach a sermon on the Eve of the Holy Trinity in Christ Church for which he was to have forty shillings.

* Gilbert MS., pp. 119-120.

GUILD MERCHANT IN XVII. CENTURY 153

Prior to the appointment of Mr. Glandee, an order had been made that the Accountant Master should lay out so much money as should be necessary in providing wine and other refreshments for the Eve of the Holy Trinity when the brethren were to meet decently dressed to attend the Masters and Wardens to Christ Church in their gowns to hear a sermon and return to the Tholsell according to ancient custom.*

The sum of £30 was voted by the Guild on 13th October, 1679, towards the repairing and beautifying of the King's Chapel in Christ Church and the erecting of a seat fit for the grandeur of the Chief Magistrate and officers of Dublin.

In the closing years of the seventeenth century a number of French Protestants found their way to Dublin, driven hither by the intolerant attitude adopted by Louis XIV. and his ministers towards those of the Protestant religion. Several petitions were presented by the refugees to the Guild Merchant praying to have free liberty of trading in Dublin—a privilege which was granted.

The tradition of the Guild's activity in the cause of charity was carried on by the Guild Merchant in the seventeenth century. At the Midsummer Assembly in the year 1668 a petition was presented by certain of the brethren that a grant should be made "lest so pious a work as the building of the Alms house now in hands should be discontinued for want of the necessary supply of money for erecting the fabrick thereof." It was ordered by the Assembly that the fines of freemen, admitted that

Charity of Guild.

* Gilbert MS., p. 141.

day, should be bestowed towards the building of the Hospital.

Reference to the municipal records reveals the fact that in this year a committee was appointed by the Common Council of Dublin to take steps for the erection of an hospital for "the pore and aged, as well men as women, and the fatherless and motherless children that have not freinds nor estates to live uppon"—a project which resulted in the foundation of The Hospital and Free School of King Charles II., Oxmantown, Dublin, popularly known as "The Blue Coat School." A list of the first subscribers towards the building and maintenance of the Hospital, dated 15th January, 1669, is published in the Calendar of the Ancient Records of Dublin. In this list "The Trinyty Guild" are credited with the payment of the sum of £25.

At an assembly held on 12th April, 1675, it was ordered by the Masters, Wardens and Brethren of the Guild that four poor boys be placed in the New Hospital on the account of the Guild, and that £3 be given with each boy towards his present maintenance and education.

On the Christmas quarter day in the year 1696 the Guild ordered that the sum of £20 be paid to George Darby, a free brother of the Guild, in order to discharge the fees due by him and procure his release from the Marshalsea prison.

One of the features which characterised the Guild Merchant in the seventeenth century was the rise to power of an inner body known as the "Council of the House." This Council appeared at one time to be in danger of completely dominating the affairs of the Guild to the

GUILD MERCHANT IN XVII. CENTURY 155

exclusion of the ordinary brethren. The general executive power became vested in this body.

Council of the House. The first mention of the Council appears in the record of a meeting held on 14th January, 1655, when an order was made that a certain number of persons be appointed the Council of the Guild to assist the Masters and Wardens when required. Sixteen persons were appointed to form the first Council.*

In April 1657 a petition was presented by certain of the brethren, stating that, in their opinion, the affairs of the corporation might not be so well carried on by the whole number of the brotherhood as by a select number to be chosen thereout, as the whole corporation could not meet as often as business required. The petitioners therefore requested that a certain number might be elected a Council of the House, and that the others should forbear their attendance in the hall, save only on Quarter days and at such other times as they should be required by the Masters and Wardens. The prayer of this petition was answered by the appointment of a Council of twenty-four. The names were given in the original record but do not appear in the Gilbert transcript.

The movement towards the concentration of power in the hands of the Council is well exemplified in a by-law made in January 1663. A Petition was presented praying that a Council might be appointed consisting of forty-eight persons, to be added to the Aldermen and Sheriffs' Peers, to attend all Assemblies, that so the younger brethren might not be troubled to attend upon all meetings

* Gilbert MS., p. 148.

of the Guild. It was ordered, accordingly, that for the future the number to sit in the Assembly of the said Guild should not exceed forty-eight brethren, besides the Aldermen and Sheriff's Peers, and that the Assembly so modelled should have full power to make and repeal all laws belonging to the Guild. It was further provided that the forty-eight brethren should be nominated by a committee.

Fortunately for the welfare of the Guild Merchant this oligarchic by-law was repealed in July 1664.

The by-laws already referred to do not indicate the tenure of office of the Council members. In the year 1665 a Council was appointed to hold office for the ensuing year. This democratic step was counterbalanced by a provision that the members of the Council should be nominated by the Masters and Wardens. The number of persons appointed was fifty which points to a considerable guild membership.

A further attempt to strengthen the position of the Council was made in the year 1673 by a law which reads as follows* :—

" Upon petition of certain of the brethren praying that there might be a Council chosen out of the brethren of this Guild, to act in the intervals of assemblies, for that this Corporation is grown very numerous, it would be inconvenient that they should be all warned to appear upon every occasion. It is therefore ordered this day the Masters and Wardens, all the Aldermen and Sheriff's Peers, so many as are free of this Guild and 40 more to be chosen by the Masters and Wardens out of the Brethren

* Gilbert MS., p. 156.

GUILD MERCHANT IN XVII. CENTURY

of this Guild, are hereby apptd. to be of the Council of this Guild for the ensuing year, nine whereof shall be a quorum, one Master and one Warden to be always two to act in the intervals of the assemblies."

Six years later a law was made excluding the general body of brethren from participation in the Guild's affairs, save on the occasion of the Michaelmas Quarter Assembly. The record of this law appears as follows in the Gilbert transcript of the by-laws:—" Upon petition of certain of the Brethren stating that this corporation is become so very numerous consisting of upwards of 400 brethren that should they all meet there is not a Hall large enough to contain them, besides the prejudices that younger brothers that are newly out of their time of apprenticeship sustain in the loss of their time, by appearing every quarter day before they have had any experience in the world; and praying that a law might be made that a certain number of the brethren of this guild that may best spare their time in the service of the Corporation might be chosen and such only be summoned to meet and act in Quarter Assemblies and By Assemblies and that they be empowered to make such laws, admit brethren, and do all things requisite for the good government of this Guild . . . It was ordered that the Lord Mayor the Masters and Wardens all the aldermen and Sheriffs Peers who are free of this guild and three score more of the brethren be elected by the Masters, Wardens and Council to act as aforesaid whereof 30 to be a quorum, one Master and one Warden to be always two." A proviso was added that on the occasion of the Michaelmas Quarter Assembly it should be lawful for all the brethren to meet at the election of the

Masters, Wardens and other officers of the guild, and to hear all acts, laws and orders that had been made at the foregoing three quarter assemblies.

Although, according to this law, the brethren had become so numerous that there was not a hall in Dublin large enough to accommodate them, yet the Guild was not always in such a flourishing condition. During the early Cromwellian period, owing to scarcity of numbers, the Guild Merchant had admitted persons from other guilds contrary though it was to the ancient by-laws to admit such, save under the prohibitive fine of £40. In the year 1656 the Guild had become sufficiently strong to check recruitment from external sources. A by-law of that year recites that "whereas this Guild is now plentifully replenished with brethren and the times, through the mercy of God amended, it is therefore ordered that from next Midsummer Assembly the said laws be put into force and that from that time none of any other corporation or handicrafts trade shall be admitted into this Guild unless upon the special fine of £40 Irish."

At the same Assembly another by-law was made dealing with the admission of strangers who were not members of other guilds "upon grants especial." This bye-law deserves to be quoted in full as it makes mention for the first time of the admission of members by special grace, a practice which was ultimately to have disastrous consequences for the Guild. Hitherto membership had been gained by the tedious process of apprenticeship, or by the rights of birth or marriage. Now the guild recognised a new form of admission—

Admission by Special Grace.

GUILD MERCHANT IN XVII. CENTURY

by special grace. This by-law is recorded as follows:—

"Certain brethren setting forth that where as there was an Act of Assembly formerly made that no person should be admitted to the brotherhood of this guild under the fine of £4 and for as much as at the present there are many intruders upon the said Guild who upon pretence thereof intrude presuming to come in upon the same fine wch if not prevented will be very injurious to the apprentices of this Guild who serve out their times with their masters for the gaining of their freedoms and for as much as this Guild consists of many brothers who have many apprentices who will be daily coming out of their time And for the stock of this Guild is but little by reason of the many disbursements and small receipts And praying that from henceforth no person shall be admitted a brother of this Guild upon grants especial under the fine of £10 provided that respect may be had unto such as have served some part of their time of apprenticeship with a brother of this Guild. It is ordered 14th April 1656 that the above petition be agreed to."*

By an old guild law of the fifteenth century it was provided that persons should be admitted as brethren at the quarterly assemblies only. The guild authorities appear to have departed for a time from this rule and admitted brethren on "unusual" days, a practice which might lead to great abuse. It was ordered, accordingly, in the year 1667, that if any of the Masters or Wardens, should admit persons to the freedom of the Guild except on Quarter Days, in full assembly, they should pay a fine

* Gilbert MS., pp. 128–9.

of £100 and be banished from the freedom of the corporation.

The Common Council of Dublin at their Michaelmas Assembly in the year 1675 ordered that the Masters of the several corporations of the city should not for the future admit any person to be Quarter brother or a sworn brother of any corporation until he should be first free of the city.

Only two of the Guild by-laws of the seventeenth refer to apprentices and both deal with the provision of stocks for their punishment. The earlier of these laws is as follows:—

Stocks for Apprentices. "Certain of the brethren setting forth that whereas there are several misdemeanours committed by apprentices belonging to this Guild and that they escape unpunished by reason that there are no stocks made for the punishment of such offenders in the hall, as is usual in the halls of other corporations—It is ordered the 14th of April 1656 that a pair of stocks be provided for the punishment of such apprentices as shall offend from time to time."

Military Training of Members. The enjoyment of the guild franchise, with which the civic franchise was associated, entailed upon the guildsman certain civic duties, chief amongst which was that of taking part in the defence of the city. In the latter half of the seventeenth century this duty became confined to that of undergoing a slight amount of military training on days appointed.

Reference to the "soldiers of the Trinity Guild" appears in an entry dated 12th March, 1603, recorded in

GUILD MERCHANT IN XVII. CENTURY

the Gilbert transcript as follows:—For as much as the soldiers of the Trinity Guild are drawn away out of this city and only 12 men and an officer are left to guard the Castle and the Lord Deputy and Council have commanded that bedding be provided for that number—It is ordered that two beds shall be provided by this guild and the Mayor to provide the rest of the bedding among the corporations; said beds to be only a flock bed, a caddowe and a pair of sheets for each bed."

The Gilbert MS. contains the following entry under date, 9th May, 1608:—" According to a warrant of Mr. Mayor for charging of 40 men upon this company for the ancient raising out unto the general hosting cessors were appointed for that purpose."

Two entries dealing with the military training of the guildsmen appear under date, 21st April, 1623 namely:—
" At a meeting of the Masters, Wardens and brethren this day it is agreed that Mr. William Bushop alder^n. shall be chosen Captain of the Trinity Guild, Patrick Gough ald^n. Lieutenant and Thomas Tailor ancient and they to execute their several offices on the field on mustering days accordingly."

" It is also ordered the same day that whosoever misses the attendance of the colours belonging to the Guild on days appointed being therto required shall for every time offending pay as a fine 5s. Irish from thence forth for one whole year provided he or they be between the age of 60 and 16 years."

The following Order signed by the Mayor of Dublin appeared in the Guild records:—" Wheras it hath binn an ancient and laudable custome that the yong men within

M

this Cittie and Liberties have fowre tymes in the yeare binn drawne out into the fields, in a Corporation way and manner for the exercising them in armes to be the better trayned up for the defence of this Cittie in his ma^{ties}. service the wch. custome hath for a long tyme binn discontinued by reason of the late warres and disturbances. I doe nevertheless intend to revive the said customes and in order thereunto I doe hereby require you to give timely notice and sumonses unto all the brothers of this Corporation except the Aldermen and Sheriffs-Peers that they and every of them and their men servants from sixtiene to sixtie yeares of age in their best apparell and wth. compleate armes, doe appeare at and with the cullers of the Corporation on the first day of May next by six of the clocke in the morning either at ye Hall or in such other convenient place as you their Master shall appoynt to the end you may take your march to Oxmantowne Greene wth. the rest of your Corporation according to order on Station days and herein you may not faile; dated the 22d of April 1665."*

Frequent mention is made about this time of an old custom whereby the members of the Trinity and other Guilds marched in battle array on every Easter Monday from Dublin to Cullenswood as a defiant commemoration of a battle fought at the latter place between the citizens and certain Wicklow clans in which battle the citizens had suffered severely. The day was long known in Dublin as " Black Monday."

This annual demonstration appears to have been attended sometimes with a lack of orderliness and discipline. In

* Gilbert MS., pp. 139–140.

the year 1671 the Lord Mayor ordered that the Trinity Guild should proceed as usual to Cullenswood on Easter Monday. The Masters of the Guild were required by the order to take great care that no disturbance, disorders, debauchery or other profanation be committed, to the dishonour of God or scandal of the government, but that all should demean themselves as becometh sober citizens and good Christians.

The Guild records of the year 1676 embodied an Order from the Lord Mayor addressed to the Masters and Wardens, the preamble of which recites that the Masters of the several corporations of the city had requested an alteration of the time and place of this annual event. The Order proceeds:—

"These are therefore to authorize and require you to give timely notice and warning unto all and every the brothers and Members of your corporations, that they and every of them and men servants, above the age of 16 and under the age of 60 do prepare themselves, and on May day by 9 of the clock in the morning do meet or repair to the colours of their corporation wth compleat arms in the best apparel to the end they may take their arms in marching to St. Stephen's Green, the place appointed, according to their order on Station days, to be there by 10 of the clock and exercise their several companies until 4 of the clock in the afternoon at which time they are to march back into the city in good order and discipline. And you are likewise to take care that no disorder be committed in your Corporation which may tend to the scandal of the good government of this city and to return afterwards unto me the names of such members of your corporation as shall refuse or neglect their duty therein to the end they may be punished for their disobedience; and for so doing this shall be your warrant."*

A number of items of expenditure in connection with the annual commemoration occur in the Guild records. About the year 1653 an Order was made empowering the Masters " to disburse all such moneyes as shalbe fitt for buyeing of Cullors and defrayeing all such charges as shall be incident thereunto or thought so to be for the creditt of the said Guild." The following entry is dated 13th March, 1665, namely:—" A cess was this day made for raising the sum of £40 for provisions and other necessaries against Black Monday next when the Corpn. is to march to Cullens-wood." The sum of £50 was voted in the year 1677 to provide all necessary implements of war and suitable entertainment for the brethren on May day. At the same meeting £14 was ordered to be allowed the Accomptant Master for the purchase of two convenient tents for the accommodation of the brethren on May day.

A good deal of money was expended by the Guild on the entertainment of the members. In January 1655 it was ordered, by the desire of the brethren *Entertainment* of the Guild, that the sum of £5 should be *of Brethren.* expended every quarter day upon a dinner for the brethren. In May 1666 the Accomptant Master was authorised to lay out so much money as should be thought necessary in providing wine and other refreshment for the Eve of the Holy Trinity. In October 1677 it was ordered that a sum not exceeding £10 should be allowed the Master for the expenses of the

* Gilbert MS., p. 160.

GUILD MERCHANT IN XVII. CENTURY

day's entertainment on the occasion of the late perambulating the franchises and liberties of the city. The sum of £20 was voted in the year 1683 for necessaries in connection with the riding of the franchises and the entertainment to be provided on that occasion for the Masters, Wardens and Brethren.

Guild Expenditure. The expenditure of the Guild Merchant during the seventeenth century extended to a variety of objects. Some of these have been indicated already, such as the charitable works of the Guild, the defence of the City and the entertainment of the members. Others will now be briefly referred to.

According to an entry which appeared in the old Record Books of the Guild bearing date 16th June, 1626, the sum of £1,000 English was to be lent to His Majesty for the furtherance of his service by the whole city. Of this sum two-thirds or 1000 marks was to be levied off the brethren and sisters of the guild. Cessors were appointed to raise the guild's contribution.

In the same year the expenditure of a sum of £64 was sanctioned by the Guild to be used " in prosecuting suite to his Majesty and the Lo^{rs} to prevent the hurte intended to this Company or Corporacon and alsoe to this cittie by Samuel Smyth and diviers officers of the customs heer whoe have laboured to obtain newe graunts from his majesty to preiudice the said corporacons."*

About this time the Guild appear to have been in funds and it was found necessary to make provision for the safe custody of their funds and other valuables. It was ordered,

* Gilbert MS.

accordingly, in January 1627, that an iron-bound chest should be bought upon which there should be three locks, the Master for the time being to have the keeping of one key, the wardens of another, and one of the auditors to have the third key. The chest was to remain in the custody of the Master for the time being. It was ordered at the same time that the Master for the time being should compel the preceding Master to pass his account within one month from the determining of his office.

An important order was made by the Guild Merchant in January 1633 which reads as follows:—" It is ordered in this assemblie that the persons herunder named are elected and chosen Comitties to deale and undertake for the wine and aquavite lysence wth the Earlle of Carlies agent or wth eny other whoe have or may have power to lett or sett the said lysence and whate they doe therin or compound for in the behalfe of the trynitie yild it is ratified and confirmed by the said yielde and will give allowance thereunto."

On the 26th day of Nov., 1639, a cess was authorised by the Guild for the purpose of obtaining a new Charter. The original record ran as follows:—" Memorand—that the daie and yeare above written it was ordained in a full assemblie then holden that a cess shall be made throughout the whole bretheren of the Trynitie Guild towards the renewing of a newe charter in suche a manner and form as shalbe laid downe under the hand of the Right Woo^{rpll} Charles ffoster maior of the cittie of Dublin, alderman James Watson and alderman Davide Beigg masters of the Trynitie Guild, Mr. Andrewe Clercke and Mr. Sancke Sulliard Wardens wth a whole and a generall consent that six comitties shalbe herunder nominated unto whose choise and ellection it is agreed at the next meetinge that whate those Comitties doe agree upon with the consent of the guild whither it goe by a cess or not shalbe allowed."

The salaries of the Guild officers were a regular item of expenditure. In the year 1640 it was agreed that the Clerks of the Guild should have a yearly stipend of £10 to be paid out of the fines and " casualties " of the Guild. In the year 1648 there were two clerks each of whom received a salary of £5. It was decided, however, in the interests of economy, to do with one Clerk at an annual stipend of £5. In the same year it was agreed that Thomas Pursell, a brother of the house, should be appointed beadle of the house at an annual salary of 40 shillings. According to a note in the Gilbert transcript this was the first appointment of such an officer. The sum of £4 was voted in the year 1656 for the purpose of providing the beadle with a livery cloak and suit against Easter for his attendance upon the Master and Wardens and for the credit of the Corporation. In the year 1661 the sum of £5 was ordered to be paid to the Beadle in order that he might buy a " shutt and cloake " for Easter. The salary of Robert Parry, chaplain of the Guild, was fixed at £6 10s. 4d per annum in the year 1649. This amount was doubled seven years later on the appointment of Mr. Seele whose salary was fixed at 20 nobles.

The proclamation of Oliver Cromwell as Lord Protector occasioned a certain expenditure by the Guild. The following entry occurred in the original Record Book:—

" By the Mrs Wardens and bretheren of the guild of mchants held this 7th of July 1657:

168   THE GUILDS OF DUBLIN

"Wheras by order of the Right worpfull the maior of the Citty the said Corporacon is appoynted to attend on Thursday next at tenn of the Clock in the morning in compleate armes to attend the publishing of his highness
Proclamation of Lord Protector.
Lo: Protector of the three nations   It is ordered therefore that for that purpose and service Mr. John Sergeant is appoynted to bee capten Mr. John Totty Lieut and Mr. Christop. Bennet Ensigne, and that there is allowed to bee spent that daye out of the Stocke of the house wch is to be allowed Mr. Alderman Mills Accomptant M^r uppon his accompt the some of five pounds sterl. over and above the charges to bee laid out to the Srgeants and drome which is alsoe to bee allowed him."*

Several items of expenditure occur in connection with the Guild Hall.   In January 1683 an Order was made by the Guild upon a petition from certain of the brethren shewing that the great room in the Tholsell to be set apart
The Guild Hall.
for the Hall of the Guild was nearly finished and that it was conceived necessary that a noble seat should be erected therein for the Masters and Wardens and other seats for the brethren.   The Masters, Wardens and Council of the House were authorised to cause such seats to be erected in the Hall as they should think fit.

About the same time it was ordered, by the authority of the Assembly, that a petition be presented to the Lord Mayor, Sheriffs, Council and Citizens to have the same room granted to the Guild for ever.   The Masters and

* Gilbert MS., p. 133

GUILD MERCHANT IN XVII. CENTURY

Wardens were empowered in the event of receiving such grant, under the Seal of the City, as an acknowledgment of such a favour, to present and deliver up to the Lord Mayor and Treasurer of the city a certain bond, under the city Seal, for £200 lent by the Guild to the City in the year 1643. The Accomptant Master was likewise authorised to have inscribed over the gate of the said Hall under the Coat of Arms of the Guild the words "Trinity Guild Hall."

In July 1684 the Guild ordered that the inner room belonging to the Hall should be wainscotted with deal at a cost not exceeding £10, the said room to serve as a with-drawing room for the Guild Hall. A subsequent Order directed that the Great Hall be ceiled with parquetage with an oval feston and four compartments with small festons, the same to be guilded, and the plain ceiling painted.

In order to complete these works a self-denying ordinance was passed by the brethren in the following terms:—

"Upon petition of certain of the brethren shewing that last Midsummer there was an act made for ceiling the Hall with a noble ceiling suitable to the wainscot already done and the common stock at present being at a very low ebb so that the Masters and Wardens for the future should be very frugal until such works be finished as the Corporation have granted to be done; and praying that all feasts and quarter days and all unnecessary expenses be laid aside It is ordered that all feasting and unnecessary feasts shall cease for the future (Trinity Eve's treat only excepted) until the said works be finished, and the cellar belonging to the Guild redeemed."

THE GUILDS OF DUBLIN

For the adornment of their Hall and as an emblem of their loyalty the Guild ordered in July 1683 that the King's picture should be bought. Whether the face of Charles II. ever looked down upon the assembled brethren or not is doubtful. No entry relating to the payment for this particular portrait is recorded. The allegiance of the Guild was later transferred from the Stuarts to the House of Orange. Two entries relate to the purchase of royal portraits:—

13th July 1691—" Ordered that £10 be paid to Thomas Newman for His Majesty's picture now placed in the Hall of the Guild " and on 12th October 1691—" Thomas Newman having by order of this Guild drawn the picture of her present Majesty it is ordered that he be paid £10 for the same."

The following entry dated 20th October, 1691, is of interest, namely:—" Upon petition of certain of the brethren shewing that this Kingdom being reduced to a happy and quiet peace under the conduct of his Excellency Baron de Ginkell and that we are like to reap the benefit thereof under the serene government of their Gracious Majesties The Masters Wardens and brethren of this guild have this day ordered that the sum of £40 sterl. be paid out of the common Stock of this corporation towards a noble treat, fireworks and a ball to be made by the Lord Mayor Sheriffs Aldermen Commons and Citizens to entertain the said General Ginkell and all the general officers as a mark of their respects and gratitude and that the same be allowed the accomptant master in his accompt"*.

General Ginkell Entertained.

* Gilbert MS., p. 171.

Portion of the outlay of the Guild Merchant was devoted to public purposes. In July 1653 it was ordered that two fire-engines should be purchased by Alderman Wybrants who was to receive £60 for that purpose. An entry of the year 1661 records that pursuant to a warrant from the Mayor a cess was to be made upon the brethren of the guild for the payment of £42 for the repairs of the city wall. An undated entry in the Gilbert transcript, probably of the year 1676, refers to the Artillery Yard at Oxmantown as follows:—

Public Expenditure.

" Upon reading the petition of certain of the Brethren setting forth that the Ground in Oxmantowne Green appointed by the Common Council to be an artillery yard to train up the youth of this city in military discipline is now walled in at the charge of private persons That as this Corporation has ever been ready to contribute to all public works belonging to this City it was humbly prayed that this Guild would countenance and encourage the said good work by building of a gate to the said Artillery yard . . . . It is ordered by the M^s. W^s. and Brethren of the Holy Trinity Guild of Merchants the present Quarter Assembly that a large gate of hewen stone be built for the said Artillery yard at the charge of this Guild . . . . provided the charge thereof do not exceed the sum of £50."

The close of the seventeenth century found the Guild Merchant in a strong financial position. At their quarterly meeting in July 1697 the brethren made an order that the sum of £200 be lent to the City of Dublin at eight per cent and that a bond under the City Seal be taken for the same. In October 1699 it was ordered, upon a petition from certain of the brethren shewing that the £200 stock of the Guild had lain dead about three months, that a committee consisting of the Masters and Wardens and six of the Brethren of the Council of the House should be appointed to treat with any person that would take the said £200 at interest upon such security as they should approve but at not less than six per cent.

The records of the Guild Merchant dealing with the revenue of the fraternity were much scantier than those dealing with expenditure. The Guild had a constant source of income in the contributions paid by the brethren every quarter and known as "quarterage."

Guild Revenue. An undated entry of the period 1667-8 appearing in the Gilbert transcript records that the quarterage of every brother was raised from 6d. to 12d. per quarter. At the same time it was ordered that all brethren who had not borne office should pay an equal share to make up the salary of £10 payable to the Beadle. Fines were paid on admission to the brotherhood. These fines varied in amount and ranged from twenty shillings to forty pounds.

A certain revenue was derived from the fines or amercements imposed upon those who offended against the Guild by-laws. Some of these fines were considerable in amount. In the case of William ffrain, a Merchant brother of the guild who was found by a Jury in the year 1617 to be a great dealer for the Dutchmen, a fine of £20 was imposed. Minor breaches were met by corresponding penalties. An entry dated 13th October, 1651, that being a quarter assembly day, records that several persons were fined 5s. each for not having appeared and that certain other persons were fined from 5s. to 2s. 6d. " for not wearinge of a decent gowne but sittinge in their Cloakes."

The Guild at one time derived considerable profit from dues levied upon imported goods purchased by their members. The Egerton manuscript copy of the Guild by-laws contains the following record of a law dated 20th April, 1601, namely:—

" Wher informacon is made to this assemble that an awncient lawe greatlie benefiting this yeald by wch lawe ther was due out of ev^{r}y tun of Iorne brought to this citty by eny stranger upon his owne adventure, & bought after by a brother of this yeald, five shillings sterl. & of ev^{r}y tonn of wine five shillings sterl. & soe ratablie of all other sorte of merchaundise: wch lawe is by some ivil disposed p̄son intending the great hurt of this gwield rased & cutt out quitt of the bookes of record of the said gwield, and now the same being thought meet to be renewed," &c. It was therefore ordered that the said law should be renewed and that the said sums should be paid thenceforth to the treasury of the guild and all arrears paid up.

CHAPTER VI.

THE CRAFT GUILDS IN THE SEVENTEENTH CENTURY.

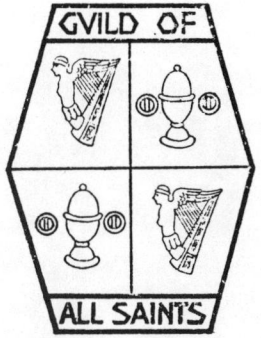

CHAPTER VI.

The Craft Guilds in the Seventeenth Century.

THE guild system in Dublin extended still further in the seventeenth century until it included practically the whole ambit of industry in the city and Liberties. During this period the close connection between the guilds and the great corporation of the city became evident. The fact at length emerges that civic administration was controlled by the representatives of the merchant and craft guilds. A change in the spirit of the Guilds, due to causes set at work in the sixteenth century became strongly marked. Racial antipathy in the guilds died only to give place to religious antipathy. A craftsman was no longer excluded from the guild because he was of Irish birth, but because he was not a member of the Established Church. In a city where a large proportion of the population professed the Catholic faith, this exclusion led to the dissociation of the guilds from a great body of craftsmen and contributed largely to the decay and final overthrow of the guild system.

Another notable feature of the seventeenth century was the association in the same guild of members practising different crafts. In the sixteenth century the masons, carpenters, heliers and joiners had formed one corporation, as did the barbers and surgeons. The latter guild in the seventeenth century included in addition the apothecaries and periwig makers. The Guild of St. Luke the Evangelist included cutlers, painter-stainers and stationers, while the bricklayers and plasterers formed one guild, as did the brewers and maltsters. Another form of association was that of the newer and less powerful guilds with older and stronger ones. Eight of the older craft guilds occupied a position of prominence. To these guilds other craft bodies attached themselves as "wings." It strengthened the position of a young guild to place itself under the *aegis* of an old and wealthy guild, and it lightened the burden of the constant levies imposed by the Common Council upon the guilds when that burden was shared with a numerous and wealthy brotherhood. In these two causes probably lies the reason of this peculiar association.

The important part played by the guilds in civic administration is clearly exemplified in the municipal records. Already it has been shown that in the year 1600 the two Houses which comprised the Common Council of Dublin were composed largely of guildsmen. The records of the seventeenth century show that the representation of the guilds was a recognised principle of the civic constitution. In the Calendar of Ancient Records of Dublin, the following record appears under the year 1627:—

Representation of Guilds on Common Council.

"Whereas the masters of the eight corporacions complained that the winges belonging to every corporacion, through over much toleracion, doe strive to have precedency in sitting in the Tholsell on the assembly daies, and offereth violence to some of the said eight masters to put them from theire places, where in reason and decensie the said eight masters should sitt together in the Tholsell on the said assembly daies, and the winges to sitt after the last master of the said eight masters: for reformacion whereof, it is ordered in this assembly that the masters of every of the eight corporacions shall hould and keepe theire places together in the Tholsell on every assembly day, and the masters of every of the winges being of the numbers shall sitt next to the last master of the said eight corporacions, and soe to continue on every assembly day, and not otherwise."

In the year 1639 the Assembly orders: "That the Maior, the threasurer, the masters of the Trinitie Guilde, Alderman Jans, Alderman Kennedy and both the Sheriffes, or any foure of them, whereof the Maior to bee one, are appointed committees to examine the rowle of numbers, and to certifie the table of aldermen which of the numbers doe absent themselves from the generall assemblies of the cittie, to the end that they may bee removed from the same; and when they shalbee soe removed, that from henceforth none be sworne of the numbers of the Trinitie Guilde above four-score and sixteene, being the two partes of the said numbers; and that hereafter, when the rest of the numbers which are of the corporacions shalbee voyde, that none of the eight corporacions and theire winges shall have above sixe to bee of the numbers, beinge the third parte of the said numbers, amounting to forty and eight; and that from henceforth none of the eight companies or the Trinitie Guilde bee sworn of the said numbers but in the presence of the Maior, one of the Sheriffes and foure of the aldermen."

At this time the civic constitution comprised the Mayor, two Sheriffs, twenty-four Aldermen, known as the " Board of Aldermen" or "Table of Aldermen," forty-eight Sheriff's Peers and Ninety-six councillors, the latter bodies being referred to familiarly as "the Forty-eight" and "the Ninety-six" and were known collectively as "the Numbers." The Common Council of which the constituent elements are above mentioned contemplated at this time, as appears from the entry above quoted, that the whole body of "the Numbers" should be drawn, as to two-thirds, from the Merchants, and, as to one-third, from the craft guilds. No record could show more clearly how closely the guild system was interwoven with the municipal system.

Under the Act of Explanation passed by a Parliament held in Dublin in the year 1665, the Lord Lieutenant and Council were empowered to make rules for the better regulating of all cities, walled towns and corporations in Ireland, such rules to have the force of law. It was not until the year 1672 that the Rules for the City of Dublin were finally issued. The "New Rules," as they were called, after providing for the approval by the Lord Lieutenant and Privy Council of the persons elected to the chief civic offices, and for the taking of the Oath of Supremacy by such officers, as well as by all those elected of the Common Council of the City and by the Masters and Wardens of all corporations or guilds, recite as follows:—

The "New Rules."

"Whereas the Common Council of the said city doth consist of a Lord Mayor and twenty-four Aldermen, who have usually sate together in one room apart by themselves and also of such who are commonly called Sheriffs-Peers not exceeding forty-eight persons, and of ninety-six other persons who are elected into the said Common-Council out of several of the Guilds or Corporations of this city, and who have usually sate together in one room apart by themselves, and have been usually called the Commons of the said city, amongst whom the Sheriffs of the said city for the time being do preside.

"And whereas we conceive it would tend to the benefit and advantage of the said city, if such persons who are chosen into the said Common Council out of the several Guilds or Corporations of this city, should be changed, and new elections made of them once in every three years, by which change a greater number of the citizens of the said city might come into the said places and be entrusted with the management of the affairs of the city," it was ordered by the Lord Lieutenant and Privy Council that the several guilds which enjoyed the right of representation should hold triennial elections of double the number of members whom they were entitled to return, that the names of the guildsmen so selected should be submitted by the Masters and Wardens of each Guild to the Lord Mayor for the time being, who was authorised and required to elect, out of the persons whose names should be so presented, the number of persons usually serving in the Common Council for each such Guild respectively. A proviso was added that this rule should not debar or hinder the Lord Mayor, Aldermen and Common-Council from exercising the power that they had formerly used of altering or changing the number of any Common-Council men usually serving for any Corporation and of distributing the same amongst any other Corporations that then were, or thereafter should be in the city, so that the whole number of persons to be chosen out of the said Corporations should not exceed ninety-six.

In the year 1688 the Common Council of Dublin enacted that "For the better regulateing of the severall corporations in the cittie of Dublin it is necessary that there be one alderman at least and a certaine number of burgesses elected by the said respective corporations, to represent the body of such corporation in the assemblies." It was accordingly ordered that the respective corporations should elect suitable representatives by the 1st day of May following. By this law members of the Guilds were made directly eligible for admission to the upper house of the Common Council, now known as the Board or Table of Aldermen, the members of which were formerly known as the "Jurats" or "Jurés."

Guilds and Board of Aldermen.

The curriers of Dublin, having been incorporated as a craft guild by William III., applied to the Common Council for the privilege of representation "pursuant to the custome of this citty," an application which was granted. The following record appears in the Calendar under date 24th April, 1696: "Whereas the master and wardens of the corporation of curriers preferred their petition to the said assembly, setting forth that his most excellent majestie, king William, had been gratiousely pleased to grant the curriers of this citty a charter under his great seale, whereby they are incorporated by the name of the master, wardens and bretheren of the guild or corporation of curriers of the cittie of Dublin, they therefore prayed this assembly, pursuant to the custome of this citty,

Curriers.

CRAFT GUILDS IN THE XVII. CENTURY 183

to allow them numbers to be of the common councill of the said citty: It is therefore ordered and agreed upon, by the authority of the said assembly, that the said corporation of curriers may have two of their numbers to be of the common councill of this cittie, to take their station gradually after the youngest corporation of this city."

At the next quarterly meeting of the Common Council a similar order was made on the application of the Master Wardens and Brethren of the Guild or Fraternity of Brewers and Malsters who had likewise been incorporated by William III. In October, 1696, the number of representatives of the Brewers and Malsters on the Common Council was fixed at four.

Composed so largely of guild representatives as the Dublin Assembly was in the seventeenth century, it represented in its economic aspect a common council of all the guilds. Many of its most important deliberations were concerned with the control of trade and industry in Dublin. Amongst the enactments of the Common Council were a number of bye laws made in the opening years of the century which affected the working of the guilds.

Control of Craft Guilds.

An entry in the Assembly Roll for the year 1604 reads: " Whear(as) the commons complained of the abuse of the tallochaunlers in exactinge of prices uppon the cittizens for candelles: it is therfore agreed, by the aucthorytie afforesaid, that in respecte of the scarsetye of talow and candelles and . . . of the prices taken by the tallochaunlers, contrarye to their chartor, that it shalbe lawfull for anye freeman of this cittie to make and sell candelles at their pleasure hensforth till Michalmas nexte; (provided) such freeman doe first come before Mr Maior and enter into recognizans with sufficient suertye not to exceede the price of six pence of the kings newe sylver for a pounde of candelles or other such . . ."

While the Common Council were always anxious to protect the members of the Guilds from any undue encroachment upon their respective spheres of industry, they were broadminded enough to welcome any extension of the work of a craft which tended to provide extra employment for the citizens. Thus, one John Handfield, a weaver, is recorded as making an humble petition to the Assembly in the year 1604 for " his freedome of the franches and lybberties of this cittie, in respecte he is skilled in . . . fustians wherin the wevers of this cittie have noe knowledge, which could hardly be graunted . . . the corporacion of wevers of this cittie: neverthelesse it is agreed, by the aucthoritie of this assemblie, that the petycioner shall have lybbertie within this cittie to make such woorke in the trade of we(aving) as is not usuallie wrought by the weavers of the cittie, he not intruding farther uppon their trade, and this lybbertie to contynue for the space of three yeares; and yf in the meane tyme his woorke and carriadge be lykede of, he shall have his freedome; other condicions he is to be tyed unto, which is to be reserved to Mr Maior, Mr Shelton, Mr. Kennedie, and Mr Cusake, to be concludid."

An important event in the history of the goldsmiths' craft in Dublin was the enactment by the Common Council in the year 1605 of a bye law requiring every goldsmith to have his own mark to be stamped upon every piece of plate wrought or offered for sale by him. This bye lawe reads as follows: "Whear(as) the commons complayned that whear(as) in tyme past there hath bene great abuse in this cittie by the indirecte and synister dealinge of the gouldsmythes, in that there hath for many yeares bene divers parcelles of plate made of every base and corrupt silver, notwithstanding they have by credible reporte receaved good silver of those that caused it to bee made, greatlie hinderinge the florishinge state of this commonwealth: for remedie wherof, it is therfore ordered and agreed, by the authorytye afforesaid, that every gouldsmyth that shall exercyse that trade within this cittie shall have a speciall marke to stampe all suche plate as he shall woorke or sell; and withall that the Mayor and constables of the Staple yearly shalbe saymasters of all plate wrought or to be soulde from the first of Januarie next within this cittie, and that a stampe shalbe made with the figures of a lyon, an harpe and a castell, and the same to be locked by, the seale of the Staple, with which stampe all plate to be soulde by anie gouldsmyth in this cittie shalbe marked before the same shalbe putt to be soulde; and if anie gouldsmyth, after the first daie of Januarie next, shall sell, or putt to be soulde, anie plate not marked with his owne marke and the stampe afforesaid, that the same shalbe forfeited, and the said gouldsmyth fined in the some of five shillinges for every ownce of plate soulde by him, and nof stamped and marked as afforesaid; the said fine to be levied of his goodes, by warrant from the Mayor and recorder of the cittie, uppon presentment therof by twelve men sworne before them at their generall quarter sessions.

Goldsmiths' Marks.

And, further, wee doe agree that the Mayor and constables of the Staple shall call to their assystance, for the towch and tryall of the said plate when the same shalbe stamped, the preferrer of the bill, or some other that hath skill in suche woorke; and that tryall shalbe made before they putt the stampe to anie parcell of plate; and if by suche tryall or uppon towch therof it appere to be corrupte, mingled with baser, or not made alltogither of as pure silver as the silver standart coyne nowe current in this kingdome, that then every suche parcell of plate to be forfeited, the one moyetie therof to the Mayor and constables of the Staple, and the other moyetie to the use of the Mayor of the cittie; of the which moyetie the Mayor and constables of the Staple shall yealde an accompte yearly, after theire yeare is ended, before the cittie auditors. Further, wee doe agree that for every parcell of plate to be towched and stamped before the said Mayor and contables of the Staple, as afforesaid, they shall have allowance, of an halfe pennie for every ounce, to be paide by the gouldsmyth that have or goeth aboute to sell the same, and the moyetie of the allowance to bee given by them to the presenter of the bill, and whosoever else shalbe assystinge them in that towch and tryall by their appoyntment. And, further, that the preferrer of the bill, or whosoever else the Mayor and constables of the Staple shall call to their assystance, shalbe sworre for the carefull and honest and true tryall of every parcell. And if anie parcell wherunto the stampe shalbe putt shall prove corrupt or mixed with baser metall, and not meete to be stamped, that then the preferrer of the bill, or whosoever shalbe assystant to the said Mayor and constables, shall forfeit twentie poundes for every parcell soe stamped, toties quoties, and endure imprysonment for six monthes uppon complaynte made unto the Mayor of the cittie, and that therfore the Mayor and constables of the Staple shall keepe note in writing of all suche parcelles as they shall stampe, and the names of suche persons as they shall call to theire assystance."

A bye law made in the year 1606 reveals the fact that for some time past country butchers had been established in Dublin. They had, doubtless, been invited in by the Common Council in order to reduce the exorbitant charges of the city butchers. The latter made an humble request to the Assembly that they might be permitted " to cutt and karve their meate in the countrye shamels as they weare accustomed, and that a certaine houer might be laid downe for the countrye bouchers to departe the markett "; upon which Petition it is ordered that " the cittye bouchers shall keape their standing as nowe they doe in the towne shambles, and that the countrye bouchers contynue in the common shambles untill two of the clocke in the afternoone and noe longer; and yf they doe contrarye, the former lawes in that case provided to be putt in execution."

A few months later the Common Council was again called upon to regulate the butcher craft, when a prohibition was issued against any butcher purchasing or renting more than one board in the flesh shambles, it being shown that the " boordes of this cittie shamelles " had of late by purchase " come into a feawe nomber of the bouchers handes."

One of the functions fulfilled by the guild system was the stocking of the city with essential commodities at reasonable prices, each guild being responsible for the stock of the commodity in which its members dealt or worked. In the case of meat the country butchers were from time to time called in to supply the deficiency. Stanihurst in his "Description of Dublin, 1577" had stated: "Their shambles is so well stored with meat, and their market with corne, as not onelie in Ireland, but also in other countries, you shall not see anie one shambles, or anie one market better furnished with the one or the other, than Dublin is."

A Guild Function.

An important regulation in the interests of the citizens generally was that made in the year 1616 requiring craftsmen to have all the necessary tools and implements of their craft. The law is thus recorded:—

"Wheareas the commons, by their humble petycion preferred unto this assembly, praieth a lawe should be made that all carpinters, masons, bricklaiers, heliers, plasterers, and such others of their corporacions whatsoever, should have all necessary towles and furnytures of all sortes fitting their severall professions or trades, whearby the cittysens hiring any such artyficers heerafter may be better served then heertofore they have bene: it is therfore ordered and agreed, by the aucthorytie of this assembly, that the heliers, and others thartyficers above named, shall have lathers, ropes, trouelles, scaffoldes and all other instrumentes necessary for thexecucion of their severall trades, wherby noe inhabitant within this citty shalbe driven to provide anything for building or reparacions but materialls onelye.

Craftsmen to have Necessary Tools.

CRAFT GUILDS IN THE XVII. CENTURY

And yf any of the artyficers aforesaid shall from hensfoorth offend contrary to this lawe, then every such artyficer, for every daie that he shall woorke, using any the said instrumentes (not being his owne or provided by himselfe) shall forfeit twelve pence, sterling, a day to the cittye, and thoffendors to be imprisonid by Mr Maior for the tyme being, upon complaint therof made, untill he paie the same."

An excellent example of the manner in which the Common Council checked practices of the Guilds which were considered detrimental to the interests of the citizens generally is provided by a law passed in the year 1620 which is thus recorded: "Forasmuch as certaine the commons by theire peticion exhibited to the said assembly, complained of the manifold abuses of the carpinters, masons, heliers, and such other corporacions of this cittie, who have unlawfull lawes made amongst themselves, that none of them shall intermedle nor take in hand what woorke soever the other hath taken in hand, uppon a penaltie to be inflicted on the offendor, albeit the woorke should lie undone, and the partie not able to performe the same, whereby many of them doe compound and undertake many mens woorkes, as well in towne as in the countrie, and oftentimes more then they cann well performe, and thereby mens woorkes soe compounded for stands long undone and theire woorkes spoyled, theire howses ruinated, and the offendor walking the streetes litle regarding the domadges of the partie offended: for the avoyding of which inconvenience dailie hapning by the common abuse of woorkmen before complained of, it is agreed and established,

An Abuse Checked.

by thaucthoritie of the said assembly, that uppon complaint made to the master of the company whereof the offendor is member, the master shall presentlie releeve the peticioners in allowing and appointing others to finish the woorkes of such as shall leave theire woorkes undone as before, and yf the said master shall neglect to performe the same, then is Mr. Maior for the time being to punish the said master by fine of twentie shillinges, sterling English mony, and imprisonment, and to take order also for the releefe of the partie offended."

An interesting account of a proposal to remove the herring fishing industry from Clontarf to Ringsend in the year 1622 and of the support and approval given to the said proposal by the Common Council is contained in the Calendar of Dublin Records, namely:

Herring Fishing at Ringsend. "Whereas Edward Gough and James Sedgraw, of Dublin, merchants, by theire peticion exhibited to the said assemblie, have shewed that, to prevent the greevous exaction and uncivill opposicion of George Kinge, of Clontarfe, gentleman, they intend to deale with Sir Thomas Fitzwilliams touching the Ringes End, whereunto they intend, for the utilitie of the common wealth, to draw the heareing fishing and the access of fishers and merchants; for the better effecting whereof, and of a convenient place for the said fishing, they humblie praied that tharticles hereunder written might be by act of the said assembly approved and confirmed, videlicet, that all carmen in and about the cittie shall give three daies worke to draw sand and stones to assist the making of a banke or furlong at Ringes End for thencouradgment of many fishers there to come, which (God willing) the peticioners intend to make as convenient as Clontarfe, whereunto the cittie carmen may well contribuit in respect they have noe passadge to Clontarfe.

" Item: That all boats or barques comeing there haveing ballast shall dischardge the same where the peticioners shall appoint, uppon paine of forfeiture of X.s. sterling.

" Item: That all shipps and barques which cometh there shall give two cocke boates loaden with stone and sand for theffecting of the said worke, and that every gabart or lighter which apperteineth to the cittie shall give one loade of sande, doung or stone for the said woorkes.

" Item: That accordingly the act made in the yeare of Mr. Richard Browne, late Maior, may be confirmed, whereby none of the waterbayliffes shall demaund custome of any boates or barques there comeing concearning fresh fish.

" Item: That forasmuch as strangers and merchants cannott performe theire fishing without cowpers, which for the most part each man bringeth with himselfe, that it may be lawfull for all cowpers to woorke there dureing the heareing fishing, without any disturbance of the free cowpers of this cittie, whoe are not able to serve merchants and strangers, neither do they make theire barrells according theire bonds when they were admitted freemen, which is, that they shall pyn and twigg theire caskes.

" Item: That the masters of the company of bakers, butchers and cookes, and theire companies, shall sell bread and flesh, raw and dressed, at the said place, paying unto the peticioners for the roome they tooke there some resonable rent towards theire great rent and chardges.

"And, lastly, that theis constitucions may be published by proclamacion, and to make known that the forsaid peticioners, for the better encouradgment of the merchantes and strangers resorting thether, will take of every fishing boate which cometh there, for theire tieth fish, ten shillinges, sterling, and for theire place on land (yf they purpose to make fish) V.s. each barque or boate, dureing the seazon, and yf they will not compound, then each boate shall pay but quarter tieth, whereas they doe paie at Clontarfe halfe tieth, which amounteth uppon many barques and boates (to) V.s. sterling.

"It is therefore ordered, enacted and established, by thaucthoritie aforsaid, that the forsaid articles shalbe confirmed and approved. Provided alwaies that the Maior and recorder for the time being shall have the ordering of all matters and controversies that shall arise there, and that the cittizens shall paie noe more duties then as the Maior and recorder shall sett downe."

Assaying of Leather.
The attention of the Common Council having been directed to certain abuses in the tanning industry, it was ordered in the year 1659 that leather should be sold only in the corn market on fixed days, while an old law requiring all leather offered for sale to be assayed and sealed was renewed. The order made is thus recorded:—

"Whereas likewise certaine of the said commons preferred peticion unto the said assemblie, sheweinge that the tanners of this cittie, or some of them, and others exercisinge the trade or misterie of tanninge leather, doe putt theire keeves or fatts in tannhills, whereby leather doth receave unnaturall heates, and doe use hott woozes in tanninge of leather, the which unlawfull practise is prejudiciall unto the commonwealth, and ought not to bee used in any well governed corporacion; and forasmuch as there is noe publique market place appointed in this cittie for vieweinge and assayinge of leather, whereby the tanners and others exercisinge the trade of tanninge doe take advantage and thereby are imboldened to putt to sale theire deceiptfull leather in theire houses, yards, backsides and other obscure places, not dareinge to adventure theire said leather to the viewe of the markett, and that for remedy of the forsaid frauds and deceipts used and practised in leather, the said commons humbly prayed this assemblie to appointe a markett place where tanned leather shalbee putt to sale as it is in London and other citties and townes in England, and that noe leather bee putt to sale in the markett of this cittie, or elsewhere within the said cittie or liberties thereof, but it shall first bee assayed and tryed, and then sealed with the cittie seale by an officer appointed, which officer is to have paied him for his service the usuall (fee) formerlie accustomed to bee paied, and that there may bee two markett dayes weekelie appointed as it is in London: it is therefore ordered and agreed uppon, by the forsaid authoritie (for preventing the inconveniences and deceipts aforsaid) that all such tanned leather which shalbee sold in this cittie shalbee brought everie Munday and Friday weekely into the corne markett, and there exposed for sale, and in noe other place, and that the said tanned hides shalbee first viewed and assayed by the assay master of this cittie in the said markett place before the same shalbee sold, and noe where else; and if any tanner or any other shall expose any tanned leather to sale in any other place of the said cittie, or before it shalbe sealed, that the parties soe exposeinge the said leather to sale shall forfeite the somme of two shillings and sixe pence, sterling, for everie hide which shalbee exposed to sale in any other place of the said cittie and liberties thereof, or not sealed as aforsaid; the said fines to bee levyed of the goodes of the partie offendinge, on the Maiors warrant, by sale of the said goodes, restoreinge the overplus to the owner; the said penaltie to bee disposed for the use of the poore of the said cittie."

The Common Council were always prepared to lend a ready ear to any lawful complaints of the guildsmen, such as competition on the part of non-members. The corporation of "tallow chandlers and soapboylers" having presented a petition in the year 1675, complaining that persons not free of the corporation daily intruded on the corporation and used the trade proper for the brethren of the said corporation, contrary to the tenor of their charter, it was ordered by the Common Council that the said charter should be enrolled in the city records and that the Lord Mayor should take steps to prevent such intrusion for the future.

From time to time the Common Council were called upon to adjudicate in cases of disputes between the guilds as to their respective spheres of industry.

Disputes between Guilds. Thus in the year 1677 the painterstainers of the Guild of St. Luke the Evangelist having complained to the Assembly that divers members of the corporation of plasterers of the City of Dublin did exercise the art of painting work, it was ordered that such of the corporation of plasterers as had been accustomed to lay colours and paintings in oil should have liberty, during residence, to continue to do so, upon payment for each person of twenty shillings to the corporation of paper stainers and that for the future no other person or persons whatsoever should use or exercise painting or laying colours in oil, but members of the corporation of paper stainers, their servants and apprentices.

A great deal of friction appears to have been occasioned in this period owing to encroachment by members of one guild upon the province of another. A further cause of discord was occasioned by the admission to the membership of certain guilds of craftsmen who had no connection with the craft with which the particular guild was originally associated. Both these grievances are mentioned in the following entry in the Calendar of Dublin Records under date 1682, namely: "Whereas the severall corporations of this cittie not being confined to the particular kinds of trades and misteries whereof they are members, is the cause of many mischiefes, troubles, and animosities, which dayly happen in this citty and ends in suites at law, to the great expence of money and time, and that from the same fountain proceeds a noe lesse injury, where a corporation, as the chirurgeons and severall others, admit members of other trades, such as apothecaries and vintners, or indeed any other trade that will apply themselves to them, to be free of them, and soe the corporation that is injured is forced to implead the person soe admitted, whoe by the others being wrongfully protected, animosities and troubles doe arise, which, if rules were laid downe by this assembly for ascerteining limitts to each corporation, would be prevented, and alsoe that handicraftsmen being suffered to trade as merchants enjoy all the privileges of a merchant, is alsoe a great and double injury, both to the merchants and to the cittie revenue in the branch of the cittie customs . . ." It was accordingly ordered by the Common Council that each corporation should be summoned before the Lord Mayor and Table of Aldermen, the Sheriffs being present, " to be heard what they allege concerning the premises," and that such rules and orders should be made by the Lord Mayor, Table of Aldermen and Sheriffs for the regulation of each corporation as would prevent such mischief in the future.

The Common Council in the year 1695 on behalf of certain of the guilds whose interests were concerned ordered that a petition be presented to the Irish House of Commons opposing the confirmation by Act of Parliament of the charter lately granted to the physi-

Opposition to Physicians' Charter

cians. The entry in the municipal records reads: "Whereas the phisitians are endeavouring to get their charter, which was granted them by king William and queen Mary in the fourth yeare of theire reigne, confirmed by act of parliament, and have now their petition to that purpose lyeing before the honorable house of commons; that if any such act doe pass in confirmation of their said charter it will be the ruine and destruction of severall of the corporations of this citty, for that there are such restrictions to all persons who either buy or sell any sort of medicines, oyles, spiritts or other druggs, and such grievous fines and amercements upon chirurgeons and apothecaryes for practiceing their trade

CRAFT GUILDS IN THE XVII. CENTURY

which, by their charters, they are sufficiently priviledged to doe, that many of the charters of this cittie will be made invalid or of very little use to the bretheren of the respective corporations, especially such who, besides many other severe penaltyes, are to forfeit twenty pounds for takeing an apprentice without licence from the said faculty, wh. renders them compleat masters and monopolists of all trades that they shall say in any manner to be dependant upon the said phisitians: for remedy whereof it is ordered and agreed upon, by the authority of the said assembly, that a petition be preferred to the honorable the house of commons in such manner as Mr. Recorder shall advise, for opposeing the said phisitians and obstructing them from passing the said charter into an act of parliament, or, if it must pass, that there be a saveing to the cittizens who are freemen of Dublin, and that the same be under the city seale."

A Bakers' Strike.

Towards the close of the seventeenth century the Common Council were faced with a sudden emergency—a bakers' strike—with which they successfully grappled. The Mayor of Dublin had for centuries fixed an assize of bread, that is, he had laid down a standard of quality to which the bread had to conform, a standard of weight and a standard price. The assize varied from time to time. In January, 1698-9, the bakers of Dublin, dissatisfied with the assize then in force, suddenly left off baking and endeavoured to cause the " foreign " bakers to do likewise. In the emergency the Common Council empowered the Lord Mayor to issue a proclamation allowing all persons whatsoever to bake and bring in bread, free from all quarterage and other impositions formerly imposed on " foreigners."

The sequel to this step was a petition in the month of July following from the Master, Wardens and Brethren of the corporation of bakers whereby they undertook to apply themselves with all diligence to supply the citizens with good and wholesome bread and to submit themselves to the Lord Mayor or other magistrate and accept of such assize as should from time to time be given them by him, and to duly conform to the same for the future, and they prayed accordingly that the Act of Assembly for foreigners baking at the petitioners' assize should be recalled.

The apprentice boys of Dublin came in for a good deal of attention from the Common Council, sometimes for more than the apprentices wished. A beneficent regulation, however, was that made by the civic authority in the year 1605 in the following terms:

Common Council and Apprentices. "Whear(as) certaine poore young men, being artysantes of this cittie, complayned that divers of them haveing served their apprentysehood with their masters, and after their longe service cannott be admitted to the brotherhood of theire company unlesse they doe paie fouer poundes, sterling, or give a great dinner: it is therefore ordered and agreed, by the aucthorytie afforesaid, that every young artyzant that have servid his apprentysehood shall paie in lieue of the dinner for his admittans to his brotherhoode the some of twentye shillinges, sterling, and noe more; and yf he shalbe refused to be admitted for that some by the master, wardins, and resydue of that companye where he served, that then he maye exercyse his owne trade himselfe without further admission."

A regulation not so much to their liking was the following, made a few months later, namely: "Whear(as) the commons complayned that there is spronge uppe emongest the prentyses of this cittie (in generall many) vices, and especiallie the wearing of long haire fashioned lyke ruffins, an unmeet thing to be permitted (in any civil cittie): it is therefore ordered and agreed, by the aucthorytie afforesaid that all the masters of the severall corporacions (that nowe) are or herafter shalbe, shall call before them the bretherin of their severall yealdes, and to gyve notyce (to them) to reforme as well the vice of longe haier as other fashions which many of their prentyses, contrary to the vocacion of an apprentyse, doe use in apparraile and otherwyse; and yf the masters of the said prentyses shall faile soe to doe, after warning or admonicion givin him therof by the said master of his companye, (then) he to forfeite unto the said companye, to be putt into theire common thresury, the som of twentie shillinges, sterling; and yf the master of any companye shall faile to give notyce to his said bretherin within fyften daies to reforme the said vice, the said master soe failing, to paie unto the thresorye of this cittie the som of twentye shillinges, sterling, *tociens quotiens*. And yf, within one moneth after the publyshing of this (lawe, any) prentyse, of what quallytie or condicion soever he be, serving in this cittie or within the franches or lybberties therof, shalbe fownd to wear lockes or long haire, it shalbe lawfull (to the master of that companye to) carrye the said prentyse to their hall, and there to see (him refor)med, and after to whippe him (with two) portors dysgysed, at the dyscression of the said master, (and that the) master of the said prentyse shall or (may) be committed for infringing this lawe by the master of his companye for sixe daies; and yf the master (of any) of the said companies doe neglecte the puttinge of (this lawe) in execution, he shall paie to this cittie thresurye, for the use of this cittie, twentye shillinges, sterling, for every defaulte; (and this to hold for a lawe) in this cittie against prentyses for ever."

In April, 1620, the practice of bull and bear baiting was condemned by the Common Council in the following by-law: "Forasmuch as certaine the commons complained to this assemblie against divers new vaine customes lately growne in this cittie and used by forriners and strandgers, as bull baytinges, beare baytinges and other uncivell and unlawful games and exercises, allureing unto them from all partes of the cittie other mens prentizes and servantes, who thereby fall into much vice and idlenes, to the decaie and impoverishing of theire masters and other the cittizens: wherefore and for the avoyding of such uncivell plaies and exercises, it is enacted and ordained, by the said aucthoritie, that the Maior for the time being shall from time to time restraine the common passadge of beares and bulles through the cittie, or any parte thereof, to draw prentizes or other servantes to the bayting of them, and likewise, by advise of Mr Recordor or other counsell of this cittie, punish all such offendors formerlie complained of by fine and imprisonment as he shall thinke fitt."

Later on in the century the practice of bull baiting was encouraged by the same authority. The corporation of butchers having petitioned in October, 1651, to be restored to the possession of the flesh shambles, " the forsakeing wherof hath beene occasioned through these troublesome and distracted times " it was ordered that the petitioners should " be restored to the possession of the said Fleshambles, they keeping the same in good repair, paying the rent of tenn pounds, sterling, by the yeare, and keeping upp the custome of bull-baiteings as it was aunciently used."

In the year 1671 the apprentices of Dublin took part in the pulling down of the new bridge over the Liffey, conduct which was condemned in the strongest terms by the City Fathers. Sir John Gilbert in his preface to the fourth volume of the Calendar of Ancient Records of Dublin remarks that it was apprehended that the bridge which was in progress of erection to the west of the old bridge might be prejudicial to local interests. In the disturbances some lives were lost through a conflict with the soldiery, and the structure in consequence became known as the " Bloody Bridge."

Under the by-laws of at least one Guild, apprentices were forbidden to marry. At their quarterly meeting held in January, 1700, the Master, *Apprentices* Wardens and Brethren of the Guild of *Forbidden to* Felt Makers made the following rule*: *Marry.* "And further it is also agreed on and for a law made and to be kept for the future that if any prentice whatsoever shall marry in the time of his service of apprenticeship and for that his offence if his master shall turne him out of his

---

* Original Minute Book of Guild of Felt Makers, Dublin—Public Record Office, Dublin (since destroyed).

service that then noe brother or member whatsoever of this corporation shall in any manner entertayne him for ye remaining pte of his tyme upon payne of fforfeiting ye sume of forty shill ster and it to be payed downe to ye master and wardens for ye tyme being."

A regrettable feature of the guild system in Dublin in the seventeenth century was the introduction of the policy of religious exclusiveness. Throughout the century the policy of excluding Catholic craftsmen was persisted in, while the guild members were forbidden to take Catholic apprentices. The consequence was that large numbers of craftsmen became dissociated from the guild system. This was one of the main causes which led to the decay and downfall of the guild system in Dublin.

Religious Exclusiveness.

The formal attendance of the Masters and leading members of the Guilds at the services of the Established Church was required by a civic by-law of the year 1607.

In January, 1652, the Common Council decreed that " none shalbee admitted unto the assemblies of any of the corporacions of this cittie unlesse hee bee a Protestant, and that noe freeman take any to bee an apprentise but such as are or wilbee and continue in the Protestant religion."

Owing to a complaint made in the year 1671 that many freemen of the city "who being of the Popish religion doe enterteine Papist servants and apprentices, and bring them up in the Popish religion, contrary to the antient good lawes of this citty," it was ordered that the ancient laws of the city concerning apprentices be revived and published.

CRAFT GUILDS IN THE XVII. CENTURY 203

At the Michaelmas meeting of the Assembly in the year 1678 it was ordered that "from henceforth noe person whatsoever be admitted and sworne a freeman of this cittie but who shall first take the oaths of allegeance and supremacy." Admission to the freedom of the city was at this time a condition precedent to admission to the freedom of the guilds. Earlier in this year the Common Council had inflicted a fine of £20 on the Master of the Guild of Cutlers, Painter-Stainers and Stationers for having admitted to membership of the Guild persons who had not been admitted to the freedom of the city.

During the brief reign of James II., governmental pressure was brought to bear upon the Common Council to have these restrictions removed. At their meeting held in June, 1686, the Council deliberated anxiously upon a letter received from the Lord Lieutenant commanding them to admit to the freedom of the city Roman Catholic traders and dealers without tendering the oath of supremacy. In reply to this letter the Council professed that they were "readie to yeeld all due submission and obedience thereunto" and pointed out that there had been from four to five hundred Roman Catholics admitted to freedom. They also called the attention of the Lord Lieutenant to the provision in the "New Rules" which directed that the Lord Mayor should administer the Oath of Supremacy to the Masters, Wardens and officers of corporations and all persons admitted members thereof. After further petitioning on the part of the Council, a peremptory order was received from the Lord Lieutenant to which the Council yielded unconditionally. In the following year the Common Council directed that the Acts referring to the taking of the Oath of Supremacy should be obliterated and erased from the books.

The enforced toleration of King James' reign gave place to narrow sectarianism in that of his successor. The following entry taken from the municipal records of the year 1695 illustrates the attitude adopted by the Common Council, namely: " Whereas one James Dennis, barber, was admitted a freeman of this city as a French refugee, and by the same pretence obteined his freedome of the corporation of barber chirurgeons, at which time he tooke the usuall oathes and subscribed the declaration, according to the custome of the citty; but forasmuch as the said James Dennis is a profest Papist, haveing lately declared himself as such before the right hon. the Lord Mayor and severall of the aldermen: it is therefore ordered and agreed upon, by the authority of the said assembly, that the said James Dennis be and he is hereby disfranchized from the freedom and liberty of this citty."

At the next quarterly meeting of the Assembly it was enacted that if any person, being free of the city or any corporation therein, should take any " Papist " to be an apprentice, and be convicted thereof, he should be disfranchised.

The Guilds of Dublin followed the policy adopted by the Common Council, although, be it said to their credit, a certain relaxation was practised.

The municipal records contain an entry of a Petition presented in March, 1696, by the Master, Wardens and Brethren of the Corporation of Cutlers, Painters and Stationers to have one James Malone, bookseller, a Papist, disfranchised. The Petition stated that the said James

CRAFT GUILDS IN THE XVII. CENTURY 205

Malone had been a Captain in King James' army. The petition was granted.

The Master and Wardens of the Corporation of Felt Makers petitioned in the year 1697 for the disfranchisement of two of their members, William Russell and James Potter, freemen of the City of Dublin and of the said Corporation, for having taken "Papist" apprentices contrary to the Act of Assembly passed in the year 1695. This petition was also acceded to.

A later entry records that the said William Russell, having turned off his Papist apprentice, and resolved never to do the like again, petitioned to be restored to the franchise and liberties of the city of Dublin, a request which was granted.

Catholics Admitted. Notwithstanding the sectarian policy of this period, Catholic craftsmen were not completely excluded from guild membership. Amongst the original records of the Guild of Barber Surgeons preserved in the Library of Trinity College, Dublin, is one called the "Book of Quarterages," which contains a record of the names of members of the Guild and of the quarterly payments made by them. Under date 22nd July, 1692, appears a list of thirty-seven names headed "Romans." Lists of "Roman Brothers" appear under different dates in the closing years of the seventeenth century.

In the records of the time mention is made of a class of guild brethren known as "Quarter Brothers" who are distinguished from the "free brothers" or "sworn brothers." They were craftsmen who were allowed to practise their craft on payment of a quarterly subscription to the Guild and who although admitted to membership did not enjoy the status of a free or sworn member.

In the municipal records of the year 1675 is recorded a by-law forbidding the masters of the several corporations to admit any person to be "either quarter brother or a sworne brother" of any corporation until he should be first free of the city. A later by-law of the year 1684 recites that "there are several quarter brothers whoe are admitted unto the severall corporations whoe doe not make their application nor sue for their freedome of the cittie."

It is suggested that Catholic craftsmen were admitted to membership of the guilds as "Quarter Brothers." They were thus enabled to practise their occupation under the *aegis* of the guild, but without having any voice in the guild councils.

In the "Book of Quarterages" belonging to the Guild of Barber Surgeons therein described as "the fraternitie of Barber Chyrurgions Apothecaries and Perrywiggmakers Comonly called the fraternitie or Guild of St. Marie Magdalen" appear a considerable number of entries of which the following is a type:—

"I Timothy Connor Barbor & Perukmaker doe hereby promise to pay unto the Corporacon of Barber Surgeons &c Five Shillings every Quarter untill I come in a free brother thereof and doe oblige myself my Ex^{ors} & Adm^{rs} in the penalty of Five Pounds not to keep or learn any Boy or Servant in the said Trade untill I be a free brother as aforesaid.

"Witness my hand & seale the 3d day of Aprill, 1693. Rob. Jeaye Clk.

Timothy Connor.

CRAFT GUILDS IN THE XVII. CENTURY

An outstanding feature of the guild system in Dublin in the seventeenth century was the association in the same corporation of workers in different crafts. Such a combination was not new, as already in the sixteenth century the barbers and surgeons had been united in one guild as had also the four crafts of the masons, joiners, carpenters and heliers. The seventeenth century witnessed the association of the apothecaries and periwig makers with the barbers and surgeons in one guild. The bricklayers and plasterers formed one corporation, as did the brewers and maltsters, while the Guild of St. Luke included cutlers painter-stainers and stationers.

Guilds Embodying more than One Craft.

In the above-mentioned cases craftsmen of different occupations who do not appear to have ever had a distinct guild organisation peculiar to their own particular craft were associated in one guild. A grouping of another class also took place, namely, an association of guilds, hitherto distinct, in the same corporation. The combination of the guilds probably began in the sixteenth century. It was nearly complete in the early years of the seventeenth century. This feature of the guild system was not peculiar to Dublin or Ireland. A similar development took place in other countries.*

The association of the barbers and surgeons was on a different footing from that of the others. The barbers at one time practised the art of surgery. In the time of Queen Elizabeth there were two distinct societies in Dublin, one of barbers and the other of surgeons, both practising the

* See Ashley : Economic History, Book II. ch. II., pp. 161–165.

art of surgery which societies the Queen incorporated into one body. The following extract is taken from a copy of the Charter of Queen Elizabeth to the Barber Surgeons, preserved amongst the Guild records in Trinity College Library: " And We having maturely considered how usefull and necessary it would be for preserving the health of the human body that there were more persons skilled in the art of chirurgery within the City of Dublin aforesaid, sickness and infirmities committing vast havock for the promotion and exercise of which Art the aforesaid Fraternity and Guild of Barbers was created and established by our aforesaid most beloved progenitor Henry and because there are now two distinct societies practising the said Art and faculty in our city aforesaid (vizt.) one of Barbers and the other of Chirurgeons which said Society of Chirurgeons is not as yet constituted nor incorporated into any body politick and it being necessary to blend joyn and reduce the said distinct and separate societies of Barbers and Chirurgeons into one body " the Charter proceeded to formally incorporate the society known as " The Master Wardens and Fraternity of Barbers and Chirurgeons of the Guild of St. Mary Magdalene."

The association of masons, carpenters, joiners and heliers in one guild was a natural association of men whose crafts were concerned with the building trade. The members of each individual craft were not sufficiently numerous to have their own distinct guild organisation. The craftsmen of the sixteenth and seventeenth centuries were fully conscious of the necessity and advantages of organisation. When they were not sufficiently numerous and powerful to obtain the grant of a charter of incorpora-

CRAFT GUILDS IN THE XVII. CENTURY

tion the members of one craft united with those of another to obtain the right to form a fraternity or guild, or else allied themselves to an existing guild.

Another potent cause of association, particularly the association of guild with guild, was the desire to lighten the burden of taxation. From time to time the Common Council of Dublin in their efforts to provide funds for civic needs made levies or cesses on the guilds of the city. One-third of the levy generally fell on the Guild Merchant, the remaining two-thirds being apportioned amongst the craft guilds. Guilds which were poor and weak in numbers endeavoured to associate themselves with the stronger guilds in order to lighten the burden on their members. Guilds of long standing naturally drew to themselves new associations of craftsmen. When weaker guilds thus became united with more powerful guilds they became known as " wings " to the latter bodies.

Combination of Guilds.

The following entry taken from the record of proceedings of the Dublin Assembly at their Michaelmas meeting in the year 1593 illustrates how the burden of taxation led to the union of two distinct guilds—those of the glovers and skinners, namely: " Where(as) the company of skynners hath bene of ould tyme accustomed to bere in all sesses with the company of glovers, the one halfe of theire chardge, who nowe are decayed and not of abyllytie, therefor, and forasmoche as theire trade is decayed, and that theire abyllyties is far under the abyllyties of those that in former tymes used their occupacion: it is agreed, by the aucthorytie aforsaid, that the said skynners shall from henceforth bere with the glovers in all sesses as members of that company in state of theire abyllyties."

In an earlier chapter it has been shown that before the close of the sixteenth century twenty-one different crafts had been organised under the guild system in seventeen guilds. Some time about the end of the sixteenth or beginning of the seventeenth century a combination of the craft guilds took place. The municipal records early in the seventeenth century begin to refer to "the eight corporations."

By an Order of the Common Council made in the year 1609 it was directed that St. Stephen's Green " be graunted unto the eight corporacions for twenty and one yeares for fouer shillinges, sterling, each cowe per annum; and yf the eighte corporacions shall refuse to take the same at the said rate, then the said Green to be sett accordingly to eny of the free cittizens as the Maior, Sheryfes, commons and cittizens shall make choyse of in the nexte assembly."

The following entry taken from the municipal records of the year 1618 is of interest showing that the Guild Merchant remained apart from the grouping movement :—

"Whereas the eight corporations made humble suyt to the said assembly, praieing to have a lease for foure score and nyneteene yeares uppon the Pill beyond the water at the yearly rent of XL.s, sterling: it is therefore ordered and agreed, by the said aucthoritie, that eight partes of nyne of the said Pill is graunted dureing the said yeares to the eight corporations, and the nynth parte to the Trenitie Yeald, all under the yearely rent of nyne powndes, sterling. Provided that yf the Trenitie Yeald do not take foorth theire lease, by the post assembly, of the said nynth parte, that then the corporations shall have the whole Pill uppon the said yearly rent of IX. li. sterling so as they take foorth theire lease by the post assembly."

Disputes frequently occurred between the associated guilds as to the right of precedence.

In January 1622 the Master, Wardens and Fraternity of Glovers complained to the Common Council that " the fraternity of cookes (being tyme out of mind noe other then wings unto your petitioners) have now of late taken uppon them to be the chiefe corporation, and your petitioners to be theire wings, whereas by chartor and antiquitie the peticioners can prove that they have beene alwaies one of the eight corporacions, and the cookes to be theire wings " whereupon the Common Council directed that the charters of both corporations should be perused and that an order be then made determining the difference between the two guilds.

A general order was made by the Common Council in the year 1627 determining the order of precedence of the guild representatives at the Council meetings. "Whereas," the Order reads, " the masters of the eight corporacions complained that the winges belonging to every corporacion, through over much toleracion, doe strive to have precedency in sitting in the Tholsell on the assembly daies, and offereth violence to some of the said eight masters to put them from theire places, where in reason and decensie the said eight masters should sitt together in the Tholsell on the said assembly daies, and the winges to sitt after the last master of the said eight masters: for reformacion whereof, it is ordered in this assembly that the masters of every of the eight corporacions shall hould and keepe theire places together in the Tholsell on every assembly day, and the masters of every the winges being of the numbers shall sitt next to the last master of the said eight corporations, and soe to continue on every assembly day, and not otherwise."

An important order was made at the same meeting of the Council, the preamble to which indicates the motive force at the back of the combination movement. This order reads as follows:—" Whereas the commons complained that the barbor-chirurgions, glovers and fishmoungers, together with severall other tradesmen, farr beyond many of the corporacions in abilitie, doe joyne themselves to one or twoe of the eight corporacions that have little neede of them, and by what aucthority or cullor it is not knowen, whereby the weaker sorte of the corporacions are much hurt when any cess or loane money cometh, by reason that those welthey tradesmen doe beare little or nothing, and soe the burthen comming upon the peticioners groeth very heavy, and therefore they humbly prayed that those winges and tradesmen shall ether be united to the corporacions that are poore and have most neede of them, or otherwise to be appoynted to attend theire owne charter, and soe every one to beare his parte of the chardge as becometh: it is therefore ordered, by the aucthoritie aforesaid, that the Maior, recordor and Sherriffes, or any two of thèm, whereof the Maior alwaies to be one, shall caule before them the severall corporacions of barbarchirurgions, glovers and fishmoungers and sadlers, and examin them unto what companies they doe belonge, and by what aucthoritie, and if they find them not to be legalie joyned to any company, then to certifie the table of aldermen thereof, and they to dispose and annex them

CRAFT GUILDS IN THE XVII. CENTURY

to such companies as they shall think to stand in most need of theire assistance."

For a number of years a dispute as to precedence in the Assembly and on Station Days* continued between the bakers and the barber-surgeons, " albeeit " as the municipal records of the year 1634 state, " the difference was at severall tymes heertofore debated and examined in severall assemblies, and that the said barbarchirurgions have binn found culpable in respect they are but a winge." Ten years later the Council referred the matter to the Mayor, Recorder and Sheriffs " to settle theire places accordinge to the antiquitie of their charters." An award having been made in favour of the barber-surgeons, the Common Council confirmed same, adding to their order " soe as the said corporacion of barborsurgeons have noe relacion unto nor dependence uppon any other corporacion, but that they shall beare all common chardges and cesses in this cittie as a distinct corporation."

Upon a certificate from the Recorder as to the antiquity of their respective charters, the corporation of tailors was, in the year 1651, declared entitled to precedence over the corporation of smiths. A like order was made in favour of the glovers in a contest between them and the cooks.

The combination of the guilds broke up, for a time at least, late in the century. According to the municipal records of the year 1682 the Common Council returned in that year to the old system of levying cess upon the individual guilds. Certain improvements in connection

---

* The " Station Days " specially mentioned were days associated with religious festivals, such as All Hallows Day and St. Stephen's Day.

with the Council Chamber having been decided upon, it was ordered that the charge thereof should be borne as to " ⅓ part by the corporation of Trinity Guild " and as to the other two third parts " by the nineteen corporations by equall portions."

In the case of guilds in which several distinct crafts were united the members were not free to practise any or all of the crafts at their discretion. The custom prevailed of requiring each brother upon admission to the freedom of the guild to enter into a bond under which he undertook to practise his own craft alone. Several such bonds are preserved amongst the records of the Barber-Surgeons' Guild. The following entry is taken from the "Book of Quarterages."

Craftsmen to Practise only one Craft.

" I Daniel Rowle of the City of Dublin Barber & Perukmaker doe hereby oblige myselfe my heires Executors & Administrators in the penall sum of one hundred pounds sterl. to be paid unto the Master and Wardens of the Corporation of Barbers & Chirurgeons Appothocaries & Perukmakers Dublin for the time being and their successors the Master & Wardens for the use of the said Corporation That I will not at any time hereafter intrude upon the said Corporation by practising Pharmacy or any part of Chirurgery, Phlebotomy & tooth drawing only excepted, within the County of the said Citty or five miles distance of the said Citty And I doe likewise oblige my selfe in the said penallty that I will not imploy any person to practice the same for me neither will I teach or instruct any person to trim or make Peruks unlesse the same be bound an apprentice to me for the tearme of

CRAFT GUILDS IN THE XVII. CENTURY 215

seaven yeares the same being for and in consideration of my admittance to be a free brother of the said Corporation and to practise the Art of Barbing and Perukmaking, Witnesse my hand & Seale the 5th day of October 1694

           daniel raoul

Sealed & delivered in the presence
of Boetius Clamy
 Robt. Jeaye Clk."

In guilds of this type it was the practice to select the Master and the Wardens from the different crafts composing the guild so that the chief offices should not be monopolised by any one craft. Thus it appears from a Bond, dated 1st April 1695, enrolled in the records of the Barber-Surgeons' Guild, that in that year the office of Master was held by Valentine Gill " Chyrurgeon " while the Wardens were Tym. Edge " Appothecary " and Richd. Hughes " Perukmaker." The Charter incorporating the guild of Cutlers, Painter-Stainers and Stationers dated 1670 named a Cutler as the first Master, a Painter Stainer and a Stationer as the first Wardens.*

Tanners. Certain of the guilds are mentioned for the first time by Gilbert in that portion of the Calendar of the Ancient Records of Dublin dealing with the seventeenth century. An entry dated January 1616 records the existence of the Guild of Tanners and the whereabouts of the tanners' hall. The entry reads:—" Wheareas alsoe the master and

---

* Samuel Cotten was nominated as the first Master, Richard Carny, painter stainer and John North, stationer, the first Wardens. The references to the Guild of the Cutlers, Painter Stainers and Stationers otherwise known as the Guild of St. Luke the Evangelist have been taken from the original records of the Guild and are published by permission of the Guild of St. Luke, in whose possession these records are. The existing Guild of St. Luke does not claim continuity from the old Guild.

companye of tanners have bene humble petycioners to the said assembly, prayeing that there might be a place appointed for them whear they might conveniently make a passadge to their hall over Saint Awdeons arche, in regard they are abridged of thauncient passadge therunto : it is therfore ordered and agreed, by the said aucthorytie that Mr Maior, Mr. Malone, the masters of the woorkes, and Masters Sherryfes, or any three of them, shall survey a place fitt to make a waye, and there the petycioners shall make their waye uppon their owne costes."

The trade in hides having been from the earliest days one of the staple trades of Dublin, it is almost certain that the Guild of Tanners was one of the most ancient guilds of the city. According to the Report of the Commissioners on the Municipal Corporations of Ireland the tanners had a charter granted in the seventeenth year of the reign of Edward the First (A.D. 1289).

Doubts as to the existence of a guild organisation among those of the fisher craft, the presence of which might be inferred from references of the fifteenth and sixteenth centuries, are laid to rest by the specific mention of the corporation of " fishmoungers " in the municipal records of the year 1627.

In the year 1660 one Edward Batho was appointed as representative of the " corporacion of shearmen " upon a committee whose duty it was to take into consideration the levying of a cess of four hundred and fifty pounds for the purpose of obtaining from Charles II. a confirmation of the city charters and privileges. Representatives of the following guilds, all of which have been already referred to, were included in the committee by the Common

CRAFT GUILDS IN THE XVII. CENTURY

Council namely:—Trinity Guild, the Guilds of Tailors, Smiths, Barber-Surgeons, Bakers, Butchers, Carpenters. Shoemakers, Cooks, Saddlers, Tanners, Tallow Chandlers, Glovers, Weavers and Goldsmiths.

Upon a petition presented by the "master, bretheren and wardens of the fraternity or guild of St. Patricks neere Dublin" for enrolment in the records of the city as a "body politick" it was ordered by the Common Council in the year 1667. "That the petitioners be received as a body politick into this city, and that their patent be inrolled amongst the records of this city, and their stacion be next after the goldsmiths, and that there be three of the corporacion, such as shall be presented by the master and wardens of the said corporacion for the time being, admitted into the numbers of this city, that is to say, on the displaceing, removeing or death of any of the corporacion of carpenters, whoe now are of the common councell of this city from time to time as the said numbers shall become void." This is the only reference to the "Guild of St. Patricks." What the occupation of the members was is not stated. But owing to the fact that vacancies on the Common Council occasioned by the death or removal of representatives of the corporation of carpenters were to be filled by representatives of the new guild, it is probable that the members followed a cognate craft. The "Guild of Saint Patricks" may have been the Joiners' Guild which is mentioned later. The Guilds were often referred to by the name of their Patron Saint.

Guild of St. Patrick.

The feltmakers of Dublin received their charter of

incorporation from Charles II on the 8th day of October 1667. The original records of this guild unhappily perished in the destruction of the Four Courts in June 1922. A transcript of their more important by-laws was, however, made by the writer before that event.

Feltmakers.

Next in seniority to the feltmakers came the fraternity or guild of Cutlers, Painter-Stainers and Stationers, incorporated by Charter dated the 4th day of October 1670. The original record books of this Guild have survived and are in the possession of the modern Guild of St. Luke. Reference has already been made to an entry, dated 1677, in the Calendar of the Ancient Records of Dublin dealing with a dispute between this Guild and the Corporation of Plasterers.

Cutlers, Painter-Stainers and Stationers.

The latter Guild also comprised the Plasterers and Bricklayers. The united Guild was known as the Guild of St. Bartholomew.

Plasterers and Bricklayers.

In the year 1681 a Petition was presented to the Common Council showing that the pavements of the city, " being permitted to be laid and made by any persons who pretend to that worke, though never soe unskilfull, are many times soe ill done that they are soone broken up, and the streets become uneeven and very dangerous and dirtie, which would be prevented if skillfull persons were employed, and apprentices bound to and educated in that calling as in the cittie of London, where there is a corporation of paviers " it was ordered " that the

Paviers.

CRAFT GUILDS IN THE XVII. CENTURY 219

said paviers be and are hereby added as a wing unto the masons, and that noe person be for the future admitted to make any pavements but such who shall be soe incorporated, their apprentices or servants." The masons, in turn, were a branch of the carpenters' guild.

The surrender of a lease by the Master, Wardens and Brethren of the Corporation of Coopers of a parcel of land situated beyond St. James' Gate is recorded in the municipal records of the year 1695. In the Appendix to *Coopers.* the Report of the Commissioners on Irish Municipal Corporations published in the year 1835 it is stated that the coopers had a charter from Charles II. dated 1666 A.D. It is noteworthy, however, that the coopers or "hoopers" were one of the crafts which took part in the Pageant on Corpus Christi Day in the fifteenth century.

The members of another ancient craft, the curriers, do not appear to have been formally incor- *Curriers.* porated until the reign of William III. In the year 1696 they were admitted to representation on the Common Council.

From time immemorial the trade of brewing was carried on in Dublin. A curious feature of the trade was that at one time it was largely in the hands of women. The "Chain Book" of *Brewers and* Dublin, one of the oldest of the civic *Malsters.* records, mentions the penalties to be inflicted on a woman-brewer for brewing inferior ale. If convicted a third time, she was to be suspended from her occupation for a year and a day. Like the curriers, the brewers and malsters of

Dublin received a charter of incorporation from William III.

The combers make their first appearance in the municipal records in the year 1697 when they presented a Petition to be added as a " wing " to the Corporation of Weavers. The Petition is thus recorded:—" Whereas severall combers of the citty of Dublin petitioned the said assembly in behalfe of themselves and others, setting forth that they were desirous to become freemen of the citty, but the combers beeing noe corporation prayed that they might be admitted as a wing of the corporation of weavers; and whereas alsoe the master, wardens and brethren of the corporation of weavers of this cittie preferred their petition to the said assembly, setting forth for the combers trade is properly belonging to and depending on the weavers. but as yett the combers are noe corporation, though willing to become freemen of this honourable citty, a wing of the corporation of weavers, and therefore prayed they might be added to and be admitted to be a wing thereof: whereuppon it is ordered by the authority of the said assembly, that the combers be added as a wing to the corporation of weavers, and that every of them before their admission to their freedome of the said Corporation obteyne their freedome of this citty."

Combers.

A reminder that the old civic duty of taking part in the defence of the city was still enforced is provided by an Order of the Common Council dated 29th November 1678. After reciting that " all freemen of this cittie are bound, as well by bond as by the auntient lawes of this cittie, to provide and keep armes and be sworne on their knees,

CRAFT GUILDS IN THE XVII. CENTURY

with armes, which have usually been sword, muskett, or firelock, with bandeleeres, and the same to have allwayes in readines for the service of the king and defence of this cittie" it was ordered "that the Lord Mayor doe send orders to the masters and wardens of the respective corporations in this cittie to call the brothers of every corporation before them to appear in their armes, and to give account to his lordshipp who of the brothers are furnished with armes and who not, to the end the companie upon occasion may be compleated, and that course be taken with such persons who want armes as Mr. Recorder shall advise."

Arms of Guildsmen.

As an illustration of the organisation and working of the guilds a complete set of the Rules of the Guild of the Cutlers, Painter-Stainers and Stationers made in the year 1675 are here reproduced. These Rules which were made pursuant to the authority of their Charter dated 1670 were ordered to be engrafted on parchment and hung up in the Hall of the guild situate over St. Audoen's Arch. They remained in operation until the year 1767 when they were revised.

Rules of the Cutlers' Guild.

Rule I. provided for the election of the Master and Wardens on the 24th day of August in each year for the year commencing on the 18th day of October, the Feast of St. Luke, the patron saint of the guild. All members of the guild were required to attend under penalty of a fine of two shillings and six pence. Candidates were to be nominated by the Master, Wardens and Council of the guild and offered by them to the rest of the brethren for election. It was provided that the officers should be chosen one from each faculty. Upon election the officers were required to take the Oaths of Allegiance and Supremacy.

Rule II. dealt with the Council of the House and provided for election of the members by the Master, Wardens and Commonalty. The Council was to consist of 21 persons, 7 from each faculty, in addition to the Master and Wardens. The Council were empowered to assemble as often as should seem meet and to enact such laws as to the majority of them should seem proper, and to alter and repeal tne same, and to put into execution all such laws and ordinances as were or should be made. The Master and Wardens or one of the Wardens together with seven of the Council were to form a quorum.

The next three Rules provided penalties for persons chosen to office who should refuse to serve. The Rules provided that a brother who was elected Master and refused to serve in the office should pay a fine of £20 or "lye in ward." In the case of the Wardenship the penalty was £5 with the like alternative, while a person refusing to accept the office of Beadle was fined thirty shillings or imprisoned.

The date of the quarterly meeting of the guild was fixed by the sixth Rule as the "Thursday seven Night" before the usual Quarter Day of the City of Dublin.

A penalty of five shillings was fixed by the next Rule in the case of a Warden neglecting his duty on any day of attendance, no just cause for his absence being shown. The penalty for persisting in absence three times was removal from office and a fine of £5 with the alternative of "lying in ward."

Any member of the Council neglecting three times successively to attend upon being summoned was to pay thirty-eight shillings sterling or to "lie in ward," if no just excuse for his absence were alleged.

One shilling fine was ordered to be imposed upon any member neglecting to attend any meeting when summoned, or leaving a meeting without the Master's licence.

Rule X. provided that any member of the guild that should "speake evill" of or revile the Master should pay for every offence ten shillings or "lie in ward," and for a like offence against a Warden five shillings.

Due decorum at the guild meetings was ensured by the succeeding Rule which provided that if any person on any Quarter Day or other day of meeting should "sweare strike or be disturbant" he should pay for every such offence one shilling or "lie in ward."

No person was to be admitted a brother for a less sum than £4 sterling and one shilling quarterly; also at the time of admission each person was required to enter into a bond of £20 sterling to obey submit and "stand" to the laws of the guild.

Any person petitioning to be a Cutler was required to state "whether he be a short cutler or a long cutler" and if his petition were granted such person was to exercise only the trade mentioned in his petition.

One of the vital Rules of the guild was Rule XIV. namely:—"That noe cutler of this Guild shall use the marke of an other Brother of the said art or mistery but that each have a distinct marke and that every one of them give in their respective markes to the Clerke of the Guild strucke on a peece of brass or copper plate with their names thereon ingraven to remaine in the Hall of the said Guild, and allsoe the said Marks to be entered in the Booke of Enrolments of this Guild with their names annexed, and such of the Cutlers as shall at any time or times hereafter without consent strike or cause to be struck his brothers marke shall forfeit for every such offence Thirty Shillings sterl. or lye in Ward."

Equally important was Rule XV. which provided that no brother should go about to undertake any other brother's work who had contracted for same under a penalty of 38s. sterling or "lying in ward."

Rule XVI. provided that every member of the guild who should at any time employ a journeyman should within fourteen days from the commencement of such employment enter the name of such journeyman with the Clerk of the guild and pay one shilling quarterly for each journeyman, to be deducted out of the said journeyman's wages, paying always twelve pence in hand. A penalty of two shillings and six pence was fixed for breach of this Rule.

The next Rule dealt with apprentices and provided that any brother that should take an apprentice should within three months bring him before the Master and Wardens "to the intent that they may see he be of a good conversation and of the Protestant Religion; and that his indentures be drawn by the Clerk of the Guild and enrolled in the Book of Enrolments within six months after the commencement of the Indentures, any brother receiving an apprentice otherwise than as aforesaid to pay 20s. fine and the indentures to be null and void."

The succeeding Rule provided that every apprentice that had served his time before he be sworn a brother should pay 6s. 8d. and that no apprentice should set up for himself till he be sworn a brother.

The nineteenth Rule forbade any brother of the guild to sue another in any Court in Ireland without leave in writing from the Master being first obtained under a penalty of ten shillings provided the debt were under forty shillings sterling.

Every Master and Warden was required in accordance with the next Rule to deliver up on the day of their removal from office to the new Master and Wardens the patent of the guild, the books of record, "Seale of the Hall," together with the plate and other utensils, and also within 28 days to render an account of all sums received and disbursed "for the use of the Hall" to the new Master and Wardens under penalty of double the amount that should be proved to have been in their hands.

To enhance the dignity of the guild meetings was the purpose underlying Rule XXI. which provided that such of the brethren of the guild as were of the Council, whensoever they should be summoned to attend the Master, should appear in their gowns on all days of election and days of swearing the new Master and Wardens, and also on all Quarter Days and days of attendance upon the Lord Mayor of the city.

The penultimate Rule dealt with "Quarter Brothers" and provided that no person should be admitted a "quarter brother" of the guild under five shillings quarterage or without entering into a Bond for £10 sterling to pay his quarterage and "obey observe submit and stand to" the laws of the guild.

The twenty-third and last Rule made at the same

session was of purely personal application and provided that one Thomas Sisson should have liberty to embrace or refuse the office of Master or Warden so long as he by himself or anyone to his use should exercise the trade of stationer.

One of the Rules of the Cutlers' Guild deals with the registration of journeymen. The references to journeymen are strangely few in both municipal and guild records, although this class formed a vital element in the guild system. The journeyman occupied a place *Journeymen.* intermediate between the apprentice and the master. The name is a hybrid one, half French, half English, the first part being derived from *journeé*—a day. Wages being fixed at a certain rate per day, the workers who were employed at this daily rate received the name of "journeemen" with the variant spellings of "jornomen" "jornemen" and "journeymen." The journeymen of Dublin appear to have consisted of two classes—craftsmen who, having served their apprenticeship outside of Dublin, had come to the city and taken employment in the service of a Dublin master, and craftsmen who, having served an apprenticeship to a member of the guild, entered the employment of a guild brother instead of or before setting up on their own account. The latter class were entitled under the civic and guild by-laws to admission to the freedom both of the city and the guild, the former class could claim admission to the civic and guild franchise on payment of a fine of twenty shillings, pursuant to the "New Rules" made for Dublin in the year 1672.

The by-laws of the Guild of Feltmakers are exceptional

in that they make several references to the journeymen. A number of by-laws for the regulation of this craft were drawn up in the year 1668 by the Master, Wardens and Brethren. Amongst others it was provided that every " Jornoman " feltmaker who had served the full term of seven years' apprenticeship to the art and Mystery of feltmaking then residing in Dublin or the Liberties thereof or who should thereafter come and reside in the said city or Liberties and should work at the said art and mystery for the space of one month should make full proof by certificate or otherwise of such his true and full service of seven years. It was further provided that upon his admission to work at the said art and mystery every such journeyman should pay the sum of twenty shillings sterling as a fine to the Master and Wardens of the corporation for the time being for the use of the said corporation and should further pay the sum of six pence quarterly to the use of the corporation of feltmakers.

Another by-law of the same date was enacted in favour of both masters and men. It protected the latter from arbitrary dismissal by their employers, while it prevented employers from being left in the lurch by their men. The by-law provided that no journeyman at the art and mystery of feltmaking in the city of Dublin or the Liberties thereof should at any time thereafter leave his master's service without giving one month's notice, so that the master could provide himself with another journeyman. On the other hand it was decreed that no master should at any time thereafter turn off any journeyman from his service without first giving him one month's warning to provide for himself, unless they mutually agreed to part. The penalty for breach of this by-law by either master or man was a fine of twenty shillings.

Another by-law of equal date provided that if any journeyman working for a member of the Corporation of Feltmakers should refuse to pay his quarterage or arrears thereof, if any such there should be, or any other lawful dues, or should refuse to stand to and abide, or disobey the commands of the Master and Wardens of the said Corporation, he should pay for every such offence a fine of two shillings and six pence. If he should refuse to pay, no member was to continue to employ him after notice given by the Master and Wardens.

Persons following the art and mystery of feltmaking within the City of Dublin or the Liberties thereof or within four miles of the same were forbidden to employ at the art servants called " clubbs " under a penalty of £10 for each such servant so employed. The " clubbs " were probably persons who had not served a regular apprenticeship to the craft.

A special branch of the trade which would appear to have been introduced into Dublin in this period is mentioned in a by-law of the year 1668, which forbade any master or journeyman to teach or instruct any master or journeyman or any others, apprentices only excepted, in the art and mystery of making any felts or felts commonly called " castor " or " Beavor " felt upon pain of forfeiting £10 to the Master and Wardens or suffering six months' imprisonment at the choice of the person offending.

A notable feature of the guild system was that under it a high standard of competence on the part of those working at a craft was insisted upon. The records of the Guild of

CRAFT GUILDS IN THE XVII. CENTURY

Feltmakers enshrined a law dealing with the masterpiece. It was enacted by the Guild in the year 1668 that if any person or persons whatsoever following the art and mystery of feltmaking in Dublin should set up the said art and mystery before he or they should have made their "proofe peeces," the same to be brought to the Common Hall of the guild to be approved of by the Master and Wardens and Assistants for the time being or the greater part of them, that then such person or persons so offending contrary to this law should forfeit and pay to the Master and Wardens the sum of twenty shillings sterling. It was further provided that if any person should follow " Castor " and feltmaking he should make his "peeces" in both.

The Masterpiece.

That journeymen were allowed to take apprentices is evidenced by a by-law enacted by the feltmakers in the year 1698 which provided that no journeyman from and after the date of the law should " take any apprentice more than one " to be bound to work at the trade of feltmaking within three years after the said journeyman should have become a brother sworn or made free of the corporation. If two apprentices should be taken within the said period of three years the journeyman taking same was required to pay the sum of three pounds to the Master and Wardens for the use of the guild. A proviso was added that the law should not affect the existing members.

The guild records of the seventeenth century reveal the fact that the jurisdiction of certain of the guilds extended beyond the limits of the City of Dublin into the Liberties adjoining and into the country beyond.

The Master and Wardens of the Guild of Cutlers,

Painter-Stainers and Stationers were empowered by their Charter received from Charles II. to hear and determine all trespasses, extortions and defects whatsoever committed or done by any persons within the City of Dublin or Liberties or Privileges thereof, or within seven miles of the said City, using or exercising any of the arts or faculties of Cutlers, Painter Stainers or Stationers.

Guild Jurisdiction Extended Beyond City.

In the Bond entered into by Daniel Rowle, a member of the Guild of Barber-Surgeons, already quoted, the said Daniel Rowle undertook not to practise pharmacy or surgery within the County of the City of Dublin or within five miles' distance from the City. In a memorandum dated 8th June 1696 appearing in the "Book of Quarterages" belonging to the said Guild it is recorded that the Corporation of Barber Surgeons agreed with one Charles Crolly that he should have liberty to practise the "Barber and Perukmaker's trade" in the Liberties of the City of Dublin for twelve pence quarterage. The sum of £5 was paid as consideration for this grant.

The by-laws of the Feltmakers' Guild refer clearly to the jurisdiction exercised by the Guild over persons following the art and mystery of feltmaking in the City of Dublin and the Liberties thereof. As a distinction has been drawn between the "Liberties of the City" and the Liberties "adjoining" the City, such as the Liberty of St. Sepulchre where a distinct manorial jurisdiction was exercised by the Archbishop of Dublin, it is important to note that the Feltmakers' Guild claimed jurisdiction in these privileged places. The thirteenth by-law of the Guild is in the following

CRAFT GUILDS IN THE XVII. CENTURY 231

terms: " It is also established agreed and for a Law made by the Authority aforesaid and with the consent thereof That every person and persons following the Art and Mystery of Feltmaking living within the liberties of the Lord Archbishop of Dublin the Earl of Meath or any other Liberty or privileged place or places in or about this City of Dublin or within 4 miles of the same That is not nor will not become a brother or Member of this Corporation but shall stand out in contempt thereof every such person or persons as shall for the future make any manner of hats or felts and shall be found selling the same out of any such liberty or privileged place or places shall forfeit all such hats and felts and £5 sterling unto the Master and Wardens of this Corporation for the time being for the use thereof or else all such person or persons to suffer three months' imprisonment."

The limits prescribed by the charter to the saddlers were very extensive reaching to fifteen miles beyond the city, in every direction, and consequently running into several counties, and interfering with different jurisdictions.*

The twenty-second by-law of the Feltmakers' Guild affords an excellent illustration of the supervision exercised over a craft by the Guild authorities. This by-law which was enacted in the year 1668 reads:—" It is also established and agreed upon and for a law made by *Supervision* the authority aforesaid and with the consent *of Feltmakers.* thereof that from henceforth it shall and may be lawful to and for the Master and Wardens of the Corporation of Feltmakers of the City of Dublin for the time being or any two of them with the

---

* Vide Municipal Corporations Report, Appendix Vol. I., p. 275.

Master at all and every convenient time or times to search view and survey all and singular their work and workmanship of all and every person or persons whatsoever making or working or which at any time or times hereafter shall make or work any manner of hats or felts in any place or places whatsoever within the City of Dublin and suburbs thereof and within four miles of the same and all and singular hats and felts as upon any such search view or survey shall be found to be falsely deceitfully and untruly made or wrought to take seize and bring or cause to be brought to the Common Hall belonging to this Corporation and if upon view of the said Master and Wardens and six of the Assistants of the said Corporation for the time being such hats or felts so seized shall appear to them to be falsely deceitfully or untruly made and wrought that then all such hats and felts shall by the said Master and Wardens and six Assistants full and free consent be condemned to be burnt and accordingly shall be burnt in the common market place of this city on such market day or days as the Master Wardens and Assistants shall appoint for that purpose and if any brother or brothers or any member of this Corporation or any other person or persons whatsoever following the Art and Mystery of feltmaking within this city or liberties thereof or within four miles of the same shall at any time or times hereafter refuse to give the Master and any two of the Wardens of this Corporation for the time being or such as they shall appoint free liberty of ingress egress and regress into his and their respective dwelling houses or shops or workhouses or workshops to search view and survey for bad goods and to make inquiry for and concerning all such things and matters as might or shall

CRAFT GUILDS IN THE XVII. CENTURY

be for the good weal and benefit of this Corporation all such person or persons so refusing shall pay and forfeit the sum of 5s. sterling to the Master and Wardens for the time being for the use of this Corporation to be levied on their goods and chattels."*

An unusual type of fraud which came under the notice of the Guild authorities is mentioned in the records of the Cutlers' Guild. An entry dated 7 Nov., 1698, states that it was made known to the Assembly that " ye title and preface of Cockers Arithm : was printed &

A Fraudulent Arithmetic. putt to Hodders Arithmetick & thereby those were deceived y^t bought y^m for Cockers Arithmetick " that two of the brothers acknowledged the fact, but promised to destroy the remainder of the titles. At the same meeting information was given that a New Testament lately printed abounded with errors. An order was thereupon made that the Stationers should have leave to devise means to suppress the same.

The same Guild penalised bad work in the following bye law made in March 1676, namely:—" It is enacted established and for a law made that if any

Penalty for Bad Work. person of this Guild being a painter Stainer shall at any time hereafter paint or colour any oyle worke whatsoever that is to stand & be without doores in the weather and shall in Steade of an Oyle primeing use Size milke &c. or that shall not stopp the crackes or slifts in timber with oyle putty Or shall lacker any worke whatsoever that is to abide the

---

* This by-law was copied verbatim from the original record, but having been copied in shorthand it is impossible to reproduce the original spelling.

weather instead of Gold every such person or persons soe offending in all or any the aforesaid cases upon complaint thereof made to the Master and Wardens of the aforesaid Guild of such ill worke made and done whereby his Maties subjects are abused and Injured that then a view being taken by the Master and Wardens of the said Guild and two of the Bretheren of the ffaculty of Painter stainers of such insufficient worke and by them adjudged soe to be; that then and in such case the party soe offending shall for the first offence pay to the Master of the said Guild for the use of the said Corporacon six shillings eight pence sterling and for the second offence and all other more offences of this nature the full vallue of his or their worke."

Attempts on the part of individual members of this Corporation to obtain a monopoly of portion of the trade were opposed by the Guild. Such action was contrary to the fraternal spirit which had always been encouraged by the Guilds. In the Records of the Guild of Cutlers, Painter Stainers and Stationers occurs an entry under date 18th April 1685 to the effect that one Joseph Ray, a brother of the Corporation, presented a petition informing the Guild that he had been informed that Mr. Samuel Helsham, a brother of the Guild, together with Mr. Andrew Crook were passing a patent under the broad seal of Ireland for the sole printing and vending of books etc. in this kingdom with restriction to all others doing the same without their licence, as his Majesty's printer general, which privileges were destructive to the whole faculty of stationer members of this Guild; that accord-

Opposition to Monopoly.

CRAFT GUILDS IN THE XVII. CENTURY 235

ingly he had made an application to the Lord Chancellor and put in a caveat against the said patent passing the broad seal which he did because the time was short between his notice and the sealing; he accordingly prayed for the concurrence of the Guild in prosecuting the said business —a copy of the letter to the Chancellor then follows and prays relief against the patent he being a free stationer. The clause objected to was one whereby the printing of psalters, primers, almanacks and many school books was to be confined to the patentees. The Guild agreed that the patent was prejudicial to them and they resolved at the charge of the public fund of the guild to assist the said Ray in his petition and to take such other means to uphold the rights of the Guild as might be adjudged meet and convenient.

Another item from the same Records dated 9th January 1692, relates that William Wynter moved that Robert Thornton a brother of the guild had obtained a patent to be Stationer to their Majesties to severall offices with stationers ware in this kingdom payable at their Majesties charge and that the same was injurious to the stationers, brethern of the Guild; and did request leave to sue and implead said Thornton or otherwise to bring the patent in question at law in the name of the corporation: It was ordered that six persons, Stationers, therein named might have license to use the name of the Guild for said purpose provided the expence be not charged upon the Guild, nor upon any member that was not willing to contribute.

The licensing of hawkers and their employment by members of the Guild is referred to in an interesting entry dated 4th April, 1696, taken from the same source which reads:—"That no Hawker shall be admitted to sell anything aboute the Towne or Citty belonging to the Corporacon afforesd except it be such as is lycenced to sell nott above a printed sheet of paper And Every Brother y^t doth Imploy any of the said Hawkers shall Enter their names in the booke belonging to the Corporacon afforesd and shall pay for every such Hawker as they or any of them shall Imploy the sume of one shill. p quarter and that none of the said Hawkers shall sell any bound book or horne book primer Catechism Almanack Writting paper penns or Ink & Knives Sizors nor any other goods w^{t}soever that belongeth to any of the ffaculties of the said Corporacon And if any such Hawker be found to be cryeing or selling such goods as above mented & not entred to some Brother of the Corporacon afforesd shall Imeadiatly be taken up & punished according to Law."

Licensing of Hawkers.

This account of the craft guilds of Dublin in the seventeenth century may be brought to a close with an apparently insignificant item from the same Records dated 18 Jan., 1691, which recited that notwithstanding the law that none should be admitted under a fine of £4 yet if any person make application for admittance provided he should not appear to intrude on any of the three faculties, or any other guild but be content with that he is brought up to and give the usual bonds, such person might be admitted at such under fines as the Master Wardens and quorum of the Council should determine. This admission to the Guild of a craftsman who was neither a cutler, nor a painter-stainer, nor a stationer is one of the first indications of a practice which became universal in the succeeding century, namely, the admission to the craft guilds of persons not associated with the particular crafts. To this practice may be attributed partial responsibility for the downfall of the guild system.

CHAPTER VII.

THE BREAK-UP OF THE GUILDS.

CHAPTER VII.

The Break-up of the Guilds.

THE period from the beginning of the eighteenth century to the year 1840 when the guild system in Dublin finally broke up was a period of progressive decline. The guild system remained in operation for over six hundred years. So firmly was it established that it lingered on in Dublin much later than in other countries. The commerce of the city was for centuries in the hands of the Guild Merchant. All the more important crafts were organised under the guild system. Several contributory causes led to the downfall of the Dublin guilds, any one of which causes would have ultimately led to their destruction. Notable amongst these was the decay of the fraternal spirit which had at one time animated the guild brethren and the substitution for the fraternal bond of the cash *nexus* between employer and employed. In Dublin as elsewhere the spirit of capitalism made its appearance and produced on the part of the workers combinations against their masters met by repression on the part of the latter.

Causes of Downfall. The exclusion of Catholic merchants and craftsmen from the guilds, a policy which was persisted in throughout this period, was another potent cause of decline. It resulted in large numbers, in fact a majority of the merchants and craftsmen, carrying on trade and working at their crafts illicitly so far as the civic laws and guild regulations were concerned. The guilds no longer exercised a monopoly over commerce and industry. The preservation of that monopoly was essential to the life of the guilds.

Neglect of the crafts with which the guilds were associated contributed as much as any other cause to their downfall. The various guilds continued to hold their annual meetings for the election of guild officers, their quarterly assemblies for the conduct of business, and "halls" from time to time when summoned, but the minutes of the meetings held do not reveal a very close attention to the detail of craft work and the furtherance and preservation of the particular trades concerned. Rather do they seem to have degenerated into political clubs and to have made politics not business their main object. In the latter half of the eighteenth century and the early nineteenth century politics dominated the guild system.

Closely associated with this new trend in guild affairs was a practice which became prevalent in this period, namely, the admission to the Guild Merchant of persons unconnected with commerce and the opening of the various craft guilds to persons not qualified by apprenticeship to any craft. Admission to the various guilds was sought and obtained as a stepping stone to the civic franchise, the possession of which gave to the holders a voice in the selection of both municipal and parliamentary representatives. The admission to the guilds of persons thus unqualified struck at the first principle of the guild system which was an association of persons working at a particular art or craft for the promotion of that art or craft and the mutual betterment of the brethren of the guild.

The records of the guilds and the municipal records amply illustrate the operation of these causes in bringing

THE BREAK-UP OF THE GUILDS

about the downfall of the guilds. The records of the Guild of Barber-Surgeons afford evidence as to the decay of the fraternal spirit between masters and men and as to the slavish conditions of labour imposed upon the journeymen.

Decay of Fraternal Spirit.

Attempts by the latter to improve their status were met with determined opposition on the part of the masters. The following entry taken from the original records bears date 10th October, 1757, and is in these terms: " At a generall meeting of the Master Wardens and Brethren of the Corporation of Barbers Chirurgeons etc. or Guild of St. Mary Magdalene within the City of Dublin as well Quarter brothers as freemen; in order to stop and suppress unlawfull combinations entered into by the Journeymen Perukemakers and Barbers in this City for lessning their usuall hours of work, contrary to Acts of Parliament in that case made and provided—We the Master, Wardens and Brethren in full hall assembled having taken into mature consideration the evil tendency & iniquity of all such unlawfull combinations; and in order to putt an immediate stop thereto have unanimously come to the following resolutions:

1. " Resolved that any Master Barber or Perukemaker that shall employ any Journeyman, who between the 29th day of Sepr. and 25th day of March in each year, shall refuse to work at said Trade from the hour of Seven in the Morning untill nine at night, and who shall from the 25th day of March to the 29th day of Sepr. in Each year, refuse to work at said Trade from Six o Clock in the Morning (being the usuall and accustomed Hours ot

working in the said Trade) Shall for every Such offence forfeit and Pay the Sum of one pound nineteen Shillings & Eleven pence.

2. "Resolved that any Master who shall Employ any Journeyman without Enquiring from the Master with whom Such Journeyman last wrought, the reasons for his parting with Such Journeyman & whether such Journeyman has given a weeks notice to his Former Master or that shall Employ any Journeyman who has been discharged for refusing to work the Hours abovementioned shall for every such offence Forfeit and pay the like Sum of one pound nineteen Shillings & Eleven Pence.

3. "Resolved That any Master that shall Treat with or offer more Wages to any Journeyman while he is in the work or business of another Master, Shall for every Such offence forfeit and Pay the Like Sum of one pound, nineteen Shillings & Eleven Pence.

(Nos. 4 and 5 being unimportant are here omitted.)

6. "Resolved that we will to the utmost of our Power Prosecute to the utmost rigour of the Law, all Journeymen of said Trade who shall for the Future Enter into any Such unlawfull assembly or Combination, as also the Master or Masters of such House or houses wherein such unlawfull assembly shall be held, and that we will give all Due Encouragement to Such Person or Persons who shall Inform us of the Same.

7. "Resolved That all Journeymen that are longer Employed than the usuall Time of working Shall be Constantly Paid for such Extraordinary Hours the Same In Proportion as for the Day—

"In Confirmation whereof We the said Master Wardens

THE BREAK-UP OF THE GUILDS

Free and Quarter brothers Have hereunto Sett our Hands the Day and year aforesaid

"Thos. Wood—MASTER,

⎫
⎬ WARDENS."
⎭

In the following year the same Guild resolved "that this Corporation will to the utmost of their power support the said James Gaynor in the prosecution of his Journeymen and others concerned in any unlawfull assembly or Combination and also in any prosecution to be by him carryed on agt. the Master or Mistress of such House who knowingly permitted any such unlawfull assembly or assemblys." This James Gaynor was merely a Quarter Brother, yet in the matter of prosecuting his journeymen he had the whole power of the Guild at his back.

Combinations of Craftsmen.

The Common Council of Dublin were sternly opposed to combinations of journeymen formed for the purpose of improving the conditions of their employment. In the year 1769 a petition was presented by "certain of the Commons" setting forth that "an outrageous mob have of late entered into unlawful combinations, particularly the weavers, bakers and coopers of this city have quit the work of their respective employers for the purpose of advancing their wages, and have committed many acts of violence, in breaking windows and several other outrages . . ." Upon this petition an order was made authorising the Lord Mayor to issue a proclamation offering a reward for the conviction of persons concerned in the said unlawful combinations.

A payment of twenty guineas was ordered in the year 1770 to be made by the City Treasurer to the Master and Wardens of the corporation of tailors who had presented a petition setting forth that the late prosecution of combining journeymen tailors had been attended with very heavy expense to the petitioners who feared they could not complete the suppressing of the said combinations unless aided by the Corporation of the city.

Immediately afterwards the following entry occurs in the municipal records, namely: " Certain of the commons setting forth that in consequence of the bad behaviour of the journeymen coopers, the masters were obliged to invite workmen from the different parts of this kingdom, that John Dinan, amongst others, came to this city to work, who was there assaulted and wounded in a desperate manner by the journeymen of this city, insomuch that many pieces were taken out of his skull. That a reward was offered for apprehending and prosecuting riotous and combining journeymen to which they apprehend said Dinan is entitled for prosecuting Richard Woods, therefore prayed such sum for said Dinan as should seem meet." This petition was referred to a committee and meantime a payment of ten guineas was made to the unfortunate Dinan.

The substantial sum of one hundred pounds was later voted to the guild of tailors to enable them to forward a Bill, for preventing irregular risings among journeymen tailors and for regulating the hours of their work and their wages.

The exclusion of Catholic merchants and craftsmen from the guilds was persisted in during the whole of this

THE BREAK-UP OF THE GUILDS 247

period. Occasionally a little relaxation in the guild by-laws took place, as, for example, when the Feltmakers passed a resolution in the year 1764: "That for the future no objection whatsoever shall lye against any Roman Catholick Feltmaker's following the feltmaking business in all its branches within the City of Dublin and the liberties thereof and in all other places where the Jurisdiction of this corporation extends for or on account of their being of the Roman Catholic religion." The proviso was added that such Roman Catholic should have served seven years' apprenticeship, should pay his quarterage and all fines and sums of money appointed and conform to the laws and ordinances of the Guild.* The liberal spirit then evinced did not long prevail.

Exclusion of Catholics.

The by-laws of the Guilds and the oaths taken by freemen on admission were aimed at excluding Catholic boys from being initiated into the mysteries of any art or craft in the City of Dublin. One of the Rules of the Cutlers' Guild already quoted provided that any brother who should take an apprentice should within three months thereafter bring him before the Master and Wardens " to the intent that they see he be of a good conversation and of the protestant religion." In the form of oath administered on admission to the Guild of Barber-Surgeons the following passage occurs: " You shall not take any Apprentice but of the Protestant religion, and for no less term than seven years." † In the oath taken on admission to the Guild Merchant the phraseology is somewhat different,

---
* From original Records of the Guild.
† See Guild Records in Trinity College Library Minute Book 1714–1791, pp. 52–53.

being as follows: " You shall take no apprentice but if he be free born; that is to say, no bondsman's son, and for no less term than seven years." The interpretation put upon this oath was that by persons not " free born " were meant Roman Catholics.*

The sectarian policy which animated the Guilds naturally drove Catholic traders and craftsmen to follow their occupations in an illicit manner and in defiance of the guild authorities. Catholic masters sometimes took apprentices without binding them for the full term of seven years.

In January, 1707, the Common Council of Dublin ordered that a proclamation should be issued by the Lord Mayor requiring the Masters and Wardens of corporations in the city to make a return to him in writing of all the Popish dealers and manufacturers in the city and others not being free of the city who were permitted to trade therein and also of the names and numbers of the several apprentices and for what term of years they were bound to their respective masters. The Order recited that complaints had been made that Roman Catholics had taken many apprentices and for less than seven years, whereas other masters were limited to two apprentices who should serve a seven years' term.

An order made by the Guild of Barber-Surgeons in February 1714 recited that divers and sundry persons not being free of the said corporation " practised the Arts and mysteries of Chyrurgeons and Barbitonsors in private and secret places " and directed that such persons should forfeit the sum of £5 for every month during which they should so practise.

* See Municipal Corporations Report Appendix Vol. I, p. 271.

THE BREAK-UP OF THE GUILDS 249

In the Records of the same Guild the following entry occurs under date, 8th April, 1771, namely: "Thomas Hanley of Mary's Street Barber complimented with the freedom of this Guild & to have a certificate by Grace Especiall gratis: In consideration that the said Thos. Hanley hath reformed from the Errors of Popery & is also marryed to the widow of a late free brother of sd. Guild."

A like compliment was paid in April, 1772, to Francis Conway of "Colledge Green," barber, "in consideration of his having been for many years past a good Quarter brother & hath lately reformed from the Errors of Popery."

In the Records of the Goldsmiths' Guild the following entry occurs under date 2nd February, 1758, namely: "The Petcon of the Widow Hutton was read praying for Charity & would have been ord^d to pay her One Guinea had it not appeared to this House that she brought a Papist Priest to her Husband as he was dying."*

An Act of the Irish Parliament passed in the year 1793 removed restrictions on Catholics with regard to admission to corporations and guilds. Notwithstanding this Act, Catholics were rigorously excluded from both the corporation of Dublin and the city guilds. During a period of more than forty years from the passing of the Act not a single Catholic was admitted to the civic franchise.

In the Report on the City of Dublin made by the Municipal Corporations Commissioners and published in the year 1836 several references to the policy of the guilds in this matter occur. Referring to the Guild Merchant they state:—" Eleven Roman Catholics obtained

* See Journal of Proceedings 1731-1758, p. 351, in the possession of this Guild.

the freedom of this guild shortly after the relaxation of the penal code in 1793, but none have since been admitted. Roman Catholic merchants are probably deterred from applying for their freedom, by a conviction that their applications would not be successful. There are many Roman Catholic merchants of high respectability in the city of Dublin. The vast majority of the leading Dublin merchants are not members of the guild. It is generally understood that not only Roman Catholics, but also Protestants, professing political opinions at variance with those of the corporation, have been, and are, studiously excluded."

With regard to the craft guilds the Commissioners state as follows:—" The strongest sectarian feeling pervades all the guilds, and with the exception of three who by a *mandamus* (which was not defended) forced their way into the smiths', there are no Roman Catholics free of any of the guilds. Protestants of political principles different from those of the majority of the corporation are equally excluded. Mr. Jordan Lambert, one of the officers of the smiths', stated, on oath, that the guild 'did everything in their power to keep out Catholics and bad Protestants.'"

During the eighteenth century the Dublin guilds, with one notable exception, showed a gradually lessening interest in the arts and crafts with which they were associated, while municipal and national politics became objects of increased concern. By-laws dealing with the regulation of industries give place to resolutions of a controversial nature, addresses to members of Parliament and to parliamentary candidates, and votes of censure on

The Guilds and Politics.

THE BREAK-UP OF THE GUILDS

municipal representatives. Ex-Lord Mayors and ex-High Sheriffs were complimented in terms of fulsome flattery on their services while in office. Meetings of the Guilds were held at which candidates for Parliament attended and addressed the brethren. In short the craft guilds of the seventeenth century became political clubs in the eighteenth century.

The guilds, however, still continued to loom large in the public eye. On occasions such as the riding of the city franchises the various guilds made a most impressive display with their standards and gay colours. Each guild had its own distinguishing colours. After the ceremony of riding the franchises, the brethren were entertained at the expense of their respective guilds.

Riding the Franchises.

Numerous entries relating to the riding of the franchises appear in the records of the guilds. An order was made by the Guild of Cutlers, Painter-Stainers and Stationers in the year 1707 that the several brothers should appear well mounted on horseback with the corporation colours in their hats, edged with gold, at the Master's house on 5th August 1707 at three o'clock in the morning to ride the franchises. In the year 1713 the brethren of the same guild were ordered to attend the Standard at 6 o'clock on the morning of 13th August at Mr. Warden Wine's house on Lazy Hill, their hats edged with gold, bearing cockades of red, blue, and yellow, and wearing yellow gloves stitched with red silk and bound with red ribbon. The Guild of Barber-Surgeons in the year 1734 ordered that the sum of £44 and no more should be allowed to the present and future

THE GUILDS OF DUBLIN

Masters for the expenses of riding the franchises out of which sum the Master was to pay to each Warden' the sum of £3 and to furnish the Beadle with a hat and cloak as usual on such occasions.

A record of the order and procession of the guilds in connection with the riding of the franchises in the year 1767 appears in the Appendix to Volume XI. of Gilbert's Calendar of Dublin Records. It gives the names and addresses of the various Masters and Wardens and the colours of the guilds and is as follows:—

Procession of the Guilds.

I.—Merchants, or Holy Trinity Guild, blue and yellow.
    Richard French, Blind Quay, Henry Hart, Eustace Street, masters. John Booker, Essex bridge, William Coats, Bagnio slip, wardens.

II.—Tailors, or Guild of Saint John Baptist, saxon blue and white.
    Abraham Lee, Merchant's quay, master. Abraham Creighton, Big Ship street, David Bacon, Trinity lane, wardens.

III.—Smiths, or Guild of Saint Loy, black and white.
    Wm. Osbrey, Dame Street, master. Richard Nix, Dame Street, John Sheen, Dame Street, wardens.

IV.—Barber-Surgeons, or Guild of Saint Mary Magdalen, purple, cherry and white.
    Alexr Ross, Blind quay, master. Edmund Chapman, Smithfield, T. Mitchel, wardens.

V.—Bakers, or Guild of Saint Anne, orange, cherry and lemon.
    Wm. Beasley, Marrowbone Lane, master. Caleb Smalley, senior, George's Lane, warden.

THE BREAK-UP OF THE GUILDS 253

VI.—Butchers, or Guild of the B.V.M., red and white.
Gust. Wild, Channel Row, master. Edwd. Rice, Fleet Street, John Brazell, George Hamilton, New Market, wardens.

VII.—Carpenters, Millers, Masons, Healers, Turners, and Plumbers, of the Fraternity of the B.V.M. and House of Saint Thomas, Dublin, red and white.
Richard Cranfield, Hog Hill, master. Wm. Stokes, Clare Street, John Morgan, Chequer Lane, wardens.

VIII.—Shoemakers, or Guild of St. Michael, Archangel, red, blue and green.
Edwd. Clarke, Capel St. John Sherwood, Cutpurse Row, masters. Wm. Sleavin, Crane lane, James McCleary, High Street, wardens.

IX.—Saddlers Upholders Coach and Coach harness makers, or Guild of the B.V.M., crimson, white and green.
Wm. McCready, Bride Street, master. Humphrey Curtin, Mary St., John Hale, George's lane, wardens.

X.—Cooks, or Guild of St. James Apostle, orange and black.
Joseph Watson, Ormond market, master. Paul Presley, Dame Street, Terence Sherridan, Sussex St., wardens.

XI.—Tanners, blue white and yellow.
Saml. Henderson, New row, on the Poddle, master. Samuel Nesfield, T. Miller, James's Street, W. Vicars, Crooked staff, wardens.

XII.—Tallow Chandlers, or Guild St. George, blue & sky colour.

John Shandly, Pimlico, master. Robt. Ferran, Coombe, Wm. Kinsolows, Cole Alley, wardens.

XIII.—Glovers & skinners, or Guild of St. Mary, green & brick colour.

T. Tudor, Blind quay, master. J. Brooks, Palmers row, T. Barrow, Patrick St., wardens.

XIV.—Weavers, or Guild of Saints Philip & James, orange & blue.

Wm Worthington, Vicar street, master. J. Wiseheart, Corn market, J. Lynch, wardens.

XV.—Sheermen & Dyers, or Guild of St. Nicholas, blue & white.

Benjamin Houghton, Ash Street, M. T. Houston, Francis St. Stephen Mara Coombe W's.

XVI.—Goldsmiths or Guild of All Saints, red, yellow, and white.

W. Wilme, Hoey's Court, M. R. Williams, Castle St., J. Fredk· Sherwin & Benj. Wilson, Skinner row, W's.

XVII.—Coopers, or Guild of St Patrick, white & green.

J. Lane, Anglesea St., M. R. Servant, George's Lane, David Hollister, Kennedy's lane, wardens.

XVIII.—Feltmakers or Hatters, white hats with sky colour.

J. Brady, Meath St., M. Alexr Tate, Temple Bar, N. Tomkins, Church St., wardens.

XIX.—Cutlers, Painters, Paper Stainers, Printers and Stationers, or Guild of St. Luke Evangelist, crimson, lemon and sky blue.

THE BREAK-UP OF THE GUILDS

John Exshaw, Dame St., M. Sampson Silvester, Castle market, Patk. Wall, Arran quay, W's.

XX.—Bricklayers & plasterers, or Guild of St. Bartholomew blue & orange.

Edwd. Gill, Dorset St., master. Thos. Walsh, Moore lane, John Kennedy, Lazers hill, W's.

XXI.—Hosiers, or Guild of St. George, white, blue & copper colour.

Chas Grollier, Castle St., master. J. Carmichael, Castle st., Stephen Malone, Coombe, W's.

XXII.—Curriers, yellow, red & black.

Richard Ginn, Back lane, M. James Hill, Patk. Street, Arthur Ord., Nicholas Gate, W's.

XXIII.—Brewers and Maltsters, or Guild of St. Andrew, buff colour & blue.

Arthur Guinness, James's Gate, master. Forbes Jones, Ferry boat slip, Thos. Andrews, New row on the Poddle, W's.

XXIV.—Joiners, Ceilers & Wainscoters, green, yellow & white.

Wm. Adair, Fleet St., M. Wm. Jones, Charles St., J. Wright, Mary's Abbey, W's.

XXV.—Apothecaries, or Guild of St. Luke, Evangelist, purple & orange.

Edward Caddy, Smock Alley, M. J. Pentland, Church St., J. Crampton, Dame St., W's.

An anonymous poet commemorated in verse the riding of the franchises on this occasion.[*]

---

[*] Ibidem.

THE POEM.

"Thou mighty Sol, who in the East ascend
Thy beams display, and all thy glories lend,
Now, mount thy chariot, drive each cloud away,
And bright Aurora usher in this day.
  Next Neptune, god and ruler of the main,
Let not the clouds exhale one drop of rain,
Then will each Hero, at the night's approach,
Come home with dry cockades without a coach.
  And now the glorious Cavalcade's begun,
Ye Muses open all your Helicon,
Inspire my verse, and assist my song
While I relate how each troop moves along.
  The City Praetor, mounted on a steed,
With ribbons drest, leads on the cavalcade,
Before his lordship, with a solemn grace,
They bear the sword of justice and the mace,
His gown of richest scarlet in his hand
Majestical he holds the powerful wand;
In awful pomp and state, on either side,
The City sheriffs in like triumph, ride,
Attended by a band, whose gripping paw,
Poor debtors dread, and keep them still in awe.
  Next march the Guild, who plow the frothy main
In depth of winter for the hopes of gain,
To distant climes our beef and wool convey,
And barter wholesome food for silk and tea;
Fearless of rocks, they seek the unknown shore,
And bring from thence the glit'ring, tempting ore.
  The cross legged Taylors next in order go,

Who, by their arts, trim others for this show,
All other arts acknowledge and confess,
They're grac'd by them in ev'ry gaudy dress,
As well the peasant as the cringing beau,
Must from the Taylor to fair Silvia go;
No wonder then those Taylors march so gay,
Since from all others thus they bear the sway.

   Next march the Smiths, men bravely us'd to fire
Without whose aid all arts must soon expire
Before them, clad in armour in his pride
A brawny Vulcan doth in triumph ride.

   Next come the Barbers, who can soon repair
Nature's defects, and lend the bald with hair,
Suit all complections, and with little pains,
Supply the skull with wigs that lacketh brains.

   Next come the well-bred men, who know the way
To please the ladies in their bread at tea,
And with their white, their wheaten, and their brown,
Can please the palate of the lord or clown.

   Next march the Butchers, men inur'd to toil
Their brawny limbs, like champions, shine with oil,
Murder and slaughter, knocking in the head,
Are their delight, the trade to which they're bred.

   Next march the Carpenters, whose arms can rend,
The lofty pines, and make proud elms to bend.

   Next do the Shoemakers in order go,
And their dragoons do make a stately show,
Since the wide hoop exposes to the view,
The well shaped leg, silk stockings, red heel'd shoe.

   Next march the Saddlers, glorious to behold,
On sprightly beasts, their saddles shine with gold;

s

A warlike steed most proudly walks before,
Richly attir'd led by a Black-a-moor.
　Next march the cooks, who study day and night,
With costly fare to please the appetite.
With these the Vintners ride, did they refine,
As much as they adulterate the wine,
Their every muse would gladly sound,
And with what pleasure would the glass go round.
　Next march the Tanners fam'd in days of yore,
For tanning hides for shields which heroes bore;
Who has not heard of Ajax's seven-fold shield,
Which neither to the sword nor shield would yield;
And won't you as much admire, as much adore,
The tanner's hand, as his the buckler bore.
　Next march the Tallow-chandlers, who expel,
With cheerful lights, shades from the darkest cell,
Enthusiasts of inward light may boast,
But these are they, illuminate the most.
　Next march the Glovers who, with nicest care,
Provide white kid for the new married pair;
Or nicely stitch the lemon-colour'd glove,
For hand of beau to go and see his love.
　The Weavers next in order proudly ride,
Who with great skill the nimble shuttle guide;
Pity such art should meet such small reward
But what art now-a-days does meet regard.
　Sheermen and Dyers next in order come,
Men who depend entirely on the loom;
The Weaver finds employment for them both
One gives the colour, 'tother finds the cloath.
　Next march the Goldsmiths who can form and mould

THE BREAK-UP OF THE GUILDS

In sundry shapes and forms, the ductile gold;
Men call them traytors, rebels, and what not,
Nor King, nor queen they spare, all goes to pot,
No pity meets, in the devouring fire,
Monarchs, and chamber-pots, and rings expire.
    Then come the jolly Coopers, who confine,
In casks well bound with hoops the sparkling wine.
    Next march the Hatters, once a gainful trade,
When men wore finest beavers on their heads,
But now, lest weight of that the curl should harm,
Beaux strut along with beaver under arm.
    Next Printers, Stationers, Cutlers, Painters appear
Three men in shields their arms before them bear
And printing-press to show that art so rare.
    Next march the Bricklayers by whose hands arise
Hibernias towers, whose top salutes the skies.
    The Stocking-Weavers next in order come,
Who form the scarlet stocking in the loom,
With clock of gold or silver nicely wrought,
Each step fair Chloe takes, a lover's caught.
    Next march the curriers, who both cut and pare
The hides for saddler or shoe-maker.
    The Brewers next well mounted doth appear,
These are the men brew humming ale and beer.
    The skilful Joyners next in order come,
Whose chairs and tables furnish out the room,
A man in white proceeds the gallant train,
Whose ample shoulders a huge pole sustain.
    See, where the proud Apothecaries drive,
Who most by fraud and impositions thrive,
Whose monstrous bills immoderate wealth procure,

For drugs that kill as many as they cure,
Well are they plac'd the last of all the rout
For they're the men we best can live without.
  In order thus they ride the city round,
View all the limits, and observe each bound,
Then homeward steer their course without delay
And fall to drink, the business of the day,
Next morning send their horse and coutrements away.

<blockquote>Dublin. Printed by B. Corcoran, on the Inns-key near the Cloister, where may be had all sorts of Ballads and Chapmens Books, 1767."</blockquote>

It will be noticed that the number of guilds had risen to twenty-five. The Guild of Joiners was incorporated by William III. in the year 1701. The guild was admitted to representation on the Common Council by an order of the latter body made at their Michaelmas meeting in the year 1702.

The Youngest Guild.
The tale of the Dublin Guilds was made complete by the incorporation of the apothecaries by George II. in the year 1747. Until their incorporation the apothecaries had formed part of the Guild of Barber-Surgeons.

In the year 1750 the Common Council of Dublin ordered " that the corporation of apothecarys have two of their corporation, and no more, to be of the common council of this city, and take their station next after the corporation of joiners, and that the said two common council be taken out of the four numbers, which are of the said common council for the corporation of barber surgeons, who for the future are to have but two numbers to represent them in the common council."

THE BREAK-UP OF THE GUILDS

In referring to the decay of interest in their respective crafts by the Dublin guilds it was stated that there was one notable exception. This was in the case of the Guild of Goldsmiths which deserves special mention. Throughout the whole of this period the Guild of Goldsmiths exercised a continuous scrutiny and control over the manufacture of gold and silver ware in Dublin and throughout Ireland.

An Exceptional Guild.

No better account of the nature and importance of the control exercised could be given than that mentioned in the oath of the Wardens prescribed by the Charter granted to the Guild by Charles I. in the year 1625 as set forth in the Appendix to the Report of the Municipal Corporations Commissioners. The oath administered to the Wardens was as follows:—

"You, and every of you, shall swear to be true and faithful unto the King our Sovereign Lord, his heirs and successors; you shall not be against his profit nor advantage, but that ye shall be to the advancement of his crown as much as in your power shall be; furthermore, you and every of you shall duly and truly execute and perform the office of wardens of the Company of Goldsmiths and in that place or office whereunto you and every of you are now appointed, you and every of you shall faithfully and uprightly behave yourselves. Ye shall therein to every person and persons who shall bring or cause to be brought unto your hands, within your office, any manner of silver plate to be tried or touched, or any weight, called Troy weight, to be asseized according to his Majesty's standard, use yourselves in the due execution of the same according to right, equity and justice; and also that you, or any of you, do not sett, or by your powers do not suffer to be sett, the King's Majesty's stamp, called the Harp Crowned, now appointed by his Majesty, on no manner of plate of silver unto you brought unto your said office by any manner of person or persons, unless the said silver-plate be in every part and parcel thereof according to his Majesty's standard, called eleven ounces two pennyweights; and in case it be under, and not of the said fineness, you and every of you shall cause it to be broken ere ever it pass your hands, whose plate or of what value soever it be. And you, and every of you, shall also make true and diligent search from time to time, as often as need shall require, for all deceivable wares of gold and silver, and do and perform all other things whatsoever touching the said office, according to the law, and according to the purport of his Majesty's grant, in that behalf made unto the said Company of Goldsmiths, without fear, favour, love, hatred or affection, by you or any of you to be borne to any manner of person or persons. So help you God, and the contents of this Book."

Terms of Goldsmiths' Charter. The Charter further directed that the Wardens should have scrutiny or assay of all gold and silver wrought or offered for sale in Dublin, and in all fairs and markets throughout Ireland, and should correct and punish all delinquencies therein, with the aid, if necessary, of the Mayor and Sheriffs of Dublin, and of the magistrates of fairs and markets elsewhere, with power to break all deceptive wares, and to punish the makers and vendors thereof; and to punish all makers and vendors of deceptive

THE BREAK-UP OF THE GUILDS

gold, silver, gems, precious stones, pearl, or coral, according to the laws, statutes, and ordinances in that behalf named, and to seize, break and render unsaleable any deceptive wares as aforesaid: that they should cause all wares wrought within three miles of Dublin to be assayed in their common hall, and, if found correct, to be stamped with their mark; that the goldsmiths in all towns in Ireland should observe the regulations of Dublin; that one or two goldsmiths from every town in which the art is practised should proceed to Dublin to make themselves acquainted with the touch of gold and silver, and with the punch, a crowned harp; that no goldsmith should work up or sell wares of gold of less value than 22 carats, and should not use "sotheraumell or stuffings" in their works beyond what was necessary for their finish; that they should not charge beyond the rate of 12d. the ounce for gold, beyond the fashion, above what it would be valued at the King's mint, under forfeiture of the value of such article; that they should not make or sell any wares of silver of less value than 11 ounces and 2 pennyweights, nor take beyond the rate of 12d. for every pound weight of silver wares, besides the fashion, more than its value at the King's mint, and should not expose for sale any silver wares until the workman thereof should have affixed his own private mark on such part as could conveniently bear it, under penalty of forfeiture of the ware; that the wardens should have power to seize wares deceptively stamped, and confiscate same, and that one half of the forfeiture should go to King, and the other half to the person who had been injured by the fraud; that no one should be admitted to the freedom of the company until he should have proved the service of an apprenticeship of seven years, and that he had wrought a piece of work of silver called his "masterpiece," to be approved of by the wardens for the time being. It further ordained that the Wardens and company should be obedient to all regulations to be thereafter made respecting the art by the Lord Lieutenant and Privy Council.*

From time to time various Acts were passed by the Irish Parliament imposing duties on gold and silver wares imported unto or wrought in Ireland, which duties were to be collected by the Guild officers. By an Act of Parliament 23 & 24 Geo. III, c. 23 three *Gold* standards of fineness were established, *Standards.* namely of not less than 22, 20 and 18 carats of fine gold in every pound weight Troy. This Act regulated the marks to be put by the makers on gold manufacture for the several standards, and required that it should be stamped at the assay office in Dublin, with a harp crowned, or at the assay office in New Geneva, in the County of Waterford, with a like harp, and a bar across its strings, excepting however, rings and small articles. It further directed that persons manufacturing gold should enter impressions of their new marks or punches, with their names and places of abode, in either of those assay offices, upon paying five shillings to the assayer or wardens, who were required to make the impressions on pewter or copper, and to make entries of the marks, names and places of abode in a book to be kept for that purpose.

*See Appendix to Report of Municipal Corporations (Ireland) Commissioners Vol I, p. 280'

THE BREAK-UP OF THE GUILDS

The records of the Guild of Goldsmiths show how faithfully the Guild officers fulfilled the duties imposed upon them by their charter. Owing to the precious nature of the metals used the temptation to fraud was stronger than in the case of craftsmen working on less valuable material. Various fraudulent devices were from time to time adopted, but there were few if any that could evade the vigilance of the Assay Master and his assistants. That the work done by the gold and silver smiths of Dublin in the eighteenth century reached such a high standard was due in no small part to the manner in which the guild officers fulfilled their trust.

Work of the Guild.

A form of fraud which was commonly attempted is illustrated by the following entry dated November 1731, namely:—" John Gyles brought a second time two p(air)s of spurrs the boddys 16 peny weight worse then standard, the tackle a peny w^t better, to the assay office in order to be touched, and that the tackle might bring of the spurrs, wch is an intended fraud for wch offence the Corporation have now fined him twenty shills and it is ordrd that if, ever he comitts the like offence again to be psecuted wth the utmost severity of Law att the Corporation expence."

A more ingenious fraud was that mentioned in an entry dated April 1733 when it was ordered " that Mr. John Moore be fined twenty shillings for designing to put a piece of touched plate at the bottom of a silver cupp, foot & handles were six peny weight worse then standard."

In January 1737 " Jacob Lyons a Jew was fined five shillings for workeing and makeing up two small pear of silver Buckles fourteen peny weight and a halfe worse then standard." Nothing daunted by this exposure and fine, Jacob continued manufacturing silver buckles of less than the standard fineness. In the following year a fine of ten shillings was imposed upon him.

The work of a Limerick goldsmith is mentioned in an entry dated 17th January, 1738, which reads:—"A silver waiter being brought to the Hall to be touched and six silver Tea spoons sent with it by John Robinson of the City of Limerick Goldsmith. And upon Tryal the Waiter was found six penny weight worse and the two spoons five penny weight and a half better by which it appeared to the Hall that it was an intended fraud not only on the Publick but on the Hall. It is therefore ordered that the said Waiter be broke. And it being proposed that the said Robinson should be fined. The question was whether it should be 20s. or 10s." By a majority the fine was fixed at the latter amount.

Another item illustrating the jurisdiction of the guild over gold and silver work wrought throughout Ireland is dated 1st August, 1739. At a "Hall" held this day it was ordered " that Mr. Archdell go to Mullingar to Prosecute Baldwin Potter for counterfeiting the Hall mark and striking it on two spoons And the Expence of Lawyers fees is left to the discretion of Mr. Archdell and that the Clerk do attend him."

In the year 1758 a warrant was granted for the arrest of one Dennis Kehoe with power to search his house, owing to the fact that two pairs of silver buckles which he had exposed for sale were found to be considerably under the standard and to have had " the Duty & Touch cast thereon wth Intend to defraud his Majesty of his Duty

THE BREAK-UP OF THE GUILDS

and to Impose thereby on the Publick." Several pairs of buckles of base silver were found in a glass case in the shop of the said Kehoe as a result of the search made.

The records of the Guild of Goldsmiths contain a set of Articles drawn up for the regulation of *The Assay Master.* the important office of Assay Master in the year 1736 in which year a vacancy in the office occurred. The articles were:—

" First that such Brother as puts in to be assay master must be duly elected by the whole house.

" Secondly that after such election the Brother so elected to finde security of one thousand pound ster. for the due execution of his office and safety of the plate lodged in the Hall or assay office and the Corporation part of the assay money.

" Thirdly that all assays be taken in at the assay office before nine o'clock each assay day.

" Fourthly that the assay master shall take no more than two pence for every assay of silver plate as well from strangers as Brothers—one shilling for every gold assay & one shill^g for every parting assay.

" Fifthly that the assay master shall in consideration of his Care and paines in the assaying the silver plate [have] one halfpenny of currant money for every ounce of plate by him assayed.

" Sixthly That twelve pound a year be paid by the sd. assay master out of his halfe penny p ounce for the use of the Corporation.

" Seventhly that the scrapeings taken of the plate not exceeding six grains on ye pound weight in ord^r to try and assay the plate shall be restored to the owner or so much thereof as can be preserved.

"Eighthly That the assay mast. acc^t everry Quarter & pay unto the Corporation their share or part of the touch money.

"Ninthly That the assay master if a shoppkeeper shall not buy nor sell any manner of plate or silver during his continuance in sd. office nor shall after a Limitted time wch will be granted him by the Corporation keep open shopp nor worke up nor cause to be wrought up any man^r of gold or silver plate.

"Tenthly That the Brother who shall be elected assay master if not a shoppkeeper nor now following the Goldsmith trade shall not keep or sell any sort of Liquors, and be also subject to all the above articles."

The amount of "Touch Money" collected by the Assay Master in the year 1736 was £172 9s. 4d. one half of which was retained by the Assay Master for his emolument, the other half being paid over to the Master on behalf of the guild.

In the records of the other craft guilds and of the Guild Merchant from the beginning of the eighteenth century onwards the references to the regulation of industry and commerce are few and far between. The bulk of the minutes of the proceedings at the guild meetings is taken up with matters of minor importance, often having no bearing upon the purposes for which the guilds were originally formed. A few instances of trade regulation, however, deserve mention.

Control Exercised by Other Guilds.

The original books of proceedings of the Guild

THE BREAK-UP OF THE GUILDS

Merchant recorded a petition presented by a member in the year 1701 praying pardon for having entered as his own the goods of a stranger in the Custom House, serious offence and one directly contrary to guild regulations, The entry appears in Gilbert's transcript as follows:—

"To the Rt. Worshipful the Masters, Wardens, and Brethren of the Trinity Guild of Merchants, Dublin.

"The humble petition of Mathias Boults Humbly sheweth:

"That your petitioner, with his family, came over from Holland about three years past and taking up his residence in this City was soon after admitted to the liberties and franchizes thereof and also to be a member of this Worshipful Corporation. That your petitioner being altogether a stranger to the customs of this city and unacquainted with the English tongue was prevailed with to enter the goods of one Mr. Meyers (a foreigner) in the Custom House as belonging to your petitioner; whereof your petitioner being now made sensible is heartily sorry for the said offence and submits himself to your Worships.

"Now forasmuch as your petitioner was ignorant of the manner of dealing in such cases, and never intended any wrong either to His Majesty or the Brethren of this Guild, He humbly prays your Worships to consider his case and circumstances and to pass by this ignorant mistake of his and he will take care never to offend in the like again.

And your petitioner shall pray &c
Mattys Boults."

"8th Sept 1701. Upon consideration of the above petition of Mathias Boults by the Masters Wardens and brethren of Trinity Guild of Merchants this day assembled in their

Common Hall It is ordered and agreed that the petitioner do, for the said offence, pay into the poor box, the sum of £4 12s. in regard he is a stranger and not acquainted with the manner of dealing in this city and not understanding well the English tongue. And in case he shall ever hereafter commit the like crime, that he be disfranchised the city and corporation & never to be restored again to the freedom of same."*

The original Minute Book of the Guild of Barber-Surgeons for the period 1714 to 1791 contains the following entry under date October 13th, 1718:—

"Whereas many great frauds and abuses are daily committed and practiced in and about the City of Dublin by divers persons who sell hairs therein *False Hair.* (vizt.) by mixing of hairs cutt off of several heads together tho of different colours, mixing bleached hairs horse hairs and live hairs together and by giving false colours to hairs by dipping and dyeing the same and by other irregular and unfair management and do also lett down the same by falsely and unfairly tying the same all which and the like knavish and unfair doings of the said persons sellers of hairs tend to the great loss and abuse of the Brethren of this corporation in particular and to the wearers of wiggs in general . . ." It was thereupon ordered that all such persons should be proceeded against with the utmost severity that the law would allow in such cases.

A by-law of the Guild of Feltmakers made " att a publique Hall " held on 7th May, 1719, dealt with the question of journeymen quitting their masters' service,

* Gilbert MS. Charleville Mall Library, Dublin.

THE BREAK-UP OF THE GUILDS

leaving work undone. The by-law recited that whereas several Journeymen had left their masters' service, before they had finished the several works they had been doing for their masters, and had gone to work out of the city, to the great prejudice of their several masters, and for the prevention thereof for the future it was agreed unto and for a law made that no brother of the Corporation should forever thereafter employ such journeyman going away as aforesaid until such journeyman should make satisfaction to such master as he should have quitted and left as above mentioned and should pay all such dues to the said corporation as the said journeyman should owe.

Journeymen Leaving Employment.

An order was made by the Guild of Cutlers, Painter-Stainers and Stationers in May 1725 to the effect that no brother should in future bind books with the grain of sheep leather and that every person contravening the order should be prosecuted and that upon conviction of the offender the sum of five shillings should be given to the informer. In the following month the Guild ordered that such persons as had books bound with the grain of sheep skin should bind the same over again or be prosecuted as common cheats.

Books Bound in Sheep Skin.

The sale of fraudulent wigs again occupied the attention of the Guild of Barber-Surgeons in the year 1757. A resolution dated 10th October in that year reads:—
" Whereas the Corporation has received information that severall persons hawk about this Town and otherwise expose to sale unmerchantable wiggs Resolved that this Corporation will to the utmost of their power prevent

such fraudulent and unlawfull practices for the future & that they will prosecute to the utmost rigour of the Law the Makers and Venders of such unmerchantable wiggs."

The same Guild ordered in July 1760 that the advertisement against shaving and dressing wigs or hair on the Lord's Day should be published as usual and that the observance thereof be strictly enforced.

A Redeeming Feature. One redeeming feature common to the Dublin guilds in the period of their decline was that they dispensed a liberal proportion of their funds in charity.

The Guild of the Holy Trinity took a special interest in the Blue Coat School at Oxmantown towards the expenses of which several grants were made. In the year 1701 the Guild ordered that three poor boys, the sons of decayed brethren, should be put in the "Blue boy Hospital" at the charge of the Guild, and that £24 per annum should be paid to the agent of the Hospital for that purpose. Two years later it was ordered that the dinners to the brethren on Michaelmas Quarter days should be discontinued and that in lieu thereof the sum of £26 should be added to the £24 formerly granted to complete the sum of £50 to be paid yearly out of the common stock of the Guild towards the maintenance and education of seven poor orphans, sons of decayed (? deceased) brothers in the Blue Coat Hospital.

Some years later a committee was appointed by the Guild to consider a proposal for the establishment of a Mathematical School in Dublin. The committee reported in the year 1712 as follows:—

THE BREAK-UP OF THE GUILDS 273

"1st. That the upper isle on the south side of the Blue boys Hospital next adjoining the garden is made very commodious for a school with convenient lodgings and accomodation for a Master, 10 boys and a Nurse; The Governors of the said Hospital having given a grant thereof for that purpose till a more convenient place can be found out and provided.

2nd. That soon after we caused 10 boys to be placed in the said school who have ever since been maintained and instructed in the Mathematics, at the charge of this corporation, having cloathed them in seamen's habits made of blue serge and a silver badge with the Guild's crest on their breasts.

3rd. That Mr. Connor having been pleased to accept of the trouble of Head Master of the said school gratis we have on his recommendation employed Mr. Gibson under him to teach and instruct the boys in the necessary parts of the Mathematics at £30 per annum salary and a nurse to take care of them at £3 a year.

4th. That we have received contributions from several persons towards fitting up the said school and lodgings buying of instruments and furnishing all sorts of necessaries. And we do find that about £100 per annum given by this Guild will be a sufficient allowance to defray the charge of maintaining and instructing 10 boys yearly, till fit to be disposed of and put apprentice.

5thly. That Mr. Holland steward to the Blue Coat Hospital has been all along employed to manage and provide diet for the boys after the same rate and method as those of the said Hospital; for which trouble he has hitherto had no allowance, and which, in our opinion ought to be taken into consideration.

6thly. That Mr. Connor is of opinion that four of the said 10 boys are now sufficiently instructed in the necessary parts of the Mathematics to go abroad & ought to be disposed of and put apprentice to Masters of ships as soon as conveniently can be done.

7thly. We are humbly of opinion that all boys to be taken into the said School on this Guild's account ought not to be under the age of 12 years, and such as can read and write, who shall be under the management of the Governors for 8 years from the first admission, and by them only (when fit) disposed of and put out apprentice & by none else.

8thly. We are also of opinion that the Committee of the said school should consist of the Masters and Wardens for the time being and 11 brothers of this Guild or of any 5 of them to be a quorum, whereof one Master and one warden to be always two, who shall be elected every Michaelmas Quarter day and to be Sub Governors of the said School for the said year.

All which is humbly submitted to your worships consideration 13th October 1712."*

The maintenance of the Mathematical school appears to have placed too severe a strain on the resources of the Guild. In a Report submitted in January 1714 by the Committee for the Mathematical School it was represented that there were five boys (the whole number in the school) thoroughly instructed in the necessary parts of the Mathematics for the sea service and that some of them had

* Gilbert Transcript of Records of Guild Merchant, pp. 181-3.

THE BREAK-UP OF THE GUILDS 275

been qualified for two years past to be put out, but though all endeavours had been made to provide them masters, yet none could be found to take them without money which the revenues of the Guild would not at that time allow of. The Committee accordingly deemed it advisable that the schoolmaster should be discharged temporarily and the said five boys maintained in the Hospital with the blue coat boys at the charge of the Guild until they could be otherwise disposed of.

The charitable grants of the craft guilds were necessarily on more modest lines owing to their scantier resources. In the year 1740, according to the records of the Guild of Feltmakers, the annual allowance of five pounds to the Master for the expenses of dinner to the brethren on Swearing Day and first Quarter Day was withdrawn. At the next quarterly meeting it was unanimously agreed that the said sum of five pounds should be distributed yearly amongst such of the poor of the corporation as the Master, Wardens and Assistants should direct. Other entries recorded were a payment in the year 1755 of 11s. 4½d. to a journeyman who had broken his arm, a payment in the following year of £1 2s. 9d. to a journeyman "who had been for some time past sick and incapable to work" and a further payment to A. H. "an old journeyman past his labour." In the year 1757 two small payments were made to the widows of two journeymen. Amongst the payments ordered in the succeeding year was one of eight shillings to the Master "that he paid for burying Michael Travers an old Journeyman."

At a meeting of the Guild of Barber-Surgeons held in July 1758 it was ordered that William Fielding a poor brother should be put in the poor list at forty shillings a year during such time as he should continue in confinement. In March 1761 Sarah Lennon, the widow of James Lennon late a poor brother, was put on the poor list and made a pensioner of the Guild to the extent of forty shillings a year. An entry of the year 1791 records that the sum of £1 2s. 9d. was voted to Thomas Farrell a free brother of the guild " who now lyes ill of a broken legg." Later in the year a further grant of a half guinea was made to him.

The Goldsmiths were a generous body as numerous entries in their records show. One remarkable instance of systematic charity deserves mention. In the year 1742 a Petition was presented by a Mrs. Popkins praying for charity upon which the Guild ordered that the sum of four pounds a year be paid to her. An entry of the year 1744 reads:—" Ordered that the Master buys cloaths for two children of the late Mr. Popkins in such manner as he shall think proper." A similar entry appears in the following year. Finally, in the year 1748 an entry occurs: Ordered that the Master give one Guinea towards putting out Popkins's Daughter an apprentice."

The fourth principal cause assigned for the breaking up of the guild system in Dublin was the admission to the guilds of persons unconnected with the crafts with which the respective guilds were associated. In the matter of admission to the guild franchise political reasons were allowed to outweigh economic considerations. Admission to the Guild Merchant and to the craft guilds was regarded as a stepping stone to the

Admission of Non-Craftsmen.

THE BREAK-UP OF THE GUILDS

civic franchise, the possession of which entitled the holder to the parliamentary franchise. Many persons sought admission to the guilds solely for the purpose of obtaining the higher franchise. This practice, which became notoriously prevalent in the eighteenth century and in the early decades of the nineteenth century was completely at variance with the cardinal principle underlying the guild system—the association of fellow craftsmen for the regulation of their industry with a view to their mutual betterment.

Under several of the guild charters the master of an apprentice who had completed his seven years' apprenticeship was bound to bring him before the civic authorities in order that he might be admitted to the city franchise. The practice prevailed of holding an inquiry by a jury drawn from the Council as to the validity of claims for admission by right of servitude.

A case is mentioned in the Municipal Records of the year 1732 of one Nicholas Swan being admitted a freeman of the city upon a certificate signed by the Master and Wardens of the corporation of tallow chandlers to the effect that the said Nicholas Swan had served an apprenticeship to one Peter Sharp, a free brother of the said Corporation. Upon inquiry by the jury appointed "to try the worthiness" of apprentices it was found that no such apprenticeship, nor any apprenticeship to a freeman of the city, had been served. Two Common Council men who had been privy to and consented to the false certificate were, in consequence, disfranchised and removed from their places on the Common Council.

The serving of an apprenticeship of seven years to a

free brother of a guild was an admirable title to admission to the civic franchise. Other claims to admission to both guild and civic franchise were, however, admitted. The practice prevailed in many of the guilds of admitting to the freedom of the guild persons who claimed admission by right of birth or by right of marriage. In this respect the guilds adopted a similar practice to that prevailing in the corporation of Dublin. Sons of guild brethren and sons-in-law were admitted in large numbers to the guilds by virtue of these rights. Some of them, no doubt, would have had, in addition, a professional qualification, but many were admitted to the freedom of a craft guild who were unconnected with the craft. As in the case of the city corporation, so also in the case of the guilds, the practice grew up of admitting to the freedom of the guilds persons who were not qualified by birth, marriage or servitude by what was known as " grace especial." The Dublin guilds became flooded with persons admitted by " grace especial."

Under the city by-laws persons admitted to the freedom of the guilds were not allowed to be sworn as free brothers until they had been admitted to the civic franchise. The acceptance by the guilds of candidates qualified such persons for admission to the civic franchise.

A complaint was made to the Common Council in the year 1734 that Daniel Cooke, Master of the Guild of St. John the Baptist (Guild of Tailors) had sworn several persons free of the said Guild, though not admitted or sworn free of the city, which was stated to be prejudicial to the revenue and contrary to the known usage of the several corporations. Upon the hearing of the complaint

THE BREAK-UP OF THE GUILDS 279

a recommendation was made by a committee of the Common Council that the said Master should be disfranchised.

Owing to certain irregularities in the recommendation to the freedom of the city by Masters of guilds of persons who had not been admitted to the freedom of the guilds by the body of members, it was ordered by the Common Council in the year 1763 that for the future no certificate certifying the admission of any person to the freedom of a guild with a view to his being admitted a freeman of Dublin should be received, unless such certificate had been signed by the Master, Wardens and Clerk of the Guild and was to the effect that the person mentioned had been admitted free of the Guild at their quarterly meeting assembled in their Hall, and by the majority of the brethren or the usual quorum thereof.

Upon being admitted to any of the guilds, the person admitted presented a petition to the Common Council for admission to the civic franchise, which petition was based upon a certificate from the guild officers setting forth his qualification. The petition had to pass both Houses of the Common Council, namely the Board of Aldermen and the Commons. Both of these bodies claimed and exercised the right of admitting or rejecting at their pleasure all applicants for the city franchise. If a petition were rejected, the petitioner, as a rule, could not be sworn in as a free brother of the guild. In the Guild Merchant, however, brethren were sworn irrespective of their having been previously admitted to the franchise of the city.

The right of the Common Council to reject applicants accepted by the guilds was contested in the Court of

King's Bench in the year 1826, when the right was upheld.*

The arbitrary powers of the Common Council were exercised in a manner prejudicial to a large section of the community. The Commission of Inquiry into Irish Municipal Corporations reported, as already mentioned, that not a single Roman Catholic had been admitted to the civic franchise since the year 1793, when the statutory disqualification was removed.

The infiltration of the guilds by persons not qualified by their occupation to be active and interested members thereof proceeded steadily throughout the course of the eighteenth century and the early part of the nineteenth century. In the year 1835 when a special Report on the City of Dublin was published by the Municipal Corporations Commission the process was all but complete. In that year the Guild Merchant comprised about 900 brethren and one sister. The Commissioners stated that the majority of the members were unconnected with commerce, a result which they attributed to the admission by right of birth and right of marriage of persons, without reference to their being engaged in mercantile pursuits.

Referring to the Guild of Tailors the Commissioners state: "The trade is numerous in the city of Dublin, and the majority of it are not members of, or connected with the guild, and it did not appear that the trade derives the slightest advantage from the existence of the guild."

Even the Master and Wardens of the guilds were frequently unconnected with the trades which they were supposed to represent. In this connection the Com-

* See Appendix to Report of Municipal Corporations Commission, p. 18.

THE BREAK-UP OF THE GUILDS

missioners report : " The charters direct that the masters and wardens shall be chosen from the freemen, and in some instances ordain, in express terms, what in every case they plainly intend, namely, that the persons to be elected shall be of the trade over which they are to preside. This most important restriction has been, and is frequently overlooked, and the violation of it has contributed as materially as any other circumstance to the total disconnexion of the corporations from the trades which they originally comprised. An instance was mentioned to us which illustrates the consequences of such a departure from the spirit of the charters. It was stated that about thirty years ago the master of the guild of bricklayers was called upon by Government to inspect and report upon some public buildings, then recently erected, when it was discovered that the master was by profession an attorney."

The following particulars relating to the Corporation of Bricklayers and Plasterers in August 1833 are mentioned in the Commissioners' Report namely:—

Total number of members 104, of which 39 were bricklayers or plasterers, made up as follows:—

   15 Carrying on business.
   15 out of business and in other employment.
   7 working journeymen.
   2 Absent in England.
   —
   39

The unqualified members were 65 in number made up as follows:—

11 Aldermen, 2 Barristers, 13 Attorneys, 11 Clerks,

or in other employments, 6 Architects, 9 Carpenters or builders, 2 painters, 2 metal sash-makers, 1 coal factor, 1 hatter, 1 clergyman, 1 surgeon and the following :— Lord Viscount Ingestre, the Recorder, a Sheriff's Peer, the Marshal of Dublin and the Inspector of Prisons.

With reference to this analysis of the state of the Guild of Bricklayers and Plasterers the Commissioners stated that they had " no reason to believe it an unfair specimen of the state of these guilds generally."

The Reform Act of 1832 weakened the position of the guilds in their political aspect. A largely extended parliamentary franchise was created by this Act. The power of the new voters reduced that of the guild brethren to comparative insignificance.

As a result of the Report of the Municipal Corporations Commission an Act was passed for the reform of the municipal system throughout Ireland. This Act, the Municipal Corporations (Ireland) Act of 1840, struck a death blow at the guild system in Dublin. The year 1840 marks the end of the guild system. The guilds disappeared within a year or two from the passing of the Act as effectually as if they had been thereby dissolved, although the only reference in the Act is in one section which provided for the disposition of the property of the guilds.*

The secret of their dissolution lay in a provision of the Act of 1840 whereby the old civic franchise was swept away and in its place was substituted a broad democratic franchise which placed the government of civic affairs in the hands of the whole body of burgesses. By this Act

* See Appendix giving copy of Deed whereby the Guild of St. Luke divested itself of its property.

THE BREAK-UP OF THE GUILDS 283

all male inhabitant householders occupying premises of the yearly value of £10 who should have paid the rates assessed on such premises were directed to be admitted to the Roll of Burgesses. Incidentally they also acquired the Parliamentary franchise.

For more than a century the main purpose served by the guilds had been to act as a stepping stone to the civic and parliamentary franchise. Prior to the passing of the Municipal Corporations (Ireland) Act the bulk of the freemen of Dublin had been admitted through the medium of the merchant or craft guilds. This privilege of the guilds was abolished by the Act with the result that the whole guild structure collapsed.

There was one exception. Alone of all the Dublin guilds the Guild of Goldsmiths survived. Throughout the eighteenth century the officers of this guild had faithfully performed their duty of protecting the integrity and high standard of their craft. That duty the guild performs to-day.

Appendix

Deed of Assignment of Property of Guild of St. Luke.*

This Indenture made the Eighth day of April in the year of Our Lord one thousand eight hundred and forty-one Between William Milton of the City of Dublin Cutler Master of Corporation of Cutlers Painter Stainers and Stationers or Guild of Saint Luke the Evangelist Dublin and William Woodworth Cutler and William Pasley Stationer Wardens of the said Corporation of the one part and William North Cutler John Franklin Painter and William Frazer Stationer all of the City of Dublin Brethren of the said Corporation of the other part Whereas the said Corporation under a certain Indenture bearing date the 2nd day of July 1782 executed by Joseph Pemberton then of the City of Dublin Cutler to the Master and Wardens of the said Corporation are now entitled to and possessed of all that the Lower part of the new Building then lately erected by the said Joseph Pemberton laid out and designed as a Hall for the use and accommodation of the Corporation aforesaid situate lying and being at the rere of houses in Capel Street in the County of the City of Dublin belonging to the said Joseph Pemberton containing in breadth in front 33 feet 6 inches in the clear and in depth from front to rere twenty feet be the same more or less Together also with several apartments at the rere of the said intended Hall and full and free Liberty and Privilege to and for the said Master and Wardens and their successors Masters and Wardens and their and every of their followers and other persons authorised by them and also to and for the Commonalty of the said Corporation of Ingress Egress and Progress into and from the said demised premises at all times during the Term hereby granted through the Entry or passage leading to the same from Caple Street aforesaid To Hold for the residue of the term of 96 years from the first day of May then last at the yearly rent of Three pounds of the late Currency And Whereas the said Corporation is also possessed of as their property of Two Silver Cups and one Silver Cover for one of said Cups and also a Common Seal of Silver being the seal of the said Corporation and is also possessed of three Forms three Chairs and two long

* Copied from Deed in possession of the modern " Guild of St. Luke."

dale Tables And Whereas at a meeting of the said Corporation held the first day of April instant and pursuant to Notice at No. 19 Dawson Street in the City of Dublin for the purpose in full Hall assembled It was unanimously resolved and ordered that all the said property of the said Corporation and to which they were entitled should be vested in and assigned over to the said William North John Franklin and William Frazer for the purpose of selling and disposing of the same for the purpose of payment of any lawful debts due by the said Corporation and vesting the surplus if any of the money to arise therefrom in the Charity for the Protestant Orphan Society of Dublin and which was unanimously voted in pursuance of Acts 3rd and 4th of Her Majesty Victoria Chap 108 sec 216 Intitled "Acts for the regulation of Municipal Corporations in Ireland" Now this Indenture Witnesseth that in pursuance of the said Resolution and of all powers and Authorities they the said Master and Wardens enabling in consideration of Five Shillings sterling to them in hand paid by the said William North John Franklin and William Frazer on the perfection hereof the receipt whereof they do hereby acknowledge have granted bargained sold assigned and set over and by these presents do grant bargain sell assign and set over unto the said William North John Franklin and William Frazer All that and those the herein before mentioned Lower part of the new Building formerly erected by the said Joseph Pemberton and herein before particularly described and mentioned and all the Estate right Title and Interest therein and of the said Corporation together with all Leases and muniments relating thereto To have and To hold unto the said William North John Franklin and William Frazer and their assigns the said hereby assigned Lower part of said Building from henceforth for and during all the rest residue and remainder of the term of years for which the said premises are held under the demise thereof at and subject to the said yearly rent of three pounds of the late Currency upon the Trusts aforesaid as is hereinafter mentioned and for the considerations aforesaid and pursuant to the said Resolution of the said Corporation they the said Master and Wardens have granted assigned and set over and by these presents do grant assign and set over unto the said William North John Franklin and William Frazer all that the before mentioned Two silver Cups and one Silver cover for one of said Cups and also a Common Seal of Silver being the seal of the said Corporation and also three Forums Three Chairs and two long dale Tables and every part and parcel thereof To have and To hold unto the said William North John Franklin and William Frazer and their assigns from henceforth for ever Upon the Trusts and to and for the Uses and purposes aforesaid and hereinafter mentioned that is to say that they the said William North John Franklin and William Frazer do and shall with all convenient speed sell transfer and assign for the most money that can or may be had or gotten for the same to any person or persons whatsoever his or their Executors administrators or assigns all that the said lower part of said Building hereinbefore described and every part thereof and all the Right Title and Interest of the said Corporation therein under the Lease thereof and also the said two Silver Cups and one Silver Cover for one of said Cups and also a Common Seal of Silver being the Seal of the said Corporation and also three Forums three Chairs and two long dale Tables and Monies arising from such sale or sales to pay therewith and thereout all such debt and debts as is or are due or owing by the said Corporation so far as the same shall extend and the surplus of such money or monies if any to hand over or vest in the Protestant Orphan Society of Dublin or pay the same to the Trustees of the said Charity In Witness whereof the said Master and Wardens have hereunto put their hands and have caused the Common Seal of the said Corporation to be affixed the day and year first above written

Wm. Milton, Master   William Woodworth ⎱ Wardens
                                  William Pasley   ⎰

SEAL

TWO AUTHENTIC SEALS OF DUBLIN GUILDS

1. THE SEAL OF THE BARBER-SURGEONS, from the original Seal preserved in the Library of Trinity College, Dublin.

2. THE SEAL OF THE GUILD OF ST. LUKE, from a replica of the old silver Seal made some years ago from the original.

The other devices appearing in this book are made up from the Coats of Arms of the Guilds reproduced in Charles Brooking's Map of Dublin, 1728.

PRINTER'S NOTE

Owing to a change in the foliation of the book after the Index had been made it is necessary to *subtract four* from the numbers given in the Index in order to find the reference.

The printer begs the readers' forgiveness.

THE GUILDS OF DUBLIN

Subject Index

A.

Admission to guild, rights of, p. 27.
—— by grace especial, pp. 162, 282.
—— of unqualified persons, pp. 199–200, 240–241, 280–286.
—— payment in lieu of dinner on, pp. 202–203.
Aldermen, Table of, pp. 183–184.
Alms house, building of, p. 157.
Ancient, p. 165.
Apothecaries, pp. 132, 199, 210, 259, 264.
Apprentices, admission of, pp. 29, 74, 83, 125.
—— trading by, forbidden, p. 30.
—— misconduct of, pp. 29–30, 124.
—— wearing apparel, pp. 30–31.
—— enticing away of, p. 32.
—— equipment with arms, pp. 62, 127.
—— to be Protestant, pp. 152, 228, 206, 251–252.
—— Stocks for, p. 164.
—— wearing of long hair forbidden, pp. 203–204.
—— forbidden to marry, pp. 205–206.
Apprenticeship, merchants to serve, pp. 26, 28.
Aquavite lysence, p. 170.
Arrest of wrongdoers, pp. 97–100.
Artillery Yard, p. 175.
Assay Masters, pp. 114, 271–272.
Assay of leather, pp. 196–198.
Association of crafts, pp. 211–212.

Association of guilds, pp. 181, 213–217.
Attendance at meetings, pp. 23–24.
Awdeon's St., Arch, pp. 220, 225.

B.

Bakers, pp. 58, 60, 62, 64, 69, 112–113, 195, 217, 256.
Bakers' strike, pp. 201–202.
Balry, common purchase of, p. 39.
Barbers, p. 58.
Barber-Surgeons, pp. 60, 63, 76–79, 210–212, 216, 217, 218–219, 247–249, 251, 252, 255, 256, 274–275.
Base silver, p. 189.
Beadle of Trinity Guild, p. 171.
Black Monday, pp. 166, 168.
Blue Coat School, pp. 158, 276–279.
Bloody Bridge, p. 205.
Bond to practise at one craft only, pp. 218–219.
Bowiers and flaichers, p. 64.
Brethren, duties of, pp. 77–79.
Brewers and Malsters, p. 187.
Bricklayers, pp. 222, 259, 285–286.
Browders, p. 58.
Bull-baiting, pp. 204–205.
Bulring, maire of the, p. 59.
Butchers, pp. 59, 62, 95, 110–111, 118, 204–205, 257.
Butchers, country, called in, pp. 110–111.
Button-maker, p. 132.
Burial, payments for, p. 90.

U

Burial place of members of Guild Merchant, p. 155.
Burial service, p. 89.
Buyers for the city, pp. 37, 38, 140.
By Assemblies, p. 161.

C.

Caddowe, p. 165.
Caliver, pp. 102, 128.
Calledors, pp. 129–130.
Candles, price of, p. 187.
Captain of the Trinity Guild, p. 165.
Carpenters, pp. 58, 61, 65, 128, 192, 193, 257.
Catholics, admission of, pp. 207, 209–211, 251.
—— exclusion of, pp. 152, 206–210, 251–254.
Cesses on guilds, pp. 129–130, 169, 170, 218.
Chantry, guild, pp. 19, 71, 75, 76.
Chaplains, guild, pp. 75, 88, 156.
Charity, of guilds, pp. 90–91, 276–280.
Chest, guild, p. 170.
Clubbs, employment of, forbidden, p. 232.
Coal, common purchase of, pp. 39–41.
Colouring goods, pp. 43, 140–141, 273.
Colours, guild, pp. 256–259.
Colours of Holy Trinity Guild, pp. 165–166, 168.
Combers, p. 224.
Combinations of journeymen, pp. 247–250.
Common bargains, pp. 36–39, 138–140.
Common Council, representation upon, pp. 131–133, 182–187, 264.

Commons of the city, p. 185.
Common Hall, pp. 48–50, 148–149.
Cooks, pp. 58, 60, 66, 195, 215, 217, 257.
Coopers, pp. 147, 195, 223, 258.
Copps, p. 89.
Corporations, The Eight, pp. 214–217.
Corvisers, pp. 58, 109.
Council of the House, pp. 70, 158–161, 226.
Courteours, p. 58.
Craftsmen in Guild Merchant, pp. 13–15.
Cranage rates, p. 144.
Cullenswood, march to, p. 166.
Curriers, pp. 186–187, 223, 259.
Cutlers, pp. 222, 225–230, 237–240, 255, 258.
Cutlers' marks, pp. 227–228.

D.

Dean and chapter of Christchurch Cathedral, dispute with, pp. 154–156.
Defence of city, pp. 101–102, 127, 166, 224–225.
Disputes between brethren, pp. 25, 229.
Disputes between guilds, pp. 123–124, 198–199.
Dues levied by Guild Merchant, p. 177.
Dutchmen, dealer for, p. 176.
Duties of guildsmen, pp. 77–79.
Dyers, p. 258.
Dele, King and Queen of, p. 95.

E.

Eight Masters, The, pp. 182–183.
Election of guild representatives, p. 185.
Ensigne of Trinity Guild, p. 172.

SUBJECT INDEX

Entertainment of guildsmen, pp. 168–169.
Enticing apprentices, p. 32.
Enticing customers, p. 79.

F.

Feltmakers, pp. 221–222, 230–233, 234–237, 251, 258, 274–275, 279.
Fines, pp. 87, 176.
Fire engine, purchase of, p. 175.
Fishers, pp. 59, 62.
Fishmoungers, pp. 216, 220.
Flesh shambles, p. 62.
Foreigners, exclusion of, pp. 43–44, 63, 120–123.
Forty-eight, The, pp. 131–133, 184.
Freedom of city, admission to, pp. 125–127, 281–284.
French Protestant refugees, p. 157.
Fraudulent work, pp. 269–271, 274.
Fustians, making of, p. 188.

G.

Gardeners, p. 65.
Ginkell, General, entertainment of, p. 174.
Glovers, pp. 58, 61, 64, 68, 118–120, 213, 215, 216, 217, 258.
Gold standards, pp. 267–268.
Goldsmiths, pp. 58, 63, 66, 67, 72, 73, 126, 147, 258, 264–272, 287.
Goldsmiths' marks, pp. 188–191, 268.
Gowns, wearing of, pp. 24, 177.
Groceri, common purchase of, p. 39.
Guild Hall, pp. 17, 20.
Guilds, constitution of, pp. 70–72.
—— origin of, p. 6.
Guild Juries, pp. 24-25, 100, 101, 281.
Guild meetings, pp. 22–23.

Guild Merchant, charters of, pp. 18–19, 47–48.
—— function of, p. 35.
—— the parent guild, pp. 13–16.
—— Roll of Names, pp. 7–12.
Guild of the Staple, pp. 50–53.

H.

Habbirdashe, common purchase of, p. 39.
Hagardmen, p. 59.
Hall of Guild Merchant, pp. 172–173.
Hawkers, licensing of, pp. 239–240.
Heliers, pp. 65, 192, 193.
Heriot, p. 85.
Herring fishing at Ringsend, pp. 194–196.
Hoopers, p. 58.
Horn books, p. 240.
Hosiers, pp. 97–99, 259.
Hospital and Free School of King Charles II., p. 158.
Hosting, pp. 127–129.

I.

Imprisonment, power of, pp. 72, 97, 98.
Imprisonment of guild officers, p. 104.
Intermeddling in work, pp. 193, 228.
Irishmen, exclusion of, pp. 29–30, 74.
Iron, common purchase of, p. 39.
Iron, dues upon import of, p. 177.

J.

Joiners, pp. 65, 259, 264.
Journeymen, pp. 230, 231.
—— allowed to take apprentices, p. 233.

Journeymen, combinations of, pp. 247–250.
—— enrolment of, p. 228.
—— forbidden to leave without notice, pp. 231–232.
—— hours of work of, pp. 247–248.
—— quitting employment, pp. 274–275.
Juries, guild, pp. 24–25, 100, 101.
Jurisdiction, extent of, pp. 233–235.

K.
King's picture, p. 174.

L.
Liberties, jurisdiction over, pp. 234–235.
Limitation of numbers, p. 117.
Loan to Charles I., p. 169.
Loan to City of Dublin, p. 175.
Lysence, wine and aquavite, p. 170.

M.
Marshalsea prison, p. 158.
Maryners, p. 58.
Masons, pp. 58, 65, 192, 193, 223.
Master, election of, pp. 70–73, 225.
Master's Accounts, Chap. III.
Masterpiece, pp. 75, 233, 268.
Material, good, to be used, pp. 114–116.
Mayor, authority of, p. 73.
Merceri, common purchase of, p. 39.
Merchants, Ch. I., V.
Merchants of Christchurch Yard, p. 150.
Military training, pp. 127–128, 164–168, 175.
Monopoly of trade, pp. 145–148, 149, 238–239.
Musicians, Guild, p. 94.

Municipal Corporations (Ireland) Act, 1840, pp. 286–287.

N.
New Rules, The, pp. 184, 207.
Ninety-six, The, pp. 131–133, 184.
Numbers, The, pp. 183–184.

O.
Oath of guildsman, pp. 251–252.
Oath of Supremacy, pp. 184, 207–208.
Oath of warden, pp. 265–266.
Oliver Cromwell, proclamation of, p. 171.

P.
Pageant of Corpus Christi Day, pp. 57–59, 94.
Pageant of St. George's Day, pp. 94–96.
Painter-stainers, pp. 222, 225–230, 237–240.
Paviers, pp. 222–223.
Payment for purchases, p. 42.
Peyntors, p. 58.
Penalty for refusal to serve office, p. 226.
—— for absence from meetings, pp. 226–227.
Periwig makers, pp. 210, 211, 247.
Pewtrers, pp. 49, 132.
Physicians' Charter, opposition to, pp. 200–201.
Pill, lease of the, p. 214.
Pitch, common purchase of, pp. 39–41.
Plasterers, pp. 198–199, 259, 285–286.
Plate, stamping of, p. 189.
Porters, pp. 58, 109.

SUBJECT INDEX 293

Porters, Master, pp. 53–54, 142–143.
Pottell of wyne, p. 93.
Precedence of guilds, pp. 215–217.
Prices, excessive, charged, pp. 112–113.
Prices, fixing of, pp. 39, 109, 112, 113.
Punishment of offences, pp. 97, 115, 141, 227, 236–238.

Q.

Quarter brothers, pp. 151–152, 164, 209–210, 229.
Quarterage, pp. 86, 176.

R.

Ready made goods, not to be imported, p. 121.
Religious observance by guilds, pp. 75, 76, 87.
Representation on Common Council pp. 131–133, 182–187, 221, 264.
Resin, common purchase of, pp. 39–41.
Revenue of guilds, p. 32.
Riding the franchises, pp. 255–263.
Roman brothers, p. 209.
Rules of the Cutlers' Guild, pp. 225–230.

S.

Saddlers, pp. 64, 216, 235, 257.
Salaries of guild officers, p. 171.
Salt, common purchase of, pp. 39–41, 140.
Samountakers, p. 58.
Sanction of guild bye laws, p. 34.
Saymasters, p. 189.
St. John mydripis Day, p. 87.

St. Stephen's Green, grant to the Eight Corporations, p. 214.
—— military exercise in, p. 167.
Seal of guild, pp. 71, 154, 229.
Seale of the Staple, p. 189.
Sermon in Christ Church, p. 157.
Servants, pp. 29–31.
Shambles, flesh, p. 191.
Sheep fells, restriction on sale of, p. 118.
Sheermen, pp. 58, 220, 258.
Sheriff's Peers, pp. 159, 160, 184.
Shipcarpynderis, p. 58.
Shoemakers, pp. 61, 67, 70, 112, 257.
Sisters, guild, pp. 21, 89, 93, 284.
Skinners, pp. 58, 61, 64, 68, 213, 258.
Slaters, pp. 58, 65.
Smiths, pp. 58, 60, 66, 217, 256.
Special Grace, admission by, p. 162,
Staple, Guild of the, pp. 50–53.
Staple, Mayor and Constables of, p. 189.
Staple trades, p. 16.
Station Days, p. 166,
Stationers, pp. 222, 225–230, 237–240, 258, 275.
Steynors, p. 58.
Stocking of Dublin with commodities, pp. 191–192.
Stocks for apprentices, p. 166.
Suit in law with Dean and chapter of Christchurch Cathedral, p. 156.

T.

Tailors, pp. 58, 71–72, 83–104, 217, 250, 256, 284.
Tailors' Guild, property of, pp. 84–85.
Tailors' Hall, pp. 65, 103.

Tallow chandlers, pp. 61, 68, 112, 187, 198, 258.
Tanners, pp. 58, 60, 118, 196–198, 219–220, 257.
Tents, purchase of, p. 168.
Testors, pp. 86, 87.
Tholsell, sitting in, p. 182.
Timber, common purchase of, pp. 138–139.
Touch of plate, p. 190.
Tools, craftsmen to have, p. 192.
Torches, funeral, pp. 91–92.
Trading, illicit, pp. 45–46.
Trial of plate, p. 190.
Triall of Inquest, p. 29.
Trinity Chapel, pp. 154–156.

V.

Victuals, free trading in, p. 43.
Vintners admitted to Barber-Surgeons' Guild, p. 199.
Vote for repairing the King's Chapel, p. 157.
Vyntners, p. 58.

W.

Wages, rates of, fixed, pp. 109, 110.
Wardens, election of, pp. 70, 72.
Weavers, pp. 58, 61, 67, 126, 258.
Wine, common purchase of, pp. 39–42, 138.
Wine, importation of, without licence, p. 138.
Wines, dues upon importation of, p. 177.
Wings of Guilds, p. 182.
Workmanship, good, insisted on, pp. 236–238.

Index of Names

A.
Adair, William, p. 259.
Ameas, Hugh, p. 87.
Andrews, Thos., p. 259.
Archdell, Mr., p. 270.
Arnold, Francis, p. 101.

B.
Bacon, David, p. 256.
Balgreffen, p. 85.
Balrodrey, p. 85.
Barrow, T., p. 258.
Baskin, pp. 84, 93.
Bathe, Baron, p. 98.
Batho, Edward, p. 220.
Beasley, Wm., p. 256.
Beigg, Davide, p. 170.
Benett, Richard, p. 101.
Bennet, Christopher, Ensigne, p. 172.
Bicton, Patrick, p. 79.
Booker, John, p. 256.
Boults, Mathias, p. 273.
Brady, J., p. 258.
Bratton, Jhon, p. 91.
Brazell, John, p. 257.
Broocke, Richard, p. 114.
Brooks, J., p. 258.
Browne, Richard, p. 195.
Bryne, Terrence, p 72.
Buke, George, pp. 85, 98.
Bushop, William, p.. 165.
Byrne, William, p. 37.

C.
Caddy, Edward, p. 259.
Callan, Sr. Jhon, p. 88.
Carlies, Earlle of, p. 170.
Carmichael, J., p. 259.
Casse, Steven, p. 94.
Castlebragg, p. 100.
Chapman, Edmund, p. 256.
Clarke, Edward, p. 257.
Clarridge, Samuel, p. 150.
Clercke, Andrewe, p. 170.
Coats, William, p. 256.
Collier, Thomas, p. 57.
Colman, Adam, p. 72.
Connor, Mr., p. 277.
Connor, Timothy, p. 210.
Conway, Francis, p. 253.
Cooke, Daniel, p. 282.
Coulie, Patrick, p. 79.
Crampton, J., p. 259.
Cranfield, Richard, p. 257.
Creighton, Abraham, p. 256.
Crolly, Charles, p. 234.
Crook, Andrew, p. 238.
Cullenswood, p. 166.
Cune, James, p. 98.
Curtin, Humphrey, p. 257.

D.
Darby, George, p. 158.
Dele, King and Queen of, p. 95.
Dennis, James, p. 208.
Dermote, Cornelius, p. 99.
Dinan, John, p. 250.
Duffe, Nicholas, p. 103.

E.
Edge, Tym., p. 219.
Exshaw, John, p. 259.

F.
Ferran, Robert, p. 257.
ffleminge, John, p. 155.

fforster, Sr. Cristofer, p. 155.
fforster, James, pp. 86, 99.
ffoster, Charles, pp. 155, 170.
ffrain, William, pp. 140, 176.
Fielding, William, p. 279.
Fitzwilliams, Sir Thomas, p. 194.
Frap Lane, p. 85.
French, Richard, p. 256.

G.
Gaynor, James, p. 249.
Gibson, Mr., p. 277.
Gill, Edward, p. 259.
Gill, Valentine, p. 219.
Ginkell, General, p. 174.
Ginn, Richard, p. 259.
Glandee, John, p. 156.
Gough, Edward, p. 194.
Gough, Patrick, p. 165.
Greshena, Barnabe, p. 91.
Grollier, Charles, p. 259.
Gryffyne, John, p. 128.
Guinness, Arthur, p. 259.
Gyles, John, p. 269.

H.
Hale, John, p. 257.
Hamilton, George, p. 257
Hanley, Thomas, p. 253.
Handfield, John, p. 188.
Hanne, John, p. 72.
Harbart, Edwarde, pp. 85, 98.
Harris, Michael, p. 71.
Hart, Henry, p. 256.
Helsham, Samuel, p. 238.
Henderson, Samuel, p. 257.
Hill, James, p. 259.
Hollister, David, p. 258.
Hood, Jamys, pp. 85, 86, 98.
Houghton, Benjamin, p. 258.
Houston, T., p. 258.
Howth, Justice, pp. 98, 99.
Hughes, Richard, perukmaker, p. 219.

Hutchenson, Daniel, p. 146.
Hutton, Widow, p. 253.

J.
Jans, Alderman, p. 183.
Jeaye, Robt., p. 210.
Jones, Forbes, p. 259.
Jones, William, p. 259.

K.
Kardif, Thomas, p. 87.
Keatyng, Thomas, p. 76.
Kehoe, Dennis, p. 270.
Kelly, Sr. John, p. 88.
Kene, John, p. 86.
Kene, Richard, p. 90.
Kennedy, Alderman, p. 183.
Kennedy, John, p. 259.
Kinge, George, p. 194.
Kinsolows, Wm., p. 257.
Kyle, Iwo, p. 98.

L.
Lambert, Jordan, p. 254.
Lane, J., p. 258.
Latton, John, p. 72.
Lee, Abraham, p. 256.
Lennon, James, p. 280.
Lennon, Patrick, p. 101.
Lorying, Juliana, p. 76.
Luttrell, Justice, p.p 98, 99.
Lynch, J., p. 258.
Lyons, Jacob, pp. 269-270.

M.
Malone, James, pp. 208, 209.
Malone, Stephen, p. 259.
Mara, Stephen, p. 258.
Maude, Maystras, p. 85.
Mery, Rolland, p. 79.
Miller, T., p. 257.
Mills, Alderman, p. 172.
Mitchel, T., p. 256.

INDEX OF NAMES

Modier, Patrick, p. 90.
Moore, John, p. 269.
Morgan, John, p. 257.
Morris, Captaine, p. 99.
McCleary, James, p. 257.
McCready, William, p. 257.
McKneather, John, p. 146.
Mulghan, Walter, p. 76.
Mysell, Jeffrey, p. 83.

N.

Neill, Sorrey, p. 90.
Nesfield, Samuel, p. 257.
Newbery, Thomas, p. 37.
Nix, Richard, p. 256.

O.

Ord, Arthur, p. 259.
Osbrey, William, p. 256.
Oxmantowne Greene, pp. 166, 175.

P.

Palmer, James, p. 76.
Parker, Jeoffry, p. 76.
Parry, Robert, p. 156.
Pentland, J., p. 259.
Popkins, Mr., p. 280.
Potter, Baldwin, p. 270.
Potter, James, p. 209.
Pur, Maurice, p. 155.
Pursell, Thomas, p. 171.

Q.

Quaytrod, John, p. 89.

R.

Ray, Joseph, p. 238.
Rice, Edward, p. 257.
Rishe, Iwan, p. 87.
Ross, Alexander, p. 256.
Russell, Morrys, p. 91.
Russell, William, p. 209.

S.

Savage, Thomas, p. 37.
Sedgrave, Nycholas, p. 93.
Sedgraw, James, p. 194.
Seele, Mr., " minister of God's word," p. 156.
Sergeant, John, " Capten of Trinity Guild," p. 172.
Servant, R., p. 258.
Seynge, Cornell, p. 87.
Shandly, John, p. 257.
Sharp, Peter, p. 281.
Sharpe, John, p. 149.
Sheen, John, p. 256.
Sherridan, Terence, p. 257.
Sherwin, J. F., p. 258.
Sherwood, John, p. 257.
Silvester, Sampson, p. 259.
Sineclare, Jarvis, p. 146.
Sisson, Thomas, p. 230.
Sleavin, William, p. 257.
Small, Henry, p. 82.
Smalley, Caleb, p. 256.
Spenfell, John, p. 85.
Stanyhurst, Mr., p. 98.
Stappull, Edwarde, p. 91.
Stokes, William, p. 257.
Sulliard, Sancke, p. 170.
Synnagh, John, p. 37.
Swan, Nicholas, p. 281.
Sweteman of the newegate, p. 98.

T.

Tailor, Thomas, ancient, p. 165.
Talbote, John, p. 71.
Tankard, John, p. 37.
Tate, Alexander, p. 258.
Tath, John, p. 76.
Tavernere, Richard, p. 94.
Thole, Thadie, p. 126.
Thornton, Robert, p. 239.
Tomkins, N., p. 258.
Toole, Rowland, p. 86.

Totty, Lieut. John, p. 172.
Trasse, William, p. 128.
Travers, Michael, p. 279.
Tudor, T., p. 258.
Tyrrell, Sr. John, p. 138.

V.

Vicars, W., p. 257.

W.

Wall, Patrick, p. 259.
Walsh, Thomas, p. 71.
Walsh, Thomas, p. 259.
Waryng, John pp. 37, 76.
Watson, James, Master of Guild Merchant, p. 170.
Watson, Joseph, p. 257.

Whit, Bryan, p. 102.
Whit, John, p. 100.
White, John, p. 37.
White, Nicholas, p. 76.
Wild, Gust., p. 257.
Williams, Johne, p. 114.
Williams, R., p. 258.
Wilme, W., p. 258.
Wilson, Benjamin, p. 258.
Wine, Mr. Warden, p. 255.
Wiseheart, J., p. 258.
Wood, Thomas, p. 249.
Woods, Richard, p. 250.
Worthington, William, p. 258.
Wright, J., p. 259.
Wycke, William, p. 86.
Wyllms, " Capten," p. 91.
Wynter, William, p. 239.

The Weavers' Hall   The Coombe

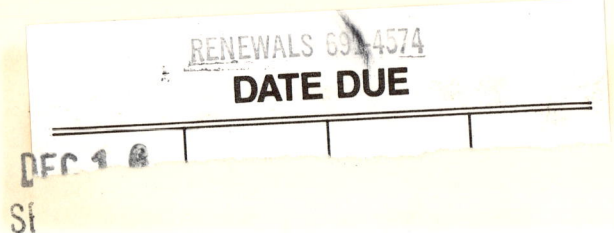